# Angel of the Battlefield

✳

*Books by Ishbel Ross*

❄

ANGEL OF THE BATTLEFIELD

REBEL ROSE

PROUD KATE

CHILD OF DESTINY

ISLE OF ESCAPE

FIFTY YEARS A WOMAN

LADIES OF THE PRESS

HIGHLAND TWILIGHT

MARRIAGE IN GOTHAM

PROMENADE DECK

# Angel of the Battlefield

## THE LIFE OF CLARA BARTON

By Ishbel Ross

ILLUSTRATED

HARPER & BROTHERS PUBLISHERS

NEW YORK

923.6
BAR

Library of Congress catalog card number: 56–6033

# CONTENTS

# ILLUSTRATIONS

*The following are grouped in a separate section after page 116*

Late in 1954 the Manuscripts Division of the Library of Congress received a new collection of Clara Barton papers from her great-niece and great-nephew, Miss Saidée F. Riccius and Hermann P. Riccius, of Worcester, Massachusetts. This added 27,000 fresh items to gifts made between 1940 and 1953 by the same donors, and by Miss Rena D. Hubbell and Mrs. Lena Hubbell Chamberlain, nieces of Dr. Julian B. Hubbell, Field Agent for the American National Red Cross from 1881 to 1904, and Miss Barton's most trusted friend and adviser to the day of her death.

With this new accession the life picture of Clara Barton seems complete and makes her one of the best documented of the nineteenth-century pioneers. From adolescence to her death at the age of ninety-one she saved letters, documents, all kinds of memorabilia, and sometimes as many as three written versions of the same story. It was her custom to sleep with candle, pad, and pencil by her cot, and her earliest drafts of the Red Cross charter and other significant papers were first scribbled in the small hours of the morning, to be developed later in her copperplate script.

Miss Barton was fortunate in having two such zealous inheritors as Miss Riccius and Miss Hubbell. Between them they have sorted out masses of documentation, annotated the material, and identified individuals figuring in the voluminous correspondence. The new collection triples the Library of Congress holding of Barton papers, and casts historical sidelights on the Civil War, the Spanish-American War, and on the contemporary political and social scene.

I am grateful to David C. Mearns, chief of the Manuscripts Division, for giving me access to the Barton papers, and to Dr. C. P. Powell, Dr. Elizabeth G. McPherson, Wilfred Langone, and Miss Joan Dodge for the splendid assistance I received all along the way. The ninety-three boxes in the new accession include correspondence, lectures, reports, diaries, photographs, documents, and clippings dating from the 1820's to 1954, with echoes long after Miss Barton's death in 1912. Most revealing of all, perhaps, are her thirty-seven diaries, thirty-five of which are in the Manuscripts Division. They light up many facets of her life and give a fresh conception of Clara Barton, the woman, aside from the official framework in which she lived.

The new collection contains such choice items as the original penciled draft of the Red Cross charter; a batch of papers labeled "Historically Important" by Miss Barton, bearing on the beginnings of the Red Cross in Europe; correspondence with Presidents Garfield, Cleveland, and McKinley, and with Henry Wilson, General Benjamin F. Butler, James G. Blaine, Susan B. Anthony, Frances Willard, Lucy Stone, and other well-known figures; the manuscript of her unfinished book on her years of teaching; and her reports on disaster operations and the Spanish-American War. Along with these papers Miss Riccius and her brother gave the Library of Congress her thirty-four badges, brooches, emblems, medals, and other decorations, picturesque testimony to the extent and variety of Miss Barton's operations.

I also wish to express my warmest appreciation to officials and staff members of the American National Red Cross for the co-operation given me in the preparation of this biography. I am particularly indebted to Ramone S. Eaton, vice-president of the organization; to Edwin H. Powers, assistant director of the Office of Public Information; and to George Korson, editor of the *Red Cross Newsletter*. The fine resources of the library in the National Headquarters were at my disposal, and I received every assistance from Chester H. Whelden, Jr., director of the Office of Research Information; his assistant, Clyde E. Buckingham; Mrs. Frances Freeland, librarian, and her associates. William R. Breyer was of much assistance with pictures.

Mrs. Laura diZerega, curator of the Museum, most helpful at every point, led me to such treasures as Miss Barton's trunk bed, her field desk, early Red Cross flags and brassards, army passes and teaching certificates, her girlhood album, and two of her most self-revealing diaries—one dated August, 1903, to June, 1904, when she was stepping out of the Red Cross, and the last of her diaries, January, 1910, to December, 1910.

I should also like to express my thanks to Mrs. W. Murray Crane for information on the earliest associations of her sister, Miss Mabel T. Boardman, with the Red Cross.

I found many interesting reminders of Miss Barton's life at her birthplace in North Oxford, Massachusetts; in the vicinity of Charleston, South Carolina; and also at Glen Echo, her former home in Maryland. I am grateful for all the help given me by Mrs. Josephine F. Noyes who, with her four sisters, now owns the house where Miss Barton passed her last years.

I am further indebted to Clarence S. Brigham, Albert G. Waite, and Miss Avis Clarke, of the American Antiquarian Society in Worcester, Massachusetts, for letters and material bearing on Miss Barton's life, and to Miss Louise C. Carruth, of the Free Public Library of Worcester.

In addition, I freely used the resources of the American History Division of the New York Public Library, and the Official Records of the Union and Confederate Armies and Navies, supplemented by information from Richard G. Wood, of the War Records Branch of the National Archives.

I. R.

# Part One

Part One

## CHAPTER I

## A TIMID CHILD

CLARISSA HARLOWE BARTON was the fifth and last child born into a vigorous New England family on Christmas Day, 1821. Her life was disciplined from the cradle and she viewed herself in retrospect as a shy and timid child. When her courage on the Civil War battlefields had become legendary and her days were starred with heroics, she often pointed out that she was not naturally "constructed that way" but was beset by fears in her childhood.

Some of these early echoes lingered on. By her own avowal Clara would rather "stand behind the lines of artillery at Antietam, or cross the pontoon bridge under fire at Fredericksburg" than preside at a public function, make a speech, or cope with a committee, all of which she did with outward calm, however.

A trim white cottage at the end of a road winding up a hill in North Oxford, Massachusetts, is recognized today as the birthplace of the woman who founded the American National Red Cross and was known to the soldiers of the Civil War as the Angel of the Battlefield. Here visitors view the small room where she was born into a bright, still world of frost and snow. She was named for an aunt baptized at a time when Samuel Richardson's heroine made parlor conversation in the American home. Before she was twenty Clarissa signed herself Clara H. Barton. By the end of the century plain Clara Barton had become a name well known to the American public.

At the age of four she was borne to school through snowdrifts on the shoulders of her brothers, Stephen and David, but the classroom proved to be the least significant part of her education. All through her early years she labored under a steady barrage of instruction at home. Her sister Sally, next in age, was ten years older than Clarissa, and all made a pet of the plain child whose bright brown eyes and heavy mop of dark brown hair were her most distinctive features.

"I had no playmates, but in effect six fathers and mothers," she recalled in later life. "They were a family of school teachers. All took charge of me, all educated me, each according to personal taste. My two sisters were scholars and artistic, and strove in that direction. My brothers were strong, ruddy daring young men, full of life and business."

But the dominant force in Clara's early training, if not in her life, was her father, Captain Stephen Barton, a keen-eyed farmer, influential in his community as selectman, moderator of town meetings, and a leader in local politics. He was philanthropic, hard working, and a confirmed warrior who had fought the Indians with "Mad Anthony" Wayne. He was present when Tecumseh was slain at the Battle of the Thames, and was party to the peace treaty signed with the Indians.

Clara always called him her "soldier father" and quoted him on the fighting front. On one of her first trips into the field in 1862 she told Chaplain Horace James, a Worcester man serving with the 57th Massachusetts Regiment, that where other little girls listened to fairy tales and Mother Goose melodies, she sat on her father's knee, or shared his blanket on the floor before the fire, and demanded more and more "stories about the war and how the soldiers lived." Characteristically, Clara added: "I early learned that next to Heaven, our highest duty was to love and serve our country and honor and support its laws."

Captain Barton pictured himself helpless and fainting from thirst in the tangled marshes of Michigan, eating dog meat to live, and drinking from the hoofprints of a horse in the sodden earth. He made Clara see the feathered arrow and tomahawk with the realism of the seasoned soldier. "Illustrations were called for, and we made battles and fought them," Clara noted.

So the twig was bent. To her dying day she was interested in military tactics and strategy. When she traveled abroad, Napoleonic landmarks were as important to Clara as Italian art or Greek sculpture. The Captain had illumined all the shades of military etiquette from her earliest years, and when the time came for her to work with army men her thoughts turned back to this indoctrination.

"Generals, colonels, captains and sergeants were given their proper place and rank," she observed. "I never addressed a colonel as captain, got my cavalry on foot or mounted my infantry." Nor is it likely that any American woman ever had more soldier friends than Clara. And none made generals do her bidding with more persistence and success.

The political images her father created for her were less abiding, except for Andrew Jackson, his own particular idol. He drilled her in Cabinet rank, and found amusement in the "parrot-like readiness" with which she lisped the names of men in public office. Such concentrated early training was strong medicine for a nervous, imaginative child who had eerie dreams, saw rams in the clouds, grew hysterical in thunderstorms, fainted when she saw an ox being killed, was too shy to make known her wants—that her gloves had worn out, that she froze in church—yet rode like a demon on horseback and had sporadic bursts of daring.

The vigorous drive around her left her some bitter dregs for the future and the feeling at times that she had been cheated out of the natural joys and diversions of childhood. But Clara remained enmeshed in family relationships throughout her life, true to the Victorian tradition. Her diaries and correspondence show the devoted care and interest she lavished on close and distant relatives, helping them with money, jobs, advice, and support through all the crises of their lives. Undeniably she had strong family feeling, but this same protective spirit was extended to friends and protégés. It was all part of the "passion for service" which Clara assessed as the governing force of her life.

In childhood she learned that she was descended from Bartons who fought on the Lancastrian side in the Wars of the Roses and that the red rose was a family symbol. Long before she heard of the Red Cross it was her custom to add a dash of scarlet to her costume. "It is my color," she would explain, swinging a scarlet scarf around her neck, often with a green dress, a favorite combination with Clara. Sometimes it was nothing more than a red ribbon at her throat or her waist. At other times it was a hood or ulster. She donned a scarlet scarf as she sailed for Cuba and the Spanish-American War. She sported a scarlet-lined cloak while she stood on a New York dock, watching grain being loaded for shipment to Russia for the famine victims of 1892. In her late eighties she was observed milking her Jersey cow, dressed in a black gown with checked apron, a brown Quaker bonnet, and a red shawl gleaming with the jewels of two of her foreign decorations. Clara loved her medals, and wore them on numerous occasions, sometimes just "to brighten up the old dress." Some had historic significance; others had purely sentimental value.

There were doctors, teachers, and landowners in her ancestry, as well as soldiers and legislators. Her great-grandmother's brother was Brigadier General Ebenezer Learned, who fought with distinction in the Revolutionary War. The Oxford branch was directly descended from Samuel Barton, who bought mills in the Huguenot settlement in 1716. They were a stern and strong-minded clan. Clara's mother, Sarah Stone—married at seventeen—was of Revolutionary stock. Long before her fifth child was born, she had developed into a shrewd and practical woman, decisive in her views, firm in her family management. Dolls were frivolity, but she taught small Clara to sew, to cook, to weave, to make soap in springtime, to cherish a small garden plot and tend her silky-haired dog, Button. The first straw bonnet Clara ever owned was made by herself. She cut the green rye, scalded and bleached it, split it into strands with her teeth, then braided and shaped it to suit her broad-boned face.

Her mother was apprehensive for her future as she watched her maneuvering soldiers with her father, doing stiff mathematical problems with her brother Stephen—"no toy equalled my little slate," said Clara—or riding a wild colt bareback at the behest of David. But before she died she observed that her youngest daughter "had come out with a more level head than she would have thought possible." Sarah's own training had taken hold. Clara found her mother's efforts "as lasting and as much honored by me as any." In fact, they had made her an orderly and accomplished housekeeper. Her knowledge of cooking and household management was invaluable to her during the Civil War and in fields of disaster.

If a soldier needed a custard, a homesick boy pined for a pie with crinkled edges, or a dry-goods box had to be covered with calico to make a chair, Clara could meet the situation. She was as much cook and provider as nurse on the battlefield as she roamed among the wounded with her mush ladle, crackers, or bread sopped in wine, the hem of her skirt pinned up around her waist, her homely face intent and purposeful under a knotted kerchief. In less warlike moments of crisis, she would instinctively scrub a floor, can fruit, "do up her laces," hang wallpaper, or bake a pumpkin pie, all far-off echoes of Sarah's early training.

Her love of animals also was traceable to her early farm days. "Button shared my board as well as my bed," she recalled of this period of her life. He was the first of many pets cherished by Clara, the most beloved being Baba, a white Arabian horse given her during the Spanish-American War; the other being her white Maltese cat, Tommy. Every animal had personality for Clara. She wrote of her army mules as if they were human beings, of the Czar's black Orloffs as if they were kings.

Her father kept blooded stock and she was only five when David first heaved her on the back of an unbroken colt, told her to hang on to the mane, and galloped beside her "over field and fen, in and out among the other colts in wild glee like ourselves." This was exhilarating sport. Eight decades later, writing the story of her childhood, Clara commented:

They were merry rides we took. This was my riding school. To this day my seat on a saddle or on the back of a horse is as secure and tireless as in a rocking-chair, and far more pleasurable. Sometimes, in later years, when I found myself suddenly on a strange horse in a trooper's saddle, flying for life or liberty in front of pursuit, I blessed the baby lessons of the wild gallops among the beautiful colts.

Clara had many chances to test her horsemanship. She had magnificent poise in the saddle and proved it as late as her eightieth year. Civil War officers found it a challenge to ride with her. During the Siege of Charleston, while stationed at Hilton Head, she rose at half past four in the morning to gallop through magnolia-scented lanes with soldier comrades. In this same general area she would jump direct from her horse with electrifying precision to the ladder of an ironclad and climb aboard. More than once she saved her skin on the battlefield by a last-minute dash on horseback when she had stayed to tend the wounded until the Confederates were close at hand.

Clara's dexterity was not confined to horsemanship. She readily abandoned hoops when there was work to be done. Instead of floating around with the leisurely grace of her contemporaries, she was lithe, firm footed, and acrobatic in movement. Washingtonians on their way to church soon ceased to marvel at Miss Barton perched on top of her boxes, bales, and bundles, setting off for the battlefields with her mule-drawn wagon trains. Soldiers invariably gave her a cheer when she gathered up her skirts and hopped up among her barrels in a crowded train, or stood knee-deep in mud directing loading operations.

But the woman Clara became had survived a lengthy toughening process from the proud, shy child whose first day in school was clouded when her teacher, Colonel Richard C. Stone, opened the "cat and dog" section of the primer for her perusal. Small Clara indignantly insisted that she belonged in the three-syllable "artichoke" division, a small pedant aggrieved by undervaluation. But she came to admire her handsome teacher, who soon moved on to another post, the Oxford High School.

When she was eight Clara was sent to board with his family and attend his school. Her parents hoped that this separation from home would strengthen the shy child and cure her of her morbid timidity. But she suffered acutely, refused to eat, grew thin and pale, and felt lost among the boys and girls of sterner fiber. At this point in her development none could detect a heroine in the making.

However, her life soon broadened through other means and the years from eight to eleven were comparatively happy and carefree. Her father sold his land on the hill to his sons and moved with his wife and Clara to a three-hundred-acre farm threaded by French River, narrow, stony, and picturesquely fringed with trees. Her sisters, Sally and Dorothy, stayed to keep house for their brothers. The elder Bartons joined forces with the widow of one of the Learneds and her four children, ranging in age from six to thirteen years.

This combination gave Clara the young companionship she needed. She raced with them in the meadows, hunted for chestnuts, played hide-and-seek in the barns, explored the thickly wooded and rocky hills, and played with the animals that abounded on the farm. Above all, she liked to ride on the sawmill carriage as it swung out twenty feet above the stream and back to the old-fashioned saw. Later her brothers built a dam across the river, when they replaced the old saw with belted "circulars" operated by water power. By chance, more than a century afterward, during the floods of 1955, a dam burst near this spot in the French River and close to Clara's birthplace. Red Cross workers soon were on hand to give aid.

She learned new arts as she watched the old farmhouse being made over. The painter taught her to grind and mix paints; to match, trim, and hang wallpaper; to use putty; to paint and varnish furniture—skills she often used in later life when putting barren lodgings or emergency quarters into shape. At this point Clara learned to milk a cow, to drive a nail with accuracy, to use hammer and saw, to throw a ball with an underswing like a boy's, and to tie square knots. But she was not allowed to skate or to dance. Skating was still taboo for girls. "When it became fashionable I had neither time nor opportunity," she commented. "Neither did I ever learn to dance."

This was more of a grief. Clara ached with longing, for "the dance was in my very feet, the violin haunted me," she wrote, when a dancing school opened in North Oxford. Her family's decision was more of a concession to local opinion than parental prejudice, at a time when a religious revival was in progress in the community and dancing was not approved. But Clara lost nothing in grace. In her late seventies she would rise from the floor like a ballet dancer without using her hands. She had learned to work, Indian fashion, surrounded by her papers, a habit acquired when she sat cross-legged in army tents.

From eleven to thirteen Clara's life took a morbid turn when she became her brother David's nurse. He was badly injured during a barn raising and for two years she waited on him hand and foot until she "almost forgot that there was an outside to the house." Month followed month while she nursed a "sleepless, nervous, cold dyspeptic." David would scarcely let her out of his sight. She gave him his medicine, applied the prescribed leeches, read to him, and tried to pull him out of his gloom.

On her tenth birthday her father had given her Billy, a high-stepping Morgan horse, and he was her chief solace during this period of confinement. On one occasion, escaping from David's sickroom, she rode him into Worcester through a blinding snowstorm. At last Clara was released when Dr. Samuel Thompson, a specialist in hydrotherapy, stepped in after a long succession of doctors, and David was given the new "steam treatment." More significant, perhaps, was the fact that leeches were abandoned and nostrums were thrown out. In three weeks he was able to return home and resume his work. Clara found him "like one come back from the dead." She was convinced that she had all but killed him with the leeches. This was her initiation into the care of the sick. It made a lasting impression.

But her own development had been checked by this unnatural life as she entered her teens. She gained only one pound in two years and lapsed back into a state of painful timidity. By this time Stephen had married Elizabeth Rich. He had sold his hill farm and moved down close to his father, buying his sawmill, water power, and adjoining timberland. Industrial life was stirring throughout New England and the Bartons all had enterprise.

Sally was now Mrs. Vester Vassall, living near by. Dorothy had become a chronic invalid. Clara herself, doing some local nursing after her experience with David, picked up a mild case of smallpox, her only serious illness except for a bout of dysentery and convulsions that nearly cost her her life at the age of five.

Aware that her education was being neglected, her family finally sent her to Lucian Burleigh's school in Oxford. He soon moved on to enlarge his own experience but continued to correspond with Clara and worry about her eternal soul. Her next instructor was Jonathan Dana, one of Oxford's most scholarly men. He had sixty pupils and she walked a mile and a half through snowdrifts to study philosophy, chemistry, and Latin with him.

She was scarcely thirteen when she started collecting the memorabilia that outline Clara in detail today. She began with a scrapbook in which she pasted verse and items that caught her fancy. She kept a sentimental album, embellished with hawthorn and wild roses. The cross-stitched bookmark still yellowing in its pages spells out the word *Friendship*, the human relationship on which Clara set greatest store and practiced handsomely. Becoming a collector early in life, she went on to keep a rounded record of a lifetime rich in experience. She also developed the habit of turning out verse, a taste that was to abide with her even in her old age. Moments of intense patriotism brought on the poetic mood—or a novel situation, such as a trip across the Sea of Marmora, dawn on a battlefield, an American tea party in London. None of it was memorable; some of it was downright doggerel, but, like Clara herself, it flashed with spontaneous vigor.

Moving deeper into her teens she became restless and questing. School was out and her life seemed unfocused. Her cousins, the Learned girls, had gone into factories, and she now hankered to work in the Satinet Mill of North Oxford, run by her brothers in partnership with two Englishmen, Paul and Samuel Parsons. Her parents thought her too small for the high looms, since she never grew beyond five feet. But Stephen, always kind to his little sister, had a low platform built for her and Clara worked for two weeks with a sense of elation as she controlled the flying shuttles of the glossy new looms. Her work ended abruptly when the factory burned down.

One decisive factor now shaped her course. Phrenology was in vogue and one of its leading exponents, L. N. Fowler, stayed with the Bartons when he visited New England on a lecture tour. Clara, ill with mumps, overheard her mother discussing her future with this authority. Sarah pictured her as the most baffling of the Barton children—not disobedient or wayward, but completely sunk in timidity and self-abnegation.

Fowler had studied Clara. He recognized her qualities and felt that life would strengthen her, but that her nature was basically sensitive and would not change materially in this respect. "She will never assert herself for herself—she will suffer wrong first—but for others she will be perfectly fearless," he predicted. "Throw responsibility upon her. She has all the qualities of a teacher. As soon as her age will permit, give her a school to teach."

This was to be Clara's occupation for years until she emerged from obscurity into a blaze of national attention, but all of her life was devoted to one form or another of public service. She regarded Fowler as one of the significant forces in her destiny and visited him later in London to tell him so. His book, Mental Science, as Explained by Phrenology, changed her thinking and her way of life. Before psychology became a popular study, Clara touched the fringes of self-analysis, and applied the principles of mind over matter to the recurrent crises of her own extraordinary life. She maintained that the important thing was to know oneself, and "to stand erect in the consciousness of those higher qualities that make for the good of humankind."

The Bartons were Universalists, liberal in faith, and in later life Clara sometimes described herself as a "well-disposed pagan." But she was proud of the fact that her father had welcomed the elder Hosea Ballou to the tall pulpit of the old Universalist Church in North Oxford, and the five-mile drive to church was a weekly rite of her childhood.

The dominant strains in Clara Barton's life can be traced quite clearly to these early days in North Oxford—to her soldier father, her practical mother, her siege of nursing David, Fowler the phrenologist stirring her psyche, her strong identification with rural life, her physical vigor and inner uncertainties. By heritage and upbringing she was none too different from many another New England girl. But Clara had a hidden drive, a resolute will, that were destined to establish her among the immortals.

## CHAPTER II

## MISS BARTON TEACHES SCHOOL

CLARA WAS eighteen when she stood before her first class, the New Testament in her hand open at the Sermon on the Mount. "All who could read, read a verse each, I reading with them in turn," she later recalled. Instinctively she had found a sure beginning, although fear and uncertainty had troubled her as she stepped lightly "over the dewy, grass road" to District School Number Nine, on a scented May morning in 1839.

The little schoolhouse was along the road from Sally's home. A clergyman, a lawyer, and a justice of the peace had just signed her first teaching certificate. Her family had helped her "to look larger and older" by getting her a tightly fitted green dress with velvet facings, longer and more adult in cut than the "two little old waifish dresses" she owned at that time.

Clara's luxuriant brown hair, her one vanity, was parted in the middle and squared back from her wide forehead. Thick clusters of ringlets hung bunched over her ears. Her high-planed cheekbones and wide mouth, curving up at the corners, gave maturity to her face. Her dark brown eyes were wise and merry. Her waist was slim, her hands noticeably small. If not a beauty, Clara looked healthy and animated, bright and sympathetic, on her first day as a teacher. Actually, in spite of the family tradition in teaching, she had no idea how to handle her pupils and was too tongue-tied to address them directly. Thus she sought refuge in the Bible.

A playground insurrection came next. Four of the rowdier boys, taller than she, were prepared to plague and drive her out as they had her predecessor. They started trouble outdoors and she promptly joined them in a game. Clara's petticoats whirled as she leaped after the ball. Her arm muscles were like steel. "My four lads soon perceived that I was no stranger to their sports or their tricks; that my early education had not been neglected, and that they were not the first boys I had seen," she commented.

They found tiny Miss Barton both strong and agile; her throw as sure and straight as theirs. After that, in her own words, they were "all children together." Yet Clara's school, at the end of the term, stood first in the district for discipline, a surprise to her since this was "an acquirement as foreign and unknown to me as Sanskrit."

She never forgot those early pupils, who wept when she left to teach at Millbury where their successors were "bright manly boys, tall graceful girls, clear-eyed, ruddy-faced and wholesome, grown on Charlton's choicest farms, and of the best blood of its earliest patriarchal days." But one of the boys was also a problem and his mother begged Clara to discipline him firmly. He towered above his teacher, was noisy, insolent, and deliberately distracted the class. At last he went too far and she drew from her desk her riding whip, a braided-leather lash four feet long with a heavily loaded handle. She explained to him that his conduct called for corporal punishment or an apology to the class.

"Not by a damn sight," he flared.

Clara whirled her whip and lashed him hard. The boys watched in awe. The girls wept. When it was over their teacher trembled with emotion. The boy finally got up from the floor and apologized to Clara and the class. She sent her pupils to the playground for the rest of the day, to picnic and enjoy themselves. The subdued boy returned with a bouquet of wild flowers for Clara. They were friends after that and she followed his successful career with appreciation. He was a youth of character and drive.

There were no more floggings at any of her schools, but Clara kept her whip in evidence, and expelled the more troublesome. Her reputation as a disciplinarian grew and she was assigned often to trouble spots in the local school system. She went from one district to another like a small dynamo, self-possessed, gaining more confidence all the time, invariably making an impression. Scores of New England youths remembered her during the Civil War as their beloved young teacher—Miss Barton the kind, Miss Barton the good. Their affectionate letters may be found today in her papers, and she wrote of them:

Scattered over the world, some near, some far, I have been their confidante, standing at their nuptials if possible, lent my name to their babies, followed their fortunes to war's gory field, staunched their blood, dressed their wounds, and closed their Northern eyes on the hard-fought fields of the Southland.

Clara caught her first whiff of the larger world at the outset of her teaching career when she went to Maine with David to be bridesmaid at his wedding to Julia Porter. She found excitement in the "gay party of ladies and gentlemen at one of the most elegant hotels in Boston"; in the steamer that took them to Portland; and the "magnificent span of horses" that drove them to the bride's home in Kennebec County. A gay winter followed in North Oxford, with many parties to celebrate the wedding of handsome David Barton. Clara's autograph album was much enriched that year with florid sentiments in masculine script.

After years of teaching in district schools, usually living at home, Clara finally told her brothers that she wished to help the factory children whose parents worked in their mills. They gave her a discarded picking room and here seventy children studied, at first in quarters lighted only through the open door. A tame crow perched on Clara's desk, and two pet goats wandered in and out at will. She conducted "concert reading and parrot spelling" with the whole street listening in. Finally her brothers, always interested in education as well as in business, built her a school of her own. She soon had 125 pupils, from "tiny fresh-aproned bits of humanity . . . to young men with sprouting beards and mustaches, ranged on the back seats."

It was a most original school, run along lines favored by Clara, who disliked school committees and functioned best when left to her own devices. She grew in force and dignity during these years of teaching but burned with discontent. She had a restless, ambitious nature, with limited chance for expression. Her father saw to it that she had good horses to ride, and she still galloped headily over the countryside. She worked for church causes, sold at fairs, distributed clothing to the needy, and kept her brothers' books. They were now prosperous businessmen, with various mills and lumber interests. She became expert at complex calculations. Years later, when directing disaster relief for the Red Cross, she astonished lumbermen with her precise computations on a million feet of lumber shipped for emergency housing.

After a decade of selfless effort, Clara decided that life was slipping away from her and the thought grew irresistibly that she must find a school that would teach *her* something. She settled on the Liberal Institute of Clinton, New York, and set off in 1850, a scarlet scarf finishing off her bottle-green costume, her cheeks ruddy in the frosty air as Stephen and David drove her to the station in a "jingling cutter." As she waved good-by they knew instinctively that she would not be back. She was twenty-nine, a mature woman shifting her course in life, none knew how greatly.

Since no past history was demanded at Clinton Institute, Clara did not disclose that she had taught for a decade. With her small stature and youthful looks she fell readily into the mold of the young student. Avid for self-improvement, she signed for every course available. "I had the habit of study," wrote Clara, "with a burning anxiety to make the most of lost time."

Her eagerness was observed by some of the junior professors at Hamilton College who tutored advanced young ladies from Clinton Institute. This brought Clara into touch with Paul A. Towne, a mathematician, and Samuel Ramsey, a divinity student at the time, both of whom were to become lifelong friends. Some believed Ramsey to be a romantic figure in Clara's life, but she indignantly denied this in a letter written in 1876 to her cousin and lawyer, Judge Robert S. Hale. She had asked him to collect a loan made years earlier to Ramsey. He had implied a love interest in Ramsey on her part. Clara quickly retorted that this was a ludicrous assumption. "I trust this letter will show you clearly that my pecuniary affairs and my heart affairs are not at all mixed," she wrote. "My observation has not been favorable to such a course of procedure."

But their association was long sustained, beginning with horseback rides together at Clinton. Later they took their meals at the same mess in Washington and often worked together over their papers in the evenings. When Clara became influential she found him government posts, in addition to lending him money. But she did both quite generally for friends and relatives throughout her lifetime. During the Civil War Ramsey worked in the Surgeon General's office and frequently helped Clara distribute her medical supplies. Later, when she was spreading the idea of the Red Cross, he assisted her with some of the documentary work. He was an expert linguist and a man of scholarly attainments.

No reverberant note of tenderness shows in the correspondence that passed between them. Most of Ramsey's existing letters to Clara contain pleas for money. Her diary comments on him are astringent, yet even after she had made legal efforts to recover some of her money their friendship continued. However, Clara's relationships were complex and sometimes hard to fathom. She was infinitely forgiving, and would rather cancel a debt than "break a man down in his business," she told Judge Hale.

Although no strong or sustained romance looms up in Clara's papers, she was obviously well liked by men, and had excellent working relations with some of the most forceful figures of her generation—great soldiers, good statesmen, men of stature. She worked with them, rode with them, talked them into doing her bidding. As her work became more demanding she surrounded herself with able young men whom she called her "boys." She used them as publicists, translators, field agents, supply distributors, or secretaries.

But marriage never seemed close to the horizon with Clara. The men in her family always insisted that she had had her share of beaux, but that none had measured up to her ideal of a husband. She told her cousin and biographer, the Rev. Dr. William E. Barton, that early in life she chose the course which seemed "more fruitful of good for her than matrimony," and she firmly believed that she "had been more useful to the world by being free from matrimonial ties."

But her twenties were filled with unrest and dissatisfaction, and her diary entries at this time suggest that she was torn by romantic longings and indecision. One suitor, whom she had met while teaching in North Oxford, went off to California in the Gold Rush of 1849. He made a fortune and begged Clara to marry him, but she refused. Nevertheless, he insisted on giving her $10,000 amassed from his "gold dust." She banked it and did not touch it for years, until she had spent all her own funds for soldier comforts and needed more for the same cause.

Her closest friend at Clinton was Abby Barker, who later married Joseph Sheldon, a judge and lifelong friend of Clara's whose home was in New Haven, Connecticut. His early interest centered on Clara, but for half a century they were a friendly trio. Judge Sheldon was to aid and advise her in her long fight to get the Red Cross established in America. He was to accompany her to Geneva for the International Red Cross Conference of 1884. He and Abby were to rejoice with her in her triumphs and help her through ill-health and misfortune. Clara was richly blessed with lifelong friends, but was ignominiously betrayed by others.

"Our excellent mother is no more," Stephen wrote to her one somber day after she had been at Clinton Institute for a year. As this calm comment on the end of a meaningful life sank into her consciousness she sought her room "without a word." She was stunned by the news. It was too late to reach North Oxford for the funeral. When she visited her home later that year she was deeply conscious of change. With Sarah gone, the family structure was shaken. Her sister Dorothy had died in 1846 and Captain Barton was showing his age. She was relieved that he had moved in to live with Stephen.

Clara saw that she was needed no longer at home. She was free at last to travel where she wished. She went with a classmate, Mary Norton, to Hightstown, New Jersey, first to visit, than to teach in a local school. Her vigorous bearing drew comment as she tramped in high rubber boots through snowdrifts, shoved wood into the tin-plate stove in the one-room schoolhouse, and drew up water from the well by windlass. Soon she was visiting parents to learn more about the children she taught. Clara had advanced views on education.

But 1852 was not a happy year for her. On March 1 she noted that "things were cheerless, outdoors and in." She mended a frock, made a nightcap, and longed for death. In bitter disillusionment, the woman who was to count her friends in thousands, all the way from Texas to St. Petersburg, wrote that she was "badly organized to live in the world or among society"; that she had grown weary of life at an age when other people were enjoying it most; that she had seldom felt more friendless; that there was not a living thing that would not be as well off without her. In short:

I contribute to the happiness of not a single object and often to the unhappiness of many and always my own, for I am never happy. True, I laugh and joke but could weep that very moment and be the happier for it. . . . How long I am to or can endure such a life I do not know—

This was not the way in which James Norton, Mary's brother, viewed her. Two months earlier he had written to Bernard Barton Vassall, Sally's son, that his Aunt Clara "got along well." One young man in particular—was it James himself?—escorted her to and from school quite frequently and Edgar Ely took her sleigh riding. He pictured the Norton family gathered around the piano, urging her to play and sing. She picked out a few notes but refused to sing. Clara was always rather tuneless, but on this occasion her thoughts, dark as night, ranged far afield, and she wrote despairingly in her diary: "Don't know why I receive no intelligence from certain quarters."

Then all entries ceased for several weeks. Obviously there had been a crisis in Clara's affairs. Late in May she resumed with the cryptic note: "Have kept no journal for a month or more. Had nothing to note, but some things are registered where they will never be effaced in my lifetime." Had Clara been crossed in love at this point?

She was well used to family badinage, and her letters to her abundant clan were always spirited, allusive, and filled with homely jokes. Her correspondence and her diaries show the two selves of Clara Barton in startling contradiction. The melancholy thread of her inner life is traceable through sixty years of diary entries, in juxtaposition to the bright and purposeful picture of her daily activities as revealed in her letters, her accomplishments, the comments of her friends, and the newspaper accounts of her successful career. By this time she was already committed to the constant note taking which was to illumine every facet of her life, reflecting her thoughts, motivations, and actions with the accuracy of a mirror, except for the periods when total silence denoted her nervous collapses.

With a fresh burst of optimism Clara decided to open a public school in nearby Bordentown. The sight of boys loafing in the vicinity of grogshops stirred her reforming spirit. She consulted Peter Suydam, the local postmaster and chairman of the school board. He looked at tiny Clara with skepticism until she assured him that she had taught for years. He told her that the boys were better candidates for the penitentiary than for school, that their parents would object to a pauper institution, and that the local lady teachers would be upset.

Clara, interested in human welfare, was quite undaunted. Her urge to be useful had become overpowering. She approached the boys themselves and found they liked the idea of a free school. She offered to teach for nothing until she had established herself. With characteristic persistence she wore down opposition until the school board gave her a teacher's certificate on July 1, 1852. A shabby old schoolhouse was assigned. Notices a foot square were posted on spare boards, street corners, fences, the market place, and tree trunks.

She was ultimately credited with being the first to open a free school in New Jersey. She was unquestionably one of the pioneers. Her first pupils were six small boys she found sitting on a fence rail outside the school and led indoors to the "pungent flavor of freshly cut southern pitch pine, and the bitter soot of the long iron stove pipe rusting for years." Soon she had sixty boys and girls, and a mixture of social classes that pleased her. She had won over a great many parents, who took their children out of private academies to attend Miss Barton's experimental school. She brought Frances Childs from North Oxford to help her teach in a hall above a tailor's shop, and installed young Jenny Suydam as a student assistant.

After school hours Clara went for long walks. She watched the wild partridge whirl by and the "silver flow of the Delaware below its rocky bluffs." She relished her picturesque surroundings and the historical associations of the town where Joseph Bonaparte, brother of Napoleon, lived for a time as the Comte de Survilliers. She found its "miles of shrubs and flowers, its walks, its rests, the ripple of brooks, and the unceasing song of birds—the repose of nature— a home fit for a King."

But, as usual, Clara was stung by yearnings that nothing around her appeased. She feared that at any moment she "might go off on a tangent," and start something new that people would judge and condemn. "Had ever one poor girl so many strange wild thoughts," she wrote, "and no one to listen or share one of them or ever realize that my head contains an idea beyond the present foolish moment." The key to Clara's future lay in this constant smoldering dissatisfaction.

Yet her school grew so fast that by 1854 a new $4,000 building was approved, seating six hundred students. Clara had become a salaried schoolmistress by this time but she found that a man must administer the flourishing institution she had created. She was assigned to second place, a bitter blow. She went out and sketched azaleas to ease her heartache when she knew this decision to be final. Worse still, the new superintendent embarked on a campaign which she took to be persecution. She wrote to Stephen that she could stand the ingratitude of the school board, but not the pettiness and jealousy shown her by the new man. The students were solidly behind her. Stephen urged her to hang on, pursuing her "straightforward, just, independent system."

But nature took a hand in the matter. That spring the damp lime dust of the newly plastered brick school affected her vocal chords. When she became too hoarse to talk she handed in her resignation. It was a tactful parting gesture, but was only half the story. Clara's later breakdowns were invariably preceded by loss of speech.

She did not know it at the time but she had left the teaching profession forever. Yet life was only beginning for her in the larger sense when she set off for Washington with Fannie Childs on a February day in 1854. She thought that a more southerly climate might help her throat, and a government clerkship put less strain on her vocal chords than teaching. Thus Clara arrived in the capital, where she was to become a formidable figure in the next half century.

Her speech quickly returned. She felt "healthy, wealthy and spunky," she soon wrote home. The break with her past had invigorated her. The rush of spring blossoms showering Washington soon after her arrival charmed her, and she noticed the flowers, the fine horses, and the graceful clump of unfinished buildings around Capitol Hill, rather than the muddy stretches and gaping vistas of the capital. She viewed the Patent Office, where she soon went to work, as a "stately marble palace with several suites of display salons, a library and in front, the courtyard with flowers and fountain." When the sun shone she lunched outdoors, watching the jets of spray shoot up like strings of diamonds, while she sniffed the near-by lilacs.

Clara's first rooms in Washington were bleak but she quickly found friends from New England. Colonel Alexander De Witt, Congressman from Massachusetts, who knew her family well, sent her to Judge Charles Mason, the liberal Commissioner of Patents, who installed her as a clerk in his department. She was assigned to copying, and her bold, clear handwriting took on the precision of copperplate under this discipline. Here was a post in which her hoarse tones did not matter but her clear script did. She was paid ten cents for a hundred words and during her first three months her pay ranged from $71 to $83 a month. When she became Mason's confidential clerk, she earned $1,400 a year, a large income for a woman in the 1850's. Her status had a permanency unknown to the wives and daughters who occasionally filled in as copyists for their menfolk but did most of their work at home.

Again Clara was pioneering where women were an unpopular factor. But she was well liked by Mason, who was interested in temperance and moral reform. He found in her a kindred spirit and since some of his clerks were intemperate and had also been selling patent secrets to outsiders, she became his "very valuable ally." She was shrewd, observant, and discreet.

The malingerers and the cheats resented both her industry and her surveillance. They hazed her to a disconcerting degree. They blew smoke in her face. They spat tobacco juice in her direction. They made jibes as she approached. Clara ignored them, "seeing only their boots," as she passed. When they attacked her personal character, Mason intervened. He challenged her defamer to show proof or resign. No proof was offered. The culprit retired.

Neither President Franklin Pierce nor Robert McClelland, his Secretary of the Interior, approved of women in government offices. In the autumn of 1855, McClelland moved to oust the copyists. "There is such obvious impropriety in the mixing of the sexes within the walls of a public office, that I am determined to arrest the practice," he wrote. Mason protested, saying that they were among his best clerks and, besides, "charity dictated their appointment and retention." He put in a special plea for Clara, praising her work.

McClelland replied that he had no objection to her employment by the Government, if only her work could be done away from the office. "It would give me pleasure to know that whilst the public business is being performed, it is made instrumental to the comfort of an aged patriot through the ministrations of a kind and dutiful daughter." Clara survived. Instead of being laid off on October 1, as McClelland had planned, she was at work in the office, on her increased salary, the most diligent of copyists. But she had felt the first chill breath of officialdom in Washington. She was to know it well before she had established the Red Cross in America.

The year 1856 was one of great political debates. When Clara could spare an hour or two she sought the Capitol galleries. The orators from New England always commanded her attention. Charles Sumner's historic speech on the Kansas-Nebraska Act was not only "an oration of greater power than any I ever knew" but it brought Clara closer to the antislavery ranks. "I have often said that *that night war began,*" she observed in later years. "It began not at Sumter but at Sumner."

She was well on her way to becoming a Republican, as the new political elements took shape and form around her. Captain Barton was a Jacksonian Democrat but Clara and her nephew, Irving S. Vassall, who had joined the family influx to Washington, watched the advent of James Buchanan with some trepidation. In the spring of 1857 Clara prepared herself for the ax to fall. "A day of general decapitation is looked for in all the offices," she noted. Colonel De Witt had not been returned to Congress and Clara felt like "weeping for a week" over this. She herself was under suspicion of harboring antislavery sentiments. Mason, who had resigned twice because of conflict with McClelland over patronage appointments, was mollified at first by President Buchanan but made his resignation final later that year. This left Clara largely to her own resources. She visited North Oxford in the spring, suffering from malaria. Her skin was saffron colored, and she felt wretched, but by summer she was back in the capital, working harder than ever and trying to protect herself at night from the "skeeters" that plagued her. She fitted nets to her windows, but the merry hum continued all through the swampy capital.

Clara did a prodigious amount of work that summer. In three

months she had burrowed through 3,500 pages of "dry lawyer writing" and out of them had filled a volume of abridgments so large that it was almost too heavy to lift. "My arm is tired, and my poor thumb is all calloused holding my pen," she commented. "I begin to feel that my Washington life is drawing to a close, and I think of it without regret."

She lived a frugal and austere life. She was up fantastically early in the morning, a lifelong habit. She washed and ironed, and scrubbed the floors of her bare rooms, snatching some time to study French. She visited the markets, bought thriftily, and was at the Patent Office by nine o'clock. She worked there until three, then took her work home and copied documents until midnight, often with Ramsey sitting across the table from her.

But the political ax fell and Clara was off the government rolls during 1858 and 1859. She went home, ill, depressed, and uncertain about her future. Her eyes gave her trouble. She suffered from "dogwood poisoning" and her voice was constantly husky. She was dismayed with the narrowness of her lot and burned with the ferments that stirred up other feminine pioneers of her era. Captain Barton's tales were still enthralling, but they were not enough.

By the summer of 1860 she was considering her old profession. She had been offered a school in Rome, New York. But Clara's outlook had changed and she wrote: "I have outgrown that, or that me. I dread the routine of such a life. I am to blame, I know, for nobody teaches so easily or has so little trouble with it." She took painting lessons and thought of teaching art and French in the South, but feared this would not be "active enough" for her taste. Stephen had migrated to North Carolina in 1857 and was building another Barton dynasty on the Chowan River. He had taken twenty helpers with him from the North and together they founded Bartonville, a community of mills, with its own schoolhouse, post office, blacksmith shop, houses, barns, lumber, and cattle.

Her political-minded relatives in North Oxford suggested a Post Office appointment. Clara also considered bookkeeping, but competition in this field was keen. Meanwhile, she kept David's books when her eyes were in fit state for close work, and considered writing to Sam Houston ("there was a *man*"), asking him for a billet in Texas. "You will laugh at my *desperate* moves but my moves have always been desperate by which I have ever accomplished anything," she wrote to her nephew Bernard. In the final analysis, she longed to get back to her desk in Washington.

At last the miracle occurred. As election time approached she was invited back to the Patent Office for patronage purposes by friends still there. Much had gone wrong during her absence, and her neat, methodical touch was welcome. Pay for copyists had been cut to eight cents for a hundred words. Economies had been enforced.

Clara found the capital gay, its people reckless, its more noted hostesses flashing their riches like peacocks in public. The split between North and South was opening wide, but she did not seem to know it and misjudged the political temper. On January 21, 1861, she wrote to her cousin, Elvira Stone, that "secession is wearing out in its infancy, and if wisely left alone, will die a natural death long before maturity."

In this same letter she said she lacked Republican friends and felt that their support would be vital with the shift of administration. Elvira knew Senator Henry Wilson well. Clara asked her to tackle him on her behalf. "I want Henry Wilson the Hon. to know me and be my friend," she wrote. "He will be the strongest man in our delegation and I want his influence. In *time* I can make friends of all of them that are worth having—but you see I have but a little time now."

In the following month Abraham Lincoln arrived in Washington and she listened attentively to the inaugural address of the man who was to change the course of American history. It was delivered in a "loud, fine voice, which was audible to many, or a majority of the assemblage," Clara wrote on March 5 to Annie Childs, sister of Frances, living in Worcester. It had gone down well with the crowd although "it will not suit your latitude quite as well, but I hope they may find it endurable."

Clara was invited to the Inauguration Ball but was unable to go because of a bad cold. She was also in a "hopeless state of semi-nudity," she confessed to Annie, who was her dressmaker as well as her friend. She had missed the last levee. Her wardrobe needed toning up, and only Annie could supply this need for Clara. But she was making headway without fashionable adornments. Mason had communicated with Sumner about Clara. Colonel De Witt had extolled her where it counted. She met several members of the delegation from Massachusetts and finally reached Henry Wilson at the Capitol late in March, 1861. This was a significant encounter, since he remained her friend and champion to the day of his death. Clara might never have become so much of a Civil War figure but for his powerful backing.

He received her with her nephew, Irving S. Vassall, in the reception gallery and "his whole aspect *changed* in an instant" when she mentioned the Patent Office. He put down his hat, arranged his coat sleeves, and "settled himself into a conversable posture, which seemed to say 'let us talk,' and we *did* talk." He told Clara that he was "fighting mad at the rottenness of things which could not be reached." He was at sword's point with her chief, Caleb B. Smith, Secretary of the Interior, and had told Mr. Lincoln that Secretary Smith was a "damned old fool," which she *couldn't* think any sin, commented Clara.

After half an hour of genial conversation they walked through the Capitol grounds together, tiny, prim Miss Barton from North Oxford, and the tall, lumbering chairman of the Senate Committee on Military Affairs. They parted at his hotel, and he paid his return call at half past eight that night, picking up the conversation where they had left off. He told her he was on his way to visit Charles Sumner and would interest him in Clara. He professed sympathy for her cause, saying that when a man came looking for a Post Office job held by a woman, he became quite angry, since it "surely was the design of the Almighty that women should *exist*, or he never would have created them"—although it was a scant chance they got, at that.

A week later Clara felt sufficiently sure of herself with Henry Wilson to write to Elvira: "How I should *like* to see that little click oppose *me* in this matter—just let them try. . . . My business is in 'good shape' and I shall succeed I think in opening the doors of the Patent Office for ladies to write like other clerks. I have all the influence of my state—personal at that."

From this time on Wilson called on Clara for a few moments nearly every day when he was in Washington. He would ring her bell in passing, and she would send a messenger and summon him if any crisis arose. He rarely failed her. Soon she was calling him a "glorious fellow" and Sumner had become her advocate, too. "From the efficient manner he has thus far proceeded, I am confident that he intends to serve my cause to the extent of his ability," she noted of the majestic Mr. Sumner.

Clara was in good spirits again. She had a cause and some power behind her to push it. Her old friends were glad to have her back. "I must confess that I fear I am getting a little dissipated, not that I drink champagne and play cards,—oh, no,—but I do go to levees and theaters," she wrote Stephen early in February. "Great acting," she commented after seeing Charlotte Cushman as Lady Macbeth. She had been to "Mr. Buchanan's *big party*" and found it splendid, with General Winfield Scott abundantly in view—"in fact, we are getting decidedly military in this region." But she missed the New England snow and longed to go sleighing.

In April Fort Sumter fell, Abraham Lincoln issued his call for 75,000 men, and the Civil War began. Captain Barton deplored the fact that the summons was not for an army of 300,000. Clara, well schooled in military operations, at once prepared herself for action. She went to the Monument Grounds with Dr. R. O. Sidney, a clerk in the Patent Office who shared her mess, and engaged in target practice, "putting nine balls successively within the space of six inches at a distance of fifty feet." Her companion indicated that he was lonely and would like to be her escort, but Clara considered his desire to call on her due solely to her "northern extraction." There would be little time in her life for dalliance from this hour on. Within a matter of months she would be introduced to the American public as the Angel of the Battlefield.

## CHAPTER III

## "MOTHER EARTH FOR A KITCHEN HEARTH"

CLARA BARTON, close to her fortieth birthday, sat in the Vice-President's chair in the Senate Chamber on an April day in 1861 and read to a group of Union soldiers as if she were conducting a class. She had a copy of the Worcester *Daily Spy* in her slim hands and was reading an account of their departure from home to join Abraham Lincoln's forces.

Actually, some were old pupils from Worcester. They were members of the 6th Massachusetts Regiment who had been attacked when passing through Baltimore and now were quartered in the Capitol, in a city unprepared for war. They lounged in the seats of the Senators or squatted on the floor, looking "tired and warm, sturdy and brave" to Clara's interested scrutiny.

"You would have smiled to see *me* and my *audience* in the Senate Chamber of the U.S.," she wrote home on April 25. "Oh! but it was better attention than I have been accustomed to see there in the old times."

At the moment she was convinced that Washington would be attacked within the next sixty days. "*If it must be,* let it come, and when there is no longer a soldier's arm to raise the Stars and Stripes above our Capitol, may God give me strength to mine."

Clara burned with patriotism and her avowed passion for service. It took many forms, but at this juncture she viewed herself merely as a "Massachusetts Yankee girl" galvanized into action from the moment she heard a rumor along Pennsylvania Avenue on April 19 that "*foreign troops* from the North, the old 6th Mass" were arriving that day.

By four o'clock she was at the depot, alert and helpful, moving about among the "ragged, bloody, draggled men, who said everything but their prayers." There were cries of recognition as men from Worcester and North Oxford recognized her. They told her that their baggage had all been seized and they had nothing but the heavy woolen clothing in which they stood.

Clara went home and tore up old sheets for towels and handkerchiefs. She filled the "largest market basket in the house" with supplies and passed most of that night at the Washington Infirmary helping to care for forty of these "well punished fellows." Next day she was in the Senate Chamber before noon catering to the appetites of scores more who were not yet "well used to hard tack." She led a parade of Negro porters laden with boxes and baskets filled with food through the streets. Clara was one of the first women to supply the troops with food and comforts. This was the beginning of her extraordinary record of service during the Civil War.

In the early weeks she roamed the hills where the men tented around Washington, distributing the supplies that came in response to an appeal she made through the Worcester *Daily Spy*. In her own words, she was "trying a very poor hand at nursing up, and comforting as well as I could, any portion of 75,000 strange, ill-convened and homesick boys." Clara called it "going out on a scout." She concentrated on the regiments of Massachusetts and New Jersey. After the first influx from New England, "the brigades of New Jersey brought scores of my brave boys . . . and the strongest legions from old Herkimer brought the associates of my seminary days. They formed and crowded around me. What could I do but go with them, or work for them and my country? The patriot blood of my father was warm in my veins."

From small beginnings her work spread out in all directions. She wrote letters for the soldiers. She notified their mothers of their condition. In turn comforts were sent to her, and families inquired about their boys. Her needs were lavishly advertised by word of mouth in New England. Churches, sewing circles, and relief committees responded with enthusiasm. A series of notebooks began to fill up with lists, addresses, and the records that were to be part of her daily life for the next half century.

When her own rooms overflowed with clothing, lint, bandages, preserved fruits, liquors, jellies, supplies of all kinds, Clara rented warehouse space and established a distributing agency. It was a "kind of tent life," according to Frances Childs, with Clara backed into a corner while all extra space was jammed with boxes. On one of her "scouts" Clara called on Colonel Stephen Miller in a sea of white tents which he told her would make good targets for the Confederates. She asked him what his men needed most.

"Tobacco," he told her without a moment's hesitation.

To Clara a man who smoked had always been accursed. Now she began to traffic freely in tobacco. She wrote to her cousin Elvira with the wry humor that often distinguished her correspondence:

It is needless to say that I trust soon to be a good judge of the product as it has become an article of commerce with me. You would smile at the sight of the half yard slabs of plug lying this moment on my table waiting for Dr. Sidney's Basket of Whiskey to arrive to accompany it to Kalorama. *Dainty gifts,* you will say, but all necessary, my dear Coz— this I conceive to be no time to prate of moral influences. Our men's nerves require their accustomed narcotics and a glass of whiskey is a powerful friend in a sunstroke, and these poor fellows fall senseless on their heavy drills.

Clara could scarcely have foreseen that she would found an organization that would send 87,000,000 packages of cigarettes abroad in the Second World War, but she had made a start. She took a practical interest in all the technical aspects of the military picture, and appraised each regiment filing up Pennsylvania Avenue. At times she wondered how long the "leaping fires and the gilded camps" on the hills would survive "the broad dark sweeping wing of war, hovering over our heads."

Clara was on the sidelines for most of the current spectacles and parades. She noted that President Lincoln and his Cabinet "looked very small" at Colonel Elmer E. Ellsworth's funeral—"no longer dignitaries but mourners with the throng." She stood at the Treasury building and glanced down the avenue to the Capitol gate, "and not one inch of earth or space could I see, only one dense, living, swaying moving mass of humanity." She wondered if *"Ellsworth dead* were not worth more to the Northern cause than the life of *any* man could be." She watched cannon being ranged for the night at Long Bridge but, like many others, believed the city's defenses to be a "mocking byword, our weakness known to everyone and our very streets lined with traitors." She wrote prophetically to the old soldier in North Oxford, whose days now were numbered:

I don't know how long it has been since my ear has been free from the roll of a drum. It is the music I sleep by, and I love it. . . . I begin to think it is useless to turn *back* for heroes, for I am satisfied that these times will bring out as brave men as ever graced the pages of history, and Massachusetts leads the van. . . . We trust we are ready to bind the wounds or bear them of our own, if necessary. I shall remain here while anyone remains, and do whatever comes to my hand. I may be compelled to *face* danger, but *never fear it,* and while our soldiers can stand and *fight,* I can stand and feed and nurse them.

After the First Battle of Bull Run, Clara wrote daily to her father, keeping him informed before she had historical perspective on what was happening. She had watched the troops "go over into Virginia from Wednesday until Saturday, noble, gallant, handsome fellows, armed to the teeth." But the chaos that followed changed her from a mild purveyor of comforts to an initiate in the bloodier aspects of war. As she watched the "shattered army streaming back into the capital" she picked out those "who looked the worst and limped the hardest" and drew them into her own quarters, to see what could be done for them. "All very new business," Clara commented.

But it was business she was learning fast—the true face of war. All through August and September she was in the city, visiting hospitals and wharves, and arranging her mounting supplies. She was constantly on the move, a small and vigorous figure meeting each emergency as it arose in the practical way that was to characterize all her later labors. She rounded up fellow lodgers, friends at the mess, and her New England relatives, to help her in her errands of mercy. The future of the Red Cross was already foreshadowed in the boxes, barrels, and bundles that Clara accumulated, dealing out supplies as fast as she could circulate.

She watched the army tighten up, the tension mount in the capital. Washington had come to life with a vengeance. Relief societies were in operation. Women circulated with delicacies for the soldiers. They attended the parades and flag raisings. They flirted and danced as well as sewed. Many now had cause to weep. Clara burned with indignation over army muddling and the lack of nurses.

She was scathing over some of the belles who were enjoying the war. "I greatly fear that the few privileged, elegantly dressed ladies who ride over and sit in their carriages to witness 'splendid services' and 'inspect the Army of the Potomac' and come away 'delighted,' learn very little of what lies there under canvas," she wrote to the Ladies Relief Committee of Worcester on December 16, 1861.

Clara also took note of the seditionists and the Rebel groups working quietly around the hospitals. When called home that winter by the news that her father was close to death, she visited Governor John A. Andrew of Massachusetts with Colonel De Witt and named several who, with or without her aid, later were arrested. Captain Barton rallied and Clara returned to Washington before Christmas with more stores collected along the way. She had done a tour of the familiar towns and villages to whip up interest in her soldier boys.

In March she was summoned home again. This time it was the end. On the 18th she read to her father news of the capture by General Ambrose E. Burnside of New Bern, North Carolina. "He said it was well and he said no more," Clara noted. He had already given her his blessing for her war work, and had urged her to go direct into the battlefields. "Soldiers, however rough, always respect a woman who deserves it," he told her with his dying breath, giving her a Masonic emblem as a talisman.

From his bedside Clara wrote again to Governor Andrew, asking him to help her get to the field. The "oak and iron constitution" of Captain Barton had worn out. His last tale of the Red Man had been told. "He is journeying home," wrote Clara. "With this, my highest duties close, and I would fain be allowed to go and administer comfort to our brave men who peril life and limb in defence of the priceless boon the fathers so dearly won."

Clara wrote that she had "none but right motives." She asked neither pay nor praise, simply a soldier's fare, and sanction to do "whatever my hands find to do." Next day Captain Barton died at the age of eighty-eight, so the old soldier did not live long enough to see his small Clarissa become one of the heroines of the Civil War.

Back in Washington she put on a strong campaign to wear down the opposition she encountered at every turn. Surgeon General

Alfred Hitchcock crisply responded on March 25 to Governor Andrew's letter: "I do not think at the present time Miss Barton had better undertake to go to Burnside's Division to act as a nurse."

But Clara argued that forty young men in that division were former pupils of hers and she knew she possessed "the entire confidence and respect of every one of them." She was always to view the soldiers as individuals, never en masse as part of an army. This gave much of her work its individual touch. It appalled her to think that the "same fair faces" that had come to her school a few years earlier, scrubbed and shining, should now lie in the mud "blood-matted and tangled, trampled under foot of man and horse, buried in a common trench." She knew every Tom, Dick, and Harry of them, and wrote to Fannie Childs: "To any other friend than you, I should not feel like speaking so freely of such things, but you, who know how foolishly tender my friendships are, and how I loved 'my boys' will pardon me, and not think me strange and egotistical."

With the persistence she later applied to founding the Red Cross in America, Clara went from one army official to another, pleading for passes, testing every possibility. She had her first success with Major D. H. Rucker, Assistant Quartermaster General in charge of transportation. She found him busy giving orders and permits at a desk behind a wicket fence with a gate in it.

"He was pressed, and anxious, and gruff, and I was very tired," Clara noted in her diary. She was so tired, in fact, that she burst into tears when he asked her what she wanted. He drew her inside his fence and told her to stop crying. He stared at her oddly when she said she wanted to get to the front. That was no place for a woman, he countered, pressing her for motive. Did she have a father or brother in the ranks?

Then Clara told him about her supplies. When he heard about her warehouse and her lodgings filled with good things from New England, he promptly gave her an order for wagons and the men to load them. "And here is your permit to go to the front," he added, "and God bless you."

Bit by bit Clara obtained all the necessary passes from the various Government departments—from the Surgeon General and from the Military Governor of the District of Columbia, as well as from Major Rucker. The last bit of red tape was cut for her in Major

General John Pope's office on August 12, the day after she made a diary entry: "Battle at Culpeper reached us. . . . Went to Sanitary Commission. Concluded to go to Culpeper. Packed goods."

Clara was now entitled to free transportation by train or steamboat. With General Pope's authorization the cycle was complete. She was well primed on procedure and the most pressing needs, for during the weeks of waiting she had inspected near-by hospitals, had visited Alexandria, and had entered into harmonious relations with Dr. Henry W. Bellows' rising organization, the Sanitary Commission. Although Clara was never officially attached to it or the Christian Commission, there was mutual assistance on different battlefields. Their workers usually found Clara playing a solitary hand, but making excellent headway with generals, brigade surgeons, and the fighting men. They often gave her supplies. She, in turn, offered a helping hand when the need arose. Clara and Dr. Bellows did not meet until years after the Civil War had ended. By that time they had another mutual interest in the Red Cross. Both tried to bring the United States into the Convention of Geneva. Dr. Bellows failed, through no fault of his own. Clara, in time, succeeded.

With her transportation assured at last, she went straight into action. "When our armies fought on Cedar Mountain, I broke the shackles and went to the field," she wrote. "And so began my work." Heading for Culpeper, she climbed over the wagon wheel and poised herself among her bales and bundles. Off rattled her mules, bearing Clara, a slight, vigorous woman of forty, without her hoop, wearing a plaid jacket, a dark skirt, and a kerchief.

Brigade Surgeon James L. Dunn, of Conneautville, Pennsylvania, who later claimed to be the first to give Clara's name and the news of her services to the public, and to call her the Angel of the Battlefield, was astounded when she appeared in front of his hospital at midnight with a four-mule team well laden with supplies. This was two days after the Battle of Cedar Mountain, and the hospital was virtually out of dressings. Clara was able to meet his immediate need. This came to be her special knack, or her good fortune—always to appear at the crucial moment, with the needed item.

"I thought that night if heaven ever sent out a holy angel, she must be one, her assistance was so timely," said the grateful Dr. Dunn.

Clara gave fainting men bread sopped in wine. She helped to staunch their wounds. After doing all she could on the field she returned to Culpeper, where she dealt out shirts to the wounded, made soup and applesauce, and produced bandages in quantity. In 1902 she pinned a Red Cross button on the armless shoulder of a Massachusetts man named Parker, whom she had found lying in a church at Culpeper, his right arm off at the shoulder. He was the first to receive a loaf of bread and a shirt from Clara, and she considered this her earliest distribution close to the scene of action. It was also the first full impact of war for her, and when a captain remarked to her, "Miss Barton, this is a rough and unseemly position for you, a woman, to occupy," Clara responded, "Is it not as rough and unseemly for these pain-racked men?"

On her return to Washington she was called to Alexandria to help the surgeons and supply bandages for six hundred wounded men just brought in from Culpeper. Conscious now of the desperate need, she wrote to the women of Hightstown to send her more supplies, saying that she had carried their gifts to the field herself. "Your wine brought strength to the fainting; your clothes staunched the blood of the dying. . . ."

Clara was on her way to Armory Square Hospital on August 30, 1862, taking a comb and other supplies to a Massachusetts youth, when she "saw everybody going to the wharf." Always on the alert, she joined the rush. The Second Battle of Bull Run had been fought with great slaughter and she knew that she would be needed. The capital was in a panic. She wrote hastily to David, Sally, and Cousin Elvira: "I leave immediately for the battlefield. Don't know when I can return. If anything happens to me you, David, must come and take all my effects home with you."

Clara was learning fast. She and her helpers, Mrs. Ada Morrell and Miss Lydia F. Haskell, an old New Jersey friend, packed that night and the supplies were loaded on a freight car at daybreak. Clara later sent back an ambulance for Mrs. Almira Fales, who missed the train. She was a "tall spare figure in rusty black" who had said to Clara: "I heard you were off for the fighting. I'd like to go with you." Mrs. Fales was one of the better-known war workers, although somewhat eccentric in manner.

The train moved off in pouring rain, with Clara and her colleagues jammed among the boxes. In her lectures after the war she often drew a humorous picture of her acrobatics on this occasion:

Our coaches were not elegant or commodious. They had no seats, no windows, no platforms, no steps, a slide door on the side, was the only entrance and this was higher than my head. For my manner of attaining my elevated position, I must beg you to draw on your own imaginations and spare me the labor of reproducing the boxes, barrels, boards and rails which in those days seemed to help me up and on in the world. . . .

It was still drizzling when the train whistled into Fairfax Station with three carloads of Barton supplies, including bandages, drugs, coffee, brandy, wines, cans of soup and beef, jellies, fruit juices, and crackers. But it was all too little for what lay ahead of Clara. As she stepped out she saw that the thinly wooded slope close to the station was alive with wounded soldiers. All day long they were borne in by the wagonload from the battlefield under flag of truce until the "whole hillside seemed to be covered with bloody men." They lay on the damp grass and fallen leaves until bales of hay were broken open and scattered over the ground. It was a somber sight in the misty half light.

Fifteen minutes after their arrival Clara and her helpers were preparing food and dressing wounds. Working with a gingham apron over her dress and a red bow at her collar she made compresses and slings, and moistened and bound up wounds. As each soldier was bandaged, he was carried by stretcher to a flat car, but Clara saw to it that he had nourishment first. She had not foreseen the need for cooking utensils and had only two water buckets, five tin cups, one camp kettle, one stewpan, two lanterns, four bread knives, three plates, and a two-quart tin dish, "with three thousand guests to serve." As she later told her lecture audiences:

I had not yet learned to equip myself, for I was no Pallas, ready armed, but grew into my work by hard thinking and sad experience. . . . I was never caught so again for later I became a notable housekeeper, if that might be said of one who had no house to keep but lived in fields and woods and tents, and wagons, with all out of doors for a cooking range, mother earth for a kitchen hearth, and the winds of Heaven for a chimney.

However, she kindled a fire, getting her first lesson in how to work up a blaze in the rain, heated soup and coffee, and every can, jar, bucket, bowl, cup, or tumbler that held the fruits and preserves from New England "became a vehicle of mercy to convey some preparation of mingled bread and wine or soup or coffee to some helpless, famishing sufferer."

When night fell there were only two lanterns and a few candles in the field. The men lay so close together that it was almost impossible to walk without stepping on a stricken soldier. "The slightest misstep brought a torrent of groans from some poor mangled fellow in your path," wrote Clara, who moved nimbly herself, carrying a flickering candle. "How we watched and pleaded and cautioned as we worked and wept that night." The merest fumble would have enveloped the wounded in flames, bedded down as they were in straw. Clara put socks on their damp feet, wrapped such blankets around them as she could muster, or covered them softly with hay. She learned some unforgettable lessons that night on the care of wounded men.

This was the spot in which she found one of her old pupils, Charles Hamilton, badly wounded. When the fair-haired boy with torn blouse and shattered right arm saw her, he threw his left arm around her neck and wept as he recalled how he used to carry her satchel home from school. "My faithful pupil, poor Charley," Clara commented. "That mangled right arm will never carry a satchel again."

It was also the battleground where she impersonated the sister of a dying youth and cradled him in her arms, until he fell asleep believing her to be his sister Mary. He had been crying for Mary for hours when a surgeon, with haggard face seen in ghastly outline through the flame of a flickering candle, approached Clara and begged her to go up the slope and help this dying boy. He was shot through the abdomen and was close to death.

Clara went to him at once, had the candle removed, and sank down beside him in the darkness. She kissed his forehead and laid her cheek against his. He ran "his cold, blood-wet hands about my neck, passed them over my face, and twined them in my hair, which by this time had freed itself from fastenings and was hanging damp and heavy upon my shoulders. He babbled on with relief."

The illusion was complete. He believed her to be Mary. She wrapped his feet in blankets, gave him such stimulants as he could take, seated herself on the ground, and held his head in her lap until he fell asleep. He became her last case that night. When he wakened he looked up, puzzled, then said to Clara: "I knew before I opened my eyes that this couldn't be Mary. I know now that she couldn't get here but it is almost as good, you've made me so happy."

He now begged to be taken to Washington by train. He had sworn to his family that he would return home, dead or alive. Clara urged that he be put on the next train leaving for the capital. The surgeon protested, saying there was room only for those with a chance to live. But when she insisted the youth, Hugh Johnson, was laid carefully on a blanket in the crowded train, with stimulants beside him. An attendant promised her that the boy would be taken to Armory Square Hospital and that his grave would be marked when he died.

She later learned when she visited the hospital that young Johnson had lasted until he was met by his mother and sister Mary. They had taken him home for burial. He became one of innumerable young men remembered by Clara to the end of her days. She mentioned him often in her lectures.

Next day she sought official permission to feed the men before they were taken from the wagons. If mixed up with those already cared for, they were apt to be overlooked and some would die in the long hours before they could reach the Washington hospitals. "This point secured," wrote Clara, "I commenced my day's work of climbing from the wheel to the brake of every wagon and speaking to and feeding with my own hands each soldier until he expressed himself satisfied."

She had able helpers in fifty prisoners for whose services she had bargained. She had them digging graves and burying the dead, carrying the wounded over the rough ground in their arms, loading cars, building fires, distributing soup. "I failed to discern that their services were less valuable than those of other men," she commented.

From Saturday to Monday Clara had scarcely touched food. She and her helpers had "just drawn around a box when air and earth and all about us shook with one mingled crash of God's and man's artillery. The lightning played and the thunder rolled incessantly and the cannon roared louder and nearer each minute." The Second Battle of Bull Run had merged into the Battle of Chantilly. Clara was not close to the scene but she caught the aftermath. "The description of this battle I leave to those who saw and moved in it, as it is my purpose to speak only of events in which I was a witness or actor," she noted in one of her lectures. But soon another wagon train of wounded arrived without warning and a waiting train of cars on the track received them. Clara by this time was nearly alone. Her worn-out assistants could work no longer. Her food supplies had dwindled. She was reduced to crackers, which were ingeniously put into haversacks, beaten to crumbs between stones, moistened with wine or whiskey, and sweetened with coarse brown sugar.

When the train left and Clara could do no more she sought rest in a tent that had been pitched for her in a hollow on the hillside. It was flooded with water. Rivulets had rushed through it for several hours. Mrs. Fales had returned to Washington. Mrs. Morrell was bunked on some boxes above the water line. Clara, utterly exhausted, sank down in a grassy morass where the water was not too deep. As she described it:

I remember myself sitting on the ground, upheld by my left arm, my head resting on my hand—impelled by an almost uncontrollable desire to lie completely down—and prevented by the certain conviction that if I did the water would flow into my ears. How long I balanced between my desires and cautions I have no positive knowledge—but it is very certain that the former carried the point. . . .

Clara was wakened by the rumbling of more wagons of wounded men. She had slept only two hours but "oh! what strength I had gained." She jumped up, her clothes dripping wet, wrung the water from her hair and skirts, and went to work again. This was the day on which General Philip Kearny's leaderless men marched past on their way to Alexandria. "All day they came, tired, hungry, ragged, defeated, retreating they knew not whither." The General had already been brought into camp—dead.

While they were still loading the wounded into the waiting train, enemy cavalry skirting the hills gave warning of the approaching Confederate forces. "But our work must be accomplished, and no wounded men—once given into our hands must be left, and with the spirit of desperation we struggled on," Clara wrote.

At three o'clock in the afternoon an officer galloped up to her and asked her if she could ride. Clara assured him she could.

"But you have no lady's saddle," he pointed out. "Could you ride mine?"

"Yes, sir, or without it, if you have blanket and surcingle."

"Then you can risk another hour," he exclaimed and galloped off.

At four o'clock he was back, riding at breakneck speed. Leaping from his horse, he warned Clara: "Now is your time. The enemy is already breaking over the hills. Try the train. It will go through unless they have flanked, and cut the bridge a mile above us. In that case I've a reserve horse for you, and you must take your chances to escape across the country."

Clara was on the train in two minutes' time. The last of the wounded were already aboard. She took charge of one carload, and Mrs. Morrell of the other. The man galloped off on horseback. As they moved away, the conductor applied a torch to a pile of combustible material beside the track. Clara's last view of the scene encompassed a blazing station and a troop of cavalry riding down the hill. The wounded were fed at Alexandria before being sent into hospitals. "I stood in my car and fed the men until they could eat no more," Clara reported.

After that she slept for twenty-four hours. She had had less than three hours' sleep from Saturday until Wednesday morning and had lived through scenes she would never forget. "Pope had been sacrificed and all the blood shed from Yorktown to Malvern Hill seemed to have been utterly in vain. . . . Washington was filled with dismay, and all the North was moved as a tempest stirs a forest," Clara commented. Now fully baptized, she felt herself to be a small part of the nation's great emergency. She was bone tired but her passion for service had found a most unexpected outlet.

Clara soon became a recognized provider for Union soldiers, an army housekeeper who cooked for the men and fed them in the field. She nourished them as much as she nursed them, although she gave aid to army surgeons, bandaged the wounded, held dying men in her arms, and even performed one minor operation. In general, she did the instinctive, sensible, and often the tender thing, giving each man what he needed. For some it was prayer. Others wanted letters sent home. Or their fears stilled. Or their pain eased. Or their hunger assuaged.

Most of the surgeons came to prize Clara. Few were churlish, for she could turn her hand to anything. She did what she liked, but she posed no female problems on the battlefield and they thought her a sensible ally of proved endurance. She learned how to light a campfire in the pouring rain, to make packing meal into gruel, to hold a candle steady while a surgeon sawed off a leg. She did not wince in a moment of horror. And she was possessed of a rare sense of humor, which she applied at times to desperate situations. Clara's quick wit and pungent repartee went down well with the soldiers. Toward the end of her life she said that of all her qualities the one that had served her best was her sense of humor. It had helped her over many rough places.

Most of the time she worked alone, meeting the immediate necessity with little regard for red tape or official procedure. As the army became better organized there was less leeway for her services. But in the early days of the war her close timing and choice supplies made her welcome everywhere. Her own sense of order and system contributed to her success. Things were perfectly packed. Her forces were concentrated. She got to the front before anyone knew what she was doing. She often had inside information and used it with discretion. In the field she effected distribution with a minimum of fuss and confusion. With Henry Wilson standing behind her, Clara had generals and brigade surgeons co-operating with her to the hilt. When she met opposition from petty officials, she promptly carried her case to the top. This was to become a lifelong habit, taking her at times as far as the inner sanctum of the White House.

## CHAPTER IV

## LANTERNS IN THE CORNFIELD

CLARA BARTON was at the battlefield of Antietam before the first gun was fired. She did not leave it until the last of the wounded had received care. She was warned on September 13, 1862, by one "whom she never dared to name" to get to Harpers Ferry without delay. There was work to be done. But the garrison there fell easily to Stonewall Jackson's men and, looking for one battlefield, Clara found another—Antietam.

On this occasion Major Rucker gave her an army wagon. No other woman was allowed to go, but Cornelius M. Welles and three other men accompanied Clara. They left on a Sunday morning, and she watched her cavalcade drive up to her door at 488½ Seventh Street with an alert sense of its novelty:

You . . . will scarcely appreciate the sensation with which I watched the approach of the long and high, white-covered, tortoise-motioned vehicle, with its string of little, frisky long-eared animals, with the broad-shouldered driver astride, and the eternal jerk of the single rein by which he navigated his craft up to my door.

Clara superintended the loading of the wagon and last of all she found niches for herself and the four men who were to go with her. It took some maneuvering to straighten out the string of restless mules and turn the corner into Pennsylvania Avenue, "in full gaze of the whole city in its best attire, and on its way to church." Clara had not given much thought to her own wardrobe that day. "I took no Saratoga trunk," she reported, "but remembered, at the last moment, to tie up a few articles in my handkerchief."

All day long they traversed the hills of Maryland and when darkness fell built a campfire, had supper, and retired for the night.

Next day they traveled through the debris of war. Dead horses lay by the wayside. Fainting men staggered along, hungry, beaten, demoralized, survivors of the battle fought the night before at South Mountain. Studying them, Clara decided that they lacked not only physical strength, but also confidence and spirit. "And why should they not? Always defeated! Always on the retreat! I was almost demoralized myself! And I had just commenced."

In her practical way she wasted no time in getting to work giving aid. At each stop made by the army train she bought all the bread the shopkeepers would sell her, then cut the loaves into slices and doled them out to the exhausted soldiers as the wagons bumped along. Soon she was sharply aware of the battle fought the night before when she "found their wheels crushing the bodies of unburied slain."

She left her wagon to clamber over hills and ledges looking for wounded survivors. "Not one remained," she noted, "and, grateful for this, but shocked and sick of heart, we returned to our waiting conveyance." She had to find her way through a drove of cattle, assigned as rations for the troops, in order to get back to her wagon. Clara was irked by her situation, conscious that in the hour of need she would be much to the rear. Ammunition came first in the train; then food and clothing; lastly, hospital supplies for the wounded. She saw how belated aid would be and resorted to strategy. When the train settled down for the night she "found an early resting place, supped by our camp fire, and slept again among the dews and damps" but only until one o'clock in the morning. At that hour she roused her party and persuaded her teamsters to pull out of line, drive through the woods, and move ahead to a better position in the regular supply train.

By daylight Clara's party had gained ten miles and was up with the artillery, in advance even of the ammunition. She followed the cannon closely all day and by nightfall found herself within range of "two armies lying face to face along the opposing ridges of hills that bound the valley of the Antietam." The smoke of a thousand campfires blurred the scene. The air was stifling and Clara had a "sense of impending doom":

In all this vast assemblage I saw no other trace of woman-kind. I was faint, but could not eat; weary, but could not sleep; depressed, but could not weep. So I climbed into my wagon, tied down the cover, dropped down in the little nook I had occupied so long, and prayed God with all the earnestness of my soul to stay the morrow's strife, or send us victory —and for my poor self—that he impart somewhat of wisdom and strength to my heart—nerve to my arm—speed to my feet, and fill my hands for the terrible duties of the coming day—and heavy and sad I waited its approach.

The Confederates opened fire at dawn and "Fighting Joe Hooker" ordered his line to advance. Clara, up on the hill with field glasses, watched the scene all around come alive as daylight spread over the winding Antietam, with the hills hazily outlined on either side. In later years, when lecturing, she grew rhetorical over "the dusty forms of 160,000 men risen like Old Scots from the heather!" Soon the smoke of battle obscured the scene as canisters and twenty-pound Parrotts mowed down the advancing men. She hurried down the hill and started her own little cavalcade when she learned that reinforcements were being sent to aid General Hooker, who was in trouble far to the right.

"Follow the cannon!" Clara ordered on this occasion, with little knowledge of where it might lead. Her wagon lumbered along for miles, winding up at the famous cornfield of Antietam and stopping "in the rear of the last gun, which completed the terrible line of artillery which ranged diagonally to the rear of Hooker's army." Clara always claimed in later years that "only a garden wall separated us."

The fighting in this area had stopped at about ten o'clock and for the last two miles they had been passing wounded men. Hundreds lay dead in the mutilated corn that half concealed the house and barn for which Clara headed. Her arms were filled with stimulants and bandages as she followed a path to a wicket gate leading into the yard, and came face to face with her friend, Dr. Dunn.

He threw up his hands in astonishment. "God has indeed remembered us. How did you get from Virginia here so soon—and again to supply our necessities? And they are terrible."

The attending surgeons had nothing but their instruments and the small amount of chloroform they had brought in their pockets. They had torn up all the sheets they could find in the house, and now lacked even a bandage, rag, lint, or string, while the wounded men were bleeding to death. Four tables had been rigged up on the piazza and on each lay a wounded soldier under chloroform. Clara saw at a glance that the surgeons were using green corn leaves for dressings on the raw wounds.

"With what joy I laid my precious burden down among them, and thought that never before had linen looked so white, or wine so red," she later recalled. Supplies were far to the rear. They could not be brought up until the fate of the day was settled, lest they fall into enemy hands. "That was the point I always tried to make," Clara maintained, "to bridge that chasm and succor the wounded until the medical aid and supplies should come up. I could run the risk; it made no difference to anyone if I were shot or taken prisoner; and I tried to fill that gap."

Her system worked miraculously on this occasion. Her men unloaded the wagon and brought up everything that "the good women of the country had provided." More and ever more of the wounded were brought in from the stripped cornstalks, and Clara flitted between the piazza where the surgeons worked and her improvised cooking arrangements. She administered chloroform under a doctor's direction until the food problem became overwhelming.

At two o'clock she was told that the last loaf of bread had been cut and the last cracker pounded. But luck was with her. She had twelve cases of wine in her supplies. By this time she had learned to rely greatly on liquor for the wounded, both as stimulant and anesthesia. It was her standard custom to give fainting men bread sopped in wine. And in later engagements she deadened their senses with liquor to tide them over their jolting journeys in wagons along rough roads.

On this occasion it developed that although nine of her cases of wine were packed with sawdust the remaining three, by chance, were lined with Indian corn meal. "My men were almost superstitious over that," Clara related, feeling that she had been blessed with a miracle. "If it had been gold dust it would have seemed poor by comparison." Moreover, three barrels of Indian meal and a bag of salt were found in the cellar of the house. There were three or four kettles in the kitchen and Clara went to work at once making gruel.

A Wisconsin surgeon who helped her that day pictured her a

score of years later as having organized an independent Sanitary Commission of one, traveling with a "Prairie Schooner" loaded with medical stores, necessities, and delicacies for the sick. This was the view he got of her at Antietam:

With sleeves rolled up to the elbows (I'm not certain whether sporting an apron or not), with dress skirt turned up and that portion which should normally constitute the bottom, pinned around her waist, a lady of pleasing countenance stood beside a huge iron kettle hung or placed otherwise over a roaring fire, using a ladle to stir something like a barrel-full of soup, which, by the frequent tasting she appeared to be seasoning, to make it palatable to the hundreds of wounded heroes. . . .

Clara came closest to losing her life at Antietam as she stooped to give a wounded man a drink. She raised him with her right arm and was holding the cup to his lips with her left hand when she felt a sudden twitch of the sleeve of her dress. In her own words: "The poor fellow sprang from my hands and fell back quivering in the agonies of death. A bullet had passed between my body and the right arm which supported him, cutting through the sleeve and passing through his chest from shoulder to shoulder."

There was no more to be done for him, so Clara left him to his rest. She never mended the hole in her sleeve. "I wonder if a soldier ever does mend a bullet hole in his coat," she speculated. There were to be others in her clothing before her war work was over.

As many of the men as possible were carried into the barn for protection from random shot, although the battle now raged distantly and to the left. There Clara found a man in agony with a ball buried superficially in his right cheek. He begged her to remove it. She said she would get a surgeon. But the youth said none would come. His was a trifling wound and they were all too busy. Clara hesitated for a moment, then took out her pocket knife and went to work, although she "had never severed the nerves and fibers of human flesh."

A sergeant from Illinois, badly wounded in the thighs, lay alongside, watching her movements with interest. He raised himself to a sitting posture to hold the patient while she removed the ball, and washed and bandaged the young soldier's face. It was not what one might call a scientific operation, Clara commented. But it seemed to give relief.

The smoke was so dense by this time as to obscure her sight. The "hot sulphurous breath of battle dried our tongues, and parched our lips to bleeding." They were in a slight hollow and stray shells burst over their heads or buried themselves in the hills beyond. A third charge toward sunset on the line of artillery covering the Union infantry proved to be a grueling experience. "The tables jarred and rolled until we could hardly keep the men on them, and the roar was overwhelming," Clara observed.

Quiet fell with nightfall, except for the groans and cries of the wounded and dying, who lay everywhere. She left the barn and found the surgeon in charge of the old farmhouse sitting at a table in deep discouragement with his head resting on his hands. The room was dark but for two inches of candle guttering beside him.

"You are tired, Doctor?" she inquired, sympathetically.

"Tired!" he exclaimed. "Yes, I am tired of this inhuman incompetence, this neglect and folly, which leave me alone with all these soldiers on my hands, five hundred of whom will die before daybreak unless they have attention, and I with no light but two inches of candle."

Clara led him to the door and pointed toward the barn where "lanterns glistened like stars" beyond the silhouetted corn. She had learned a lesson on her last battleground of the danger of using naked candle ends while caring for men lying on litters of straw, and had brought with her an abundance of lanterns as well as candles on this occasion. Her men were now on their way to light the farmhouse, too. Soon lanterns hung in the "bare old rooms, on the porches, the fences and wagons. Candles were flickering in all possible places, and the work of surgeons, doctors and helpers went steadily on all through the night."

The thirty helpers Clara had assembled carried buckets of hot gruel for miles down the line to the wounded, many of whom were dying where they fell. On the third day the regular army supplies arrived, but the Sanitary Commission was already on the scene with impressive aid. By this time Clara was utterly exhausted and all her stock was gone. Her assistants put her to bed on the floor of her wagon, wrapped in an old coverlet, and she slept like the dead while being jogged back to Washington.

She arrived home with a fever. When she finally saw herself in a mirror her face was still "the color of gunpowder, a deep blue." It took her several days to pick up strength again, but one of her first calls was on Major Rucker to tell him what she could have done with more wagons. He told her to ask for all she required in the future. By this time Major Rucker was convinced of the value and timeliness of Clara's services. She was quick moving, practical, and resourceful. The army surgeons had begun to notice her. After Antietam he made a point of giving her fleet mules with mule breakers for drivers, so as to avoid capture if possible. These men were rough but brave. The Major asked Clara always to start from his headquarters, so that he could dispatch the train and give last-minute directions to the drivers. Along with General Amos Beckwith, Commissary General, he got into the habit of adding stores to her pile. Then the tangled mass of mules would straighten out and off Clara would go for the front, usually well forewarned of direction. She became something of an advance courier. At first she took women with her, as well as men helpers, but Rucker finally told her, according to Clara, that "no other woman could stand what I would and she would become helpless on my hands and cause me more trouble instead of less."

She soon recovered from the strain of Antietam and later in October was secretly alerted to set off again. A big engagement was in prospect. It was not enough for Clara to wait until the papers informed her of a battle fought or won. She aimed to be there at the moment when help was needed and the men were borne from the field. But on this occasion she had serious trouble with her mule drivers—a sulky group who wheeled into a field at four in the afternoon and refused to budge. She took a strong hand with the leader and ordered him to move on, or she would dismiss the team and replace them with soldiers. They moved forward resentfully until darkness fell, then settled down to camp for the night.

Clara used tact with them at this point. While they were busy with their mules she collected fence rails and kindled a fire. She cooked them a supper which was fit fare for a general, they later volunteered. She joined them and cracked some of her dry New England jokes as if nothing had happened. The drivers were won by this direct approach. Later that evening as she sat by her own campfire they approached her, looking "like a band of brigands, with the red glare of the embers lighting up their bare brown faces." They apologized most humbly, telling her frankly that they had been assigned against their will; that they had seen enough fighting for men who carried whips instead of muskets; that they had never heard of a train being in charge of a woman, and had decided to break up the combination. They now assured her there would be no further trouble.

They kept their word and became Clara's trusted allies. That night the leader hung a lighted lantern on top of her ambulance. He arranged the quilts inside for her bed, assisted her up the steps, buckled the canvas snugly outside, and dampened down the fires. Then he wrapped himself in his blanket and lay down on the ground a few feet away to guard the ambulance.

Before long Clara was to have her own trunk bed, a curiosity still to be seen in the Museum of the American National Red Cross. On the outside it resembles a trunk of the period, with leather thongs and stout hinges. Opened up, it constitutes a trencher bed, with space beneath for blankets. Clara was to use it both in battle and disaster areas.

She was to need these drivers in the weeks that followed. She caught up with Burnside's troops at Berlin, where one of her mules ran off the pontoon bridge, the wagon toppled down an embankment, its bows were broken, and the progress of the army was briefly delayed while Clara's equipage was set to rights. Again she was in the "endless train of a moving army," this time crawling toward Falmouth. There were frequent skirmishes along the way and for a time the Union Army lacked a base of operations, reinforcements, and supplies. Clara again became a purveyor of comforts and necessities for the sick. Her wagons functioned as hospital, larder, and kitchen. Her helpers bought fresh provisions as they journeyed and at night they kept their fires ablaze, while food for the next day was prepared. She was attached to General S. D. Sturgis' men, many of whom were from Worcester.

"Those bright autumnal days!" she wrote with zest. "And at night the blaze of a thousand camp fires lighting up the forest tops, while from 10,000 voices rang out the never ending chorus of the Union Army: *'John Brown's Body'*. . . ."

In some respects it was an invigorating march but Clara suffered intensely from a bone felon on her hand. She had been exposed to burns, bruises, and heavy frosts. Her hand was treated on the field, but when a batch of sick soldiers was sent back to Washington from Warrenton she accompanied them, intending to round up more supplies. She left Welles to follow the army, along with George Morton, Peter Stark, John Mills, and her nephew, Stephen A. Barton, who was with the Military Telegraph Corps. He was now Stevé to Clara, to distinguish him from her brother.

She had scarcely reached the capital when a message from Welles summoned her back: "We want more liquors and something to eat. Your place is here. Hundreds of wounded men but few to work. Come." With fresh stores Clara journeyed to the headquarters of the 2nd Division, which had settled in near Falmouth, and opposite Fredericksburg. General Sturgis had a supper and a "splendid serenade" arranged for Clara, welcoming her back. On December 8, 1862, with the snow deep on the ground, she noted that she had received calls from two generals that day and their campaign plans had differed radically. "General Burnside stood a long time in front of my door today, but to my astonishment *he did not express his opinion—*STRANGE!"

The uncertainties of army life had become a commonplace to Clara but action was at hand. Late on the night of December 12 she wrote to her cousin, Elvira Stone:

Five minutes time with you!—and God only knows what the five minutes might be worth to the may-be-doomed thousands sleeping around me.

It is the night before a battle. The enemy, Fredericksburg, and its mighty entrenchments lie before us . . . the river, between. At tomorrow's dawn, our troops will essay to cross, and the guns of the enemy will sweep these frail bridges at every breath.

The moon is shining through the soft haze with a brightness almost prophetic. For the last half hour I have stood alone in the awful stillness of its glimmering light, gazing upon the strange sad scene around me, striving to say, "Thy will, oh God, be done."

As Clara described it to Elvira, the campfires blazed around her with unwonted brightness. The sentry's tread was quick. The acres of little shelter tents were dark and still as death, but the light still burned in Major General E. V. Sumner's quarters. "Already the roll of the moving artillery is sounding in my ears," wrote Clara, "the battle draws near, and I must catch one hour's sleep for today's labor."

Fredericksburg turned out to be one of the most crushing and bloodiest engagements of the Civil War for the Union forces. After Antietam, General Lee had established an army of 78,000 men on the high bluffs of the Rappahannock River near Fredericksburg. The Army of the Potomac, numbering 120,000 men under General Burnside, held the north bank at Falmouth, occupying what Clara called a "little canvas city."

On December 13 she watched the desperate efforts of the Union engineers to lay their pontoon bridge across the river. As fast as the men fastened a few boats and moved on with brace and planks they were shot down by sharpshooters concealed in fishing huts and thickets. Balls came tearing across the river, crashing through trees, hitting the windows and doors of the Lacy House, where Clara waited. "And ever here and there a man drops in the waiting ranks, silently as a snowflake," she wrote.

A group of volunteers crossed first to clear the immediate banks while the engineers completed their work. Finally Burnside, "the man of honest heart and genial face" to Clara, ordered the guns to shell the city and troops poured across under heavy fire. The Confederates, strongly entrenched, with sharpshooters firing from cellars, repulsed six assaults by the Union men before Burnside finally gave up.

When the fight was at its height Clara was summoned across the river by a courier who brought her a "crumpled, bloody slip of paper, a request from the lion-hearted old surgeon on the opposite shore carrying the pencilled message; 'Come to me. Your place is here.'"

This appeal was from an old friend, Brigade Surgeon J. Clarence

Cutter, of the 21st Massachusetts Regiment. She was nursing a Rebel officer when the note arrived. She told him she must go. Dying, the youth warned her not to cross the river; that every street and lane was a trap. She would never come out alive, he whispered. Her mule drivers, the erstwhile mutineers, offered to go in her place. But Clara, warmly hooded, set off without a moment's hesitation and at once was plunged into one of the more hazardous incidents of her life. In her own words:

In twenty minutes we were rocking across the swaying bridge, the water hissing with shot on either side. . . .

An officer stepped to my side to assist me over the debris at the end of the bridge. While our hands were raised in the act of stepping down, a piece of an exploding shell hissed through between us, just below our arms, carrying away a portion of both the skirts of his coat and my dress, rolling along the ground a few rods from us like a harmless pebble into the water.

The next instant a solid shot thundered over our heads, a noble steed bounded in the air, and with his gallant rider, rolled in the dirt, not thirty feet in the rear! Leaving the kind-hearted officer, I passed on alone to the hospital. In less than a half-hour he was brought to me—dead.

Clara worked for Dr. Cutter all that night and the following day, retreating with the troops in a great storm on the night of the 15th, when they were sure that all of their wounded were back on the Falmouth side of the river. The confusion was indescribable. Actually, every house was a hospital, and Clara, mopping up the face of a soldier lying all but dead in a Fredericksburg church, stared with amazement into the anguished eyes of Nathan P. Rice, sexton of the Old South Church of Worcester.

Moving about from point to point in the beleaguered city, she was observed by Provost Marshal Marsena R. Patrick. He took her for a resident in distress and rode up to her with the remark: "You are alone and in great danger, Madam. Do you want protection?"

Clara assured him that she believed herself to be the best-protected woman in the United States.

Soldiers standing near by heard her and shouted: "That's so!" and cheered their homely angel. The General looked confused, then saw that he was talking to Miss Barton, and quickly got the point. "I believe you are right, Madam," he said, saluting her and riding off.

The aftermath of this engagement was grim. The Minié balls had done particularly savage work. Clara had to steel herself as she viewed the terrible wounds. The icy weather was another factor. Many lay uncared for in the snow. She succored a group of Confederate prisoners whose bloody clothing was literally frozen to the ground. An ax was needed to chop them free. They were brought into a cabin and an old chimney was torn down so that the heated bricks could be piled around the half-frozen men. They were wrapped in blankets and were given hot toddy made from a stock of confiscated liquor allotted Clara by Surgeon General William A. Hammond.

At this time she worked in tents, in houses, in hotels, churches, and in Lacy House, which had been converted into a hospital. Twelve hundred men were crowded into the stately old Virginian mansion that was part of the Fitzhugh property held by crown grant since 1690. The sideboards of solid rosewood held medical supplies. The butler's pantry was a storehouse. Huge old-fashioned fireplaces warmed the icy house. The wounded lay on floors, porticoes, corridors, and stair landings. Five rested on the shelves of a large cupboard, of whom two died and three lived to be removed. "Think of trying to lie still and die quietly, lest you fall out of a bed six feet high," Clara observed, her heart full of pity.

Years later, one of Dorothea Dix's nurses, Honora Connors, recalled Clara moving about among the wounded men of Fredericksburg with vigor and cheerfulness, singing in a none-too-melodious voice: "Rally Round the Flag, Boys." She recalled her wearing a blue dress and a cap, the only record of Clara ever appearing in anything resembling a nurse's uniform. Print skirts of durable material and warm jackets, with kerchiefs or hoods, were her standard uniform for the field.

There were few entries in Clara's diary at this time, but many notations on soldiers—their names, addresses, and injuries. Beside Northern names were such entries as "William Simmons, of the 13th Mississippi, at Lacy House" and "Thomas M. Thurman from

Decatur, Miss., leg amputated." She noted that "Captain Perkins of the 57th New York" was buried underneath a spice tree on the left of the walk in front of Lacy House.

Again Clara worked with the close personal touch, viewing the army in terms of individual men, with homes, families, and best girls waiting for them. She particularly loved the 21st Massachusetts Regiment and was the lifelong friend of Sergeant Thomas Plunkett, whose blood stained the regimental battle flag later hung in the State House in Boston. Both his arms were shot away at Fredericksburg, but he planted the flagstaff between his feet and hung on to the flag with his two shattered stumps. "The 21st had never lost their colors, but they had worn them out," commented Clara.

On her return to Washington she was summoned to Lincoln Hospital, where virtually every soldier in one ward had received some service from her at Lacy House. As she entered, seventy men saluted her. Those who could stand sprang to attention. Others raised themselves feebly in their beds to honor Miss Barton.

"Every man had left his blood in Fredericksburg—every one was from the Lacy House," wrote Clara. "My hand had dressed every wound—many of them in the first terrible moments of agony. I had prepared their food in the snow and winds of December and fed them like children."

It was at Fredericksburg, after hours passed at the bedside of Lieutenant Charles Newcomb, a Harvard graduate who had returned from Europe to enlist, that Clara quietly noted: "When I rose from the side of the couch where I had knelt for hours, until the last breath had faded, I wrung the blood from the bottom of my clothing before I could step, for the weight about my feet."

Clara was in wretched condition when she returned from Fredericksburg on a chilly, dreary day and climbed the stairs to her barren quarters, "shoeless, gloveless, ragged, and blood-stained." She wept when she found a box of clothing awaiting her from her friends in Oxford and Worcester. It held hoods, shoes, boots, gloves, skirts, handkerchiefs, collars, linen, and a dress made by Annie Childs.

She was invited by messenger to the joint residence of Senator Benjamin F. Wade and Schuyler Colfax, later Vice-President, for a reception in her honor. "I had only time to lay aside my army jacket, make myself presentable, and appear. Oh, the crowd and the wonderful evening," she commented. Several days later Colfax sent cat-loving Clara a sprightly kitten bowed with ribbon, resting in a basket.

She unthawed and basked in this attention, but underneath it all lay a deep weariness. She took note of the fact that she was now called the Angel of the Battlefield, but she protested that she was only one of many. Her role had been dramatic, true, but "too many women of the Union—oh, even of the South, deserve that title. But what a tag, what a pale fancy measured by the unspeakable shambles of Antietam or Fredericksburg!" she wrote, with a strong sense of the appropriate.

Years later Clara might view some of these events in a haze of battle heroics, but at the moment she was all too well aware of the agony and bereavement surrounding the experiences in which she had shared. The Union Army had lost 12,653 men and the Confederates 5,309 in an engagement which also cost General Burnside his post. After Fredericksburg he was relieved of his command and General Joseph Hooker took his place. Clara had lost one of her best friends in the field. But she now had a host of nameless allies. The Clara Barton legend had spread quite widely among the fighting men, so that she was hailed with salutes, cheers, and waving caps when she came into view. Generals did her honor, too. When asked in later years what she considered the most memorable personal experience she had, Clara recalled an incident when the soldiers honored her with a Sir Walter Raleigh gesture as they crossed a little creek.

Clara liked to walk and often left her wagon to tramp like the marching men. She was well used to mud but on this occasion she had four wagons loaded with supplies coming in the rear. She decided to wait and cross with them instead of splashing through water a foot deep. Suddenly a company captain halted his men in midstream and shouted: "Now, boys, there stands Clara Barton. I want every one of you to kneel on your right knees and let Clara Barton walk across the stream on your left knees."

With great good will they formed a human chain. Thus Clara crossed, dry shod and deeply moved. Four years after her death, when an attempt to memorialize her was under way in Congress,

General William H. Sears, of Kansas, entered this incident on the record as one of the many occasions on which Clara Barton's presence was noticed in Civil War campaigning. The General added: "I think that Clara Barton has shown by her distinguished services and achievements that she is the greatest of all women in this country, as measured by her services to soldiers in war. . . ."

## CHAPTER V

## DEATH IN THE SANDS

CLARA BARTON sailed toward Hilton Head in South Carolina on the *Arago* on an April day in 1863. She had shifted her base of operations when David was appointed Assistant Quartermaster of Volunteers and was assigned to Port Royal. Stephen was still marooned in North Carolina, a Union man in Confederate territory.

As they neared the dock a launch came out with officers bearing the news that Admiral Samuel F. Du Pont would start an attack on Fort Sumter at three o'clock that afternoon. Clara glanced at her watch and saw that the moment had come. She felt she "should sink through the deck," not from alarm, but because her Washington friends had told her before leaving that her arrival could bode nothing but woe for Charleston. "I had never missed finding the trouble I went to find and was never late," she gravely conceded.

There was promise of brisk action in Beauregard's stronghold, but the engagement that coincided with Clara's arrival was an abortive attack, quickly repulsed by the Confederates. Clara's first experience of naval siege seemed mild after the thunderous assaults and hordes of wounded men at Fredericksburg and Antietam. "It fizzled out," she noted. But she had seen worse retreats, "if this be one." She watched the ships returning from Charleston until the harbor was filled with craft, and the wharf turned blue with the uniforms of the disembarking men. She quickly learned that most of the Union ships had been disabled in the first hour's fire. From the start Clara was convinced that the resistance of Charleston would be formidable.

But while plans went forward for a combined attack by land and sea, all was quiet at Hilton Head, and Clara found herself in the unfamiliar role of an idle and pampered woman. She was now nearing forty-two, but at few points in her arduous life does she emerge as clearly in softened feminine guise as during this summer solstice at Hilton Head. Her fame had traveled ahead of her and she was received with interest and respect. Colonel John J. Elwell, the Quartermaster, looked at the delicately fashioned woman with the strong face and tried to associate her with her letter of introduction from Major Edward C. Preston: "The smoke of battle, the roar of artillery, and the shrieks of shot and shell do not deter her from administering to those who fall."

Clara's rooms were at headquarters and she shared the officers' mess. They showered her with bouquets of roses, orange blossoms, and magnolias. They offered her saddle horses and vied for her company on early-morning rides. Colonel Elwell, a Cleveland man, was laid up with a broken leg in a starched bandage. Clara became his nurse. She read him Henry Ward Beecher's sermons, sacred verse, and chapters from Kings and Psalms. He read Tennyson's "Locksley Hall" to her. She helped him prepare his monthly report as quartermaster and they spent hours discussing battle scenes and her father. Clara usually dined with the Colonel. The mess was good, offering terrapin soup, steak and chicken, all kinds of vegetables, and excellent puddings. Together they drove in General David Hunter's carriage along the beach almost to Braddock Point, and home through the woods by way of picturesque Moss Lane.

After Colonel Elwell, her particular friend was Captain Samuel T. Lamb, the Assistant Quartermaster, whom she found "so good, and so modest, and well-bred and social and high-minded, that his acquaintance could not fail of affording pleasure to anyone, and he is an excellent friend to have." He had two sons at the post—Frank, chief telegraph operator, and Charles, clerk for his father. Her own nephew, Sam, who had broken away from his father Stephen in North Carolina, was now on the scene, too.

Captain Lamb was Clara's favorite riding companion but he had to get up at half past four in the morning to keep pace with her. Her dark hair blew from under her kerchief as she rode. Her sallow skin was becomingly tanned. On one occasion they galloped five miles in twenty minutes, crossing the creek up to their saddles in water, and ending up in the woods, where Clara, straight from her horse's back, plucked blackberries from vines twisting high up on the trees. Back at headquarters she made a blackberry shortcake with them before breakfast.

"I am enjoying such horseback rides as seldom fall to the lot of ladies," she wrote home, asking for a riding costume and a "leaping English saddle." Clara had changed her favorite bay for a jet-black horse, and she could not decide whether a black or navy-blue riding costume would look best with the new mount. All this concern on Clara's part must have astonished Annie Childs, to whom she left the decision as to "which would look the most genteel." She also wanted riding gauntlets, a slate-colored corset, some prints and ginghams, a new black veil, two dozen linen collars, and some cotton hose. Her "old extemporized rig had lasted beyond all human expectations," she observed.

It was Christmas before her things arrived, and Sam wrote North before then that Clara's attire caused him much embarrassment. She was scarcely outfitted as a New England lady should be, and needed "complete new paraphernalia." It was wounding to *his* feelings, said Sam, for his aunt to be in almost hourly contact with high commanders and representatives of the Sanitary and Christian Commissions, wearing such garments.

Both Sam and Clara welcomed the big box of attire that finally arrived. "The nicest beaver and ostrich plume that I ever saw!" Clara exclaimed with delight. Annie Childs had refurbished her handsomely. She wrote of the "splendid dress" that Annie had made and apologized for being so unfashionable in her tastes, always wanting her skirts down to her heels when no one else wore them so. She was pleased with the ruffling, the collars and cuffs—"just the thing for saddle or parlor"—and her fine new corsets. Clara was sufficiently attentive to the fit of her basque to have two little pouches, stuffed with cotton wool and finished with drawstrings, inserted in her chemises. One of these garments is still to be seen in an old trunk at her former home in Maryland.

Clara had congenial relations with the officers' wives at Hilton Head, too, and accompanied a group of them on an expedition to Paris Island. There she met Mrs. Frances Dana Gage, the suffrage worker who was to be one of her closest friends for years to come. The blackberries in this region were "dense as a black velvet carpet, the orange trees drooped with fruit and the magnolias were in bud," Clara noted, responsive to the lush beauty of her surroundings.

She visited the plantation where John Smith, the English colonist, landed in 1607, and found it the "most beautiful grove of live oaks" she had ever imagined, and a paradise of flowers. There was something idyllic about all this for Clara after the bloodshed she had seen. Such leisure, such freedom, such feminine gratification were rare in her life. But her rigid conscience soon began to trouble her. "What a life," she wrote in her diary, "and I am fearful that I should be in some other spot. . . ." And again: "I fear I may be spending time to little purpose. No one really needs me here. . . . All things conspire to give me an impression that this is not a sphere of usefulness for me. . . . I cannot feel settled to remain here without some object and I can see nothing. . . . I feel out of place. . . ."

Her moods swung back and forth. Every time the *Arago* came in she felt she should board it and leave for a more active field. Stories kept drifting in of the solitary capture of boats, and sporadic naval activity. Clara wrote to Henry Wilson describing her situation. She gave reading lessons to the Negro children at headquarters and visited the sick. She took comfort from being able to chat with three hundred convalescent soldiers on board the hospital ship *Cosmopolitan* bound for New York from Beaufort. As usual, she spotted a familiar face—Fred Davis from South Brookfield. Charles A. Page, of the New York *Tribune*, arrived with tales of Clara at Fredericksburg, quoting General Patrick as saying he had quite expected her to be shot.

Another editor friend, T. W. Meighan, wrote urging her to use her influence in favor of an immediate peace. She answered him sternly on June 24, 1863:

My business is stanching blood and feeding fainting men; my post the open field between the bullet and the hospital. I sometimes discuss the application of a compress or a wisp of hay under a broken limb, but not the bearing and merits of a political movement. I make gruel—not speeches; I write *letters home* for wounded soldiers, not political addresses. . . .

A week later Clara was riding along the Braddock Point Road with a "party of military men" when a chance remark made her feel that too much happiness had fallen to her lot. She decided then that she must return to the "stern duties of life" and give up the "gentle care" she was receiving. "I wept long and fear I was poor company," she wrote. "The moon rose high, the clouds followed a thunderstorm such as I had never seen. We tried to outride it."

Tough as she was in action, Clara wept rather readily under any form of emotional stress. Joy drew her tears as easily as sorrow. The matter soon was settled for her with the outbreak of large-scale hostilities in July. When Admiral J. A. Dahlgren, relieving Admiral Du Pont, established a beachhead on Morris Island in co-operation with the military forces under Major General Quincy Adams Gillmore, Clara knew where she was needed and headed at once for the area of trouble.

At dusk a band serenaded her at the water's edge and closed with three cheers for Miss Barton—the "Florence Nightingale of America." The officers offered her wine and lemonade. She was now the "Daughter of the Regiment," the "Angel of the Battlefield," the "Florence Nightingale of America." Clara was mildly skeptical of all this applause. It did not turn her head. "I wish I deserved all the praise they award me," she wrote in her diary.

General Gillmore, with whom she had dined a few nights earlier on the *Fulton*, gave her the necessary passes and his boat crew took her over the inlet landing on Morris Island to an advance beach hospital. They went past the old lighthouse which was being shelled from Fort Sumter at the time. "The firing was steady but not terrific," commented Clara. They turned down the beach to Dr. John C. Craven's hospital. He cleared a tent for Clara and there she met Dr. Augustus C. Barlow, whom she had also encountered at Cedar Mountain. She was with old friends again.

The preliminaries for the assault on Battery Wagner had already begun, and Clara went to work at once on the early casualties, doling out hard crackers and any supplies she could find. For the next few days they waited for the ironsides to appear over the bar. Just before the attack Clara rode to where the *Philadelphia* was berthed, to dine with the captain. He had a ladder put out for her. "I stepped from my horse to it, climbed up, dined, stayed till half past two," Clara reported. On this occasion she was given permission to leave her possessions aboard the ship because of the danger of being shelled out. But she kept herself mobile with her ambulance, horses, and her own personal saddle, always in readiness at the hospital.

Clara was never to forget the bombardment of Battery Wagner during July. She watched it from Lookout Hill. Long afterward she would describe it in her lectures, with various rhetorical flourishes:

I saw the bayonets glisten. The "swamp angel" threw her bursting bombs, the fleet thundered its cannonade and the dark line of blue trailed its way in the dark line of belching walls of Wagner. I saw them on, up, and over the parapets into the jaws of death, and heard the clang of the death-dealing sabers as they grappled with the foe. I saw the ambulances laden down with agony, and the wounded, slowly crawling to me down the tide-washed beach. . . .

Many of the men fell from the parapet into the fort. Colonel H. S. Putnam, scorched with flame and soon to die, appeared on the topmost parapet, shouting for reinforcements. Clara found among her patients Western troops, men from New England, and many of the Negro soldiers led by Colonel Robert G. Shaw.

Despite his bad leg Colonel Elwell galloped up the beach through the surf and fire under the wall of the blazing fort. Rising in his saddle, he shouted, "How goes the fight?" and cheered on the combatants. He was shot down 150 yards from the fort. Waking up some hours later in the hospital he was aware of a woman bathing his temples and fanning his face. "Clara Barton was there, an angel of mercy doing all in mortal power to soothe my pain."

Colonel Elwell credited her with saving the lives of General A. C. Voris, of Akron, Ohio, and of General M. D. Leggett, of Connecticut, in this engagement. When a shell hit General Leggett in one leg, she sprang to his side, tore off a strip of petticoat, improvised a tourniquet, and held the bleeding fragments in place until a surgeon could amputate his leg. She pressed drops of brandy between his lips during this ordeal. For years Clara wore a heavy gold chain sent to her by General Leggett after the war. Twenty years later, General John B. Dennis gave the New York *Daily Graphic* his recollections of Clara in this area. He remembered her as the only woman present, and particularly noticed her attending to the Negro soldiers. She stayed on the scene right through the shelling and helped to get the more seriously wounded sent off in ships.

Her diary thinned during these few days of concentrated effort. The only gaps in Clara's consistent record of her own life came during such periods as these, or when she was having a breakdown. Two days after the bombardment, she wrote: "Much the same calls. Did what I could. Cannot give details as I have neglected to keep up my journal in my haste to do, and all the inconveniences I have to suffer in the way of being able to get anything ready for the men to eat."

The regiments were settling in again. Clara soon found familiar faces, including Samuel Kirk, from Rhode Island, whom she called her baby, "so young but brave," his hand burned, his arm broken in three places, his little finger blown off. He wept because she could not leave in the ship with him, and she wrote to his father, preparing him for the boy's return.

That night a heavy shell landed among the men and two New Yorkers were brought in, savagely wounded. One had his leg blown off. The other's face was cut open from ear to nose "like a butchered hog," according to Clara, who was always realistic and often rustic in her similes. She thought them too desperately wounded to live. But Dr. M. J. Kittinger operated, with Dr. Barlow assisting. "I covered them with rubber blankets," Clara wrote. "It rained and was cold. I was astonished to see how comfortable they seemed after dressing and being laid away. I went in with the doctor to see them in the evening. Both were sleeping."

Difficult days now were in store for Clara. She passed the next eight months on this lonely sand bar, through operations focusing on the forts of Moultrie, Johnson, Wagner, and Sumter. It was perhaps her most sustained and arduous stretch of service. She could not vary it with trips back to Washington. The sun and sand stung her always sensitive eyes. Her feet ached from walking along the beach, or wading ankle deep in water. The nights were cold. She grew thin and haggard and had nasal and bronchial trouble. In her own words she was "scorched by the sun, chilled by the waves, rocked by the tempest, buried in the shifting sands, toiling day after day in the trenches, with the angry fire of five forts hissing through their ranks during every day of those weary months."

Three or four men assisted her. They boiled water in the lee of a sand hill. They distributed coffee and doled out dried fruits, farina, and desiccated milk and eggs. Nursing was difficult, for sand mingled with blood in every wound. Tent pins would not hold fast in the high winds and often even this light shelter overturned. Her only compensation was the occasional beauty of Morris Island—the ocean on all sides, "the water as blue as romance could paint it, and literally filled and glowing with phosphorescent light."

But in her shift from Hilton Head to the more active area of Morris Island, Clara's individualistic methods soon landed her in trouble. Dorothea Dix's nurses, well entrenched at the regular hospital, were critical, since she was a free lance working around the outskirts. A few of the doctors failed to back her up, a new experience for Clara. She was intent solely on the comfort and well-being of the soldiers, and deplored the commissariat but held her peace about it rather than cause trouble.

She was very ill herself through most of August. Her own food consisted of the "wormiest, mouldiest crackers I had ever seen an army insulted with." Her drink was the tidewater that leaked through the loose sand. But her many friends at the Quartermaster's Depot saw to it that she was properly equipped with tents and good supplies on her return to duty. On September 5 Sam wrote enthusiastically to Elvira Stone describing Clara's bountiful supplies and adding: "To think of establishing oneself in range of hostile guns, and administering comfort to the wounded and solace to the dying may be romantic, but it requires the heart and nerve that Clara alone of a thousand possesses to calmly meet the stern realities that heap themselves like thorns, in the pathway of the angel of the battlefield."

Clara was deeply hurt when her fine new tents were commandeered by some of the medical officers in an effort to freeze her out. Her friend Lamb wrote from Hilton Head that they were thieves. Colonel Elwell was incensed and urged her to return to the Port Royal area, where she would receive appropriate treatment. But Dr. Kittinger, always her ally, urged her to stay, found quarters for her to the rear of the hospital, and saw Clara re-established. It was only a temporary measure, however. On September 15 she received official notice that her services were no longer required, since the sick and wounded would be sent immediately to Beaufort. She was thanked for the benevolence that led her "to sacrifice so many comforts by residing at the actual scene of conflict," but in view of the crowded condition of the island it was thought best that she should leave for Beaufort.

Clara was outraged. She complied but balked at going to Beaufort. Instead she went back to Hilton Head and wrote the commanding general a full explanation of her position, intentions, and proposed labors. His reply was sharp and unfriendly. Her *humanity* was called to account, Clara sadly noted.

She had no wish to go to Beaufort for several different reasons. The hospitals there were supplied by the Sanitary Commission. They were also Miss Dix's province. "I should be out of place there," she maintained. Each hospital would be labeled "no admittance" to her. The surgeons "would bristle like porcupines at the bare sight of a proposed visitor." She now knew from experience that she would be coldly excluded. Should she prepare her food and thrust it against the outer walls? she asked. Should she tie her bundle of clothing and creep up and deposit it on the doorstep and slink away like a guilty mother? "I feel that my guns are effectually silenced," Clara concluded. "My sympathy is not destroyed, by any means, but my confidence in my ability to accomplish anything of an alleviating character in this department is completely annihilated."

In short, Clara had become a troublesome supernumerary in this area, with Miss Dix and the Sanitary Commission in full control. Moreover, the medical organization of the Army and Navy had strengthened with time and experience. Her methods, so effective in the field at the time of actual combat, so unorthodox in their urgency, were not attuned to hospital routine. Clara had established a world of her own on the battlefield and at times made herself answerable only to God.

She was helpless in the midst of petty bickerings and obstructionist tactics. It was not in her nature to fight back on her own behalf. By December 3 she had come to the conclusion that "between the surgical regulations and the supreme authority of Miss

Dix, what failed of being done must go undone." But her work was by no means ended. Her thoughts turned again to the North. "I must seek a freer atmosphere, where one can be allowed to work for a needy soldier without committing an indiscretion meriting disgrace."

Heading back for Washington she reflected sadly on the months of strain and hardship, and also the golden interlude that had been hers in the region of Charleston. The military picture was bleak. "We have captured one fort—Gregg—and one charnel house—Wagner—and we have built one cemetery, Morris Island. The thousand little sand-hills that glitter in the pale moonlight are a thousand headstones, and the restless ocean waves that roll and break upon the whitened beach sing an eternal requiem to the toil-worn, gallant dead who sleep beside."

But Charleston still stood firm in its defense, and wrecked Fort Sumter remained a Confederate prize.

## CHAPTER VI

## THE CONFLICT ENDS

"ABRAHAM LINCOLN's careworn face is very dear to me," wrote Clara Barton a few days after she had bowed to the "great, sad-eyed Commander" at a levee early in March, 1864. Her dignified figure was now conspicuous in any Washington gathering, for Miss Barton had achieved her own measure of fame. She made a point of attending the levees when not "out on a scout." Her political instincts were strong and she had great personal respect for Mr. Lincoln, although she was quite convinced that his wife was insane.

Clara, who was also an admirer of General John C. Frémont, and was willing to support either man, was stoutly behind the party ticket and wrote to Mrs. Gage shortly after the levee:

I *honor* Mr. Lincoln and I have believed, and still do, that his election was ordained, that he was raised up to meet this crisis, but it may also be that *no one* man could be constituted who should be equal to both the beginning and enduring of this vast, this mighty change—the same mind that could guide safely in the outset may be too slow now, for war has had its effects upon us. . . . I can trust either President Lincoln or General Frémont—on some accounts a change would be well. I think it would root out the traitors more effectually. . . .

A month later Clara sat in the gallery of the House of Representatives, watching Lincoln's rugged face with interest as he listened to the Rev. George Thompson speak. The English abolitionist, banished by Jackson in 1835, had once been mobbed, stoned, and burned in effigy in the country that now honored him. He tottered under the thunderous applause that greeted him, and Clara feared he would collapse from emotion as he faced his legislative audience, with "America free from the shackles of slavery." She was relieved when the "rich melody of his voice filled every inch of the vast Hall." Clara found his endorsement of Abraham Lincoln "one of the most touching and sublime things I have ever heard uttered."

John Brown's brother Frederick sat beside her in the gallery, "evidently proud of the gallows' rope that hung old John Brown." His eyes glistened, his lips were compressed as he applauded Thompson. Clara had always been critical of the raid and the indignation meetings that followed, but the war years had made her more tolerant of the extremists. She left the Capitol with Brown and they "took a cream at Simond's." Two days later they strolled together in the Congressional grounds. It was an idyllic spring day, and Clara, whose spirits had been low, was stimulated by this brief communion with nature. Constitutionally she preferred country to city life, fields to pavements. She often walked with her men friends early in the morning, discussing politics and army affairs in the flowering beauty of the Washington spring and summer. On this occasion she forgot the battlefields long enough to enjoy her surroundings to the full:

Before entering our ears were ravished with the melody of birds, more bewitching than can be described. . . . We sat down on the step of Wm. Wirt's monument and partook of the little breakfast we had brought and rose and roamed still on—the myrtle was in full bloom, and the daffodils were coming out. I gathered some, and also took from a tree some runners of ivy and wrapping them in a paper we turned our steps toward home.

But Clara's moods swung suicidally low that spring. She was suffering intense reaction from her stern labors in the field. "Have been sad all day," she wrote on April 18. "I cannot raise my spirits. The old temptation to go from all the world. I think it will come to that some day. It is a struggle for me to keep in society at all. I want to leave all."

Her days had been dull since her return from the South in January. She pasted white satin-striped paper on her walls, arranged her battle relics in a cabinet, and disposed her chairs for the comfort of her visitors. She darned stockings, dressed her long and lovely hair with affectionate care, and cleaned closets to pass the time. "I was never so quiet in my life," she brooded. To ease her unrest she went to market and with a fleeting sense of destiny entered a stray note in her diary: "It may be interesting at some future day to know that I paid fifty cents for a pound of butter this morning."

General Grant's arrival in town to take command of the army in person raised Clara's hopes. "This decided me to make an effort to establish myself," she wrote. "Something more active I must have." She set off for the Capitol at once to see her friend Henry Wilson. She had several matters to discuss with him. First, she wanted passes to get back into action. Next, she wanted her cousin, Corporal Leander A. Poor, appointed assistant quartermaster, with orders to support her in the field. Third, she wished to clear up her status with the Patent Office.

Clara told Wilson she was greatly mortified because the Republican party had not restored her to her old position in the Patent Office, instead of leaving her name on a negative list of temporary writers. Her actual income from this source, after she had paid a clerk named Edward Shaw for substitute work, had never been more than $25 a month, most of which had been spent on rent and army supplies. Clara was wholly without resources at this time, but "I who have run across stubble fields to carry water in hats and caps to dying men can still drink from a tin cup and be contented," she commented.

Wilson listened sympathetically and, as usual, told her that he would do what he could. But Clara's moves were uncertain. "I lack energy," she wrote. She had ceased to expect miracles. At this point the future founder of the Red Cross in America felt that she "had done with her efforts in behalf of others."

She considered the lecture platform as a source of revenue. "Sometimes I have almost a mind to go and talk like other ladies. . . . I know if I only retail what has passed under my eye it could not fail to interest." Again, she thought of writing for a living, and longed for the "power of pen to move men and women to wider, deeper thoughts and sterner actions." But early in April she wrote to Wilson: "I will find employment, satisfactory to myself, serviceable to my country and beneficial to mankind."

The rest of this letter was so bitter and unlike her that Wilson hurried round to her rooms at once and showed solicitude. She had not slept for forty hours and he found her in a bewildering mood. She showed an unexpected side of her character and was "pettish and difficult," behaving like a spoiled child. "I looked down, winked fast, bit my nails, drummed with my foot on the floor and wouldn't answer," Clara reported in her diary.

The chairman of the Senate Committee on Military Affairs was used to the vagaries of some of the sirens who haunted the Senate Gallery but he was much concerned to have sensible Clara Barton from Massachusetts behaving like a fool. However, when she wanted something her tenacity was overpowering. It was quietly exhibited, but had a toughness that none understood better than Henry Wilson. She was dogged rather than quarrelsome, an immovable force in face of opposition. He did not know, however—but Clara's diary reveals—that she kept a stern eye on him from the gallery when she sent him notes, to make sure that he read them instead of stuffing them into his side pocket, as he was apt to do when preoccupied.

Evidently her tantrum worked, for Corporal Poor received his appointment and, with a sudden change of mood, Clara decided that she "must take all steps to secure him to herself." She went straight to her old friend Rucker and a few evenings later was dining with Edwin M. Stanton. Next day she was importuning the Secretary of War by letter for a pass permitting her within army lines. She reminded him that she was not "some patriot young lady suddenly seized with a spirit of adventure." Artfully enough, she recalled her father's friendship with Andrew Jackson and her own vow to Captain Barton "to serve her country in its peril and strengthen and comfort the brave men who stood for its defence."

Dead silence ensued. There is no evidence that Stanton had warmed to Clara Barton up to this time or approved of her army operations. But he was cold to the Sanitary Commission, too. A gap in Clara's diary at this point is followed by a notation on May 2: "I was too unhappy and unsettled to write. I could get no passes and no one but myself appeared to care or think it was of much consequence."

Next day Colonel Joseph K. Barnes, the surgeon general who had succeeded Hammond, turned her down quite roughly when she sought medical supplies. Clara seemed to be out of favor with

the military authorities at this juncture. She went straight back to
Henry Wilson and her pass soon came by special messenger from
the ever-faithful Major Rucker. There was good reason to enlist
her services at this point, for Grant had just opened his campaign
in the Wilderness and the casualties were mounting. Clara was
swept back swiftly into the vortex of war. Her complaints were
heard no more. She was always at her best in action; at her lowest
ebb in periods of idleness. The Battle of Spotsylvania had changed
the picture for her entirely. Every helping hand was needed and
Clara Barton's was not the least of these.

Soon she was wading through the red mud of the boat landing at
Belle Plain, General Grant's supply base close to Fredericksburg.
Disembarking on the narrow ridge she was shocked by the scene
of mud, suffering, and confusion. The roll of wagon wheels had
ground the red clay soil to powder. Heavy rain had created a morass.
Clara viewed the entire basin as "one vast mortar-bed, smooth and
glassy as a lake, and much the color of light brick dust."

Stuck in this gluey sea were army wagons filled with wounded
men who were to be taken back to Washington by boat. They had
been driven from Fredericksburg that morning and had moved as
far ahead as the mud would allow them to proceed. Clara was outraged that the "poor mutilated starving sufferers of the Wilderness
who were pouring into Fredericksburg by thousands" should have
to undergo the added ordeal of being bumped along in army wagons
over ten miles of rough land to reach the boat landing.

She proceeded at once to tents set up on the ridge by members of
the Christian Commission, for whom she had recently been rounding up mattresses. The volunteers on this occasion were mostly
amateurs in the field, clergymen hastily summoned from their
churches by the desperate emergency. They had brought clothing,
reading matter, and crackers. Clara, experienced in such crises, took
hold at once and commandeered the services of a young minister.
Tossing him a passing bouquet, she told him that he "gathered the
brush manfully." But it took her own experienced eye to pick the
hollow beside a stump on the sopping hillside where a fire might
burn. Using two crotched sticks and a crane she soon had
camp kettles bubbling with the coffee that she had brought with
her.

The crackers were in barrels, and the young minister was at a loss as to how to distribute them. Practical Clara took two strips of linen, filled them with biscuits, and tied them, apron-wise, around her own and her companion's waists, thus leaving one hand for a kettle of coffee, and one free to pour and serve it. Thus equipped, they went down to the edge of the slope, Clara leading the way and plunging boldly into the muddy morass. It was nothing new for her to double up her skirts in the field when there was a job to be done. She noticed that the minister's pale face was now smudged with smoke; his delicate hands were grimy, but he slid cheerfully into the mud in her wake. Together they handed out coffee and crackers to as many of the wounded as they could reach close to the landing.

When Clara finally got to Fredericksburg she was startled by what she found. Stores and dwellings were barricaded. No orders had been issued to open houses and seize supplies. The city was all Secessionist, with no Union troops in occupation when the wounded were first brought in. Both the railroad and the canal leading from the city were closed. The six-mule army wagons reached so far out on the Wilderness road that Clara never found the end of them. Every wagon was loaded with wounded men. Some sat up on ammunition boxes. Amputees lay packed together like sardines. A few of the dead had been heaved out in the mud.

Clara saw at once that part of the torture for the wounded was the restless shuffling back and forth, hour after hour, of the stranded mules. She knew that this meant death for some of the amputation cases. Many of the wagons were damaged, their wheels broken, their hubs deep in mud. "You saw nothing of any animal below its knees," she observed.

This situation had been created largely through a change in orders when the army moved toward Spotsylvania. Wagons headed in another direction were ordered on to Fredericksburg, creating indescribable confusion through the sudden change in destination. A few of the "faithful Sanitary" had arrived but they were powerless. Some thirty army doctors were trying to cope with seven thousand wounded men. Most of the medical staff and all the supplies had gone on with the fighting troops. No provision had been made for such wholesale slaughter and "I believe it would be impossible to comprehend the magnitude of the necessity without witnessing it," Clara gravely concluded. She attributed much of the disorder to "improper, heartless, unfaithful officers" in immediate command of the city. One of the ranking men was convicted later as a traitor. Another dapper young captain, quartered in one of the finest mansions in town, announced in her hearing that it was a "pretty bad thing for refined people like the citizens of Fredericksburg to be compelled to open their houses, and admit these dirty, lousy common soldiers, and he *was not going to compel it.*"

The wounded were dumped in churches, factories, hotels, and public buildings, although some of the ranking officers were taken into the better homes. Clara walked into a dilapidated hotel and found five hundred men lying helpless on "bare, wet, bloody floors." As she passed they begged her for food but she did not have so much as a cracker to give them. They asked for cups that they might drink, and "I had no cup, and could get none." The pockets of some of the wounded had been ripped open by stretcher bearers who robbed them.

Clara was convinced that no hint of this confusion could have reached official Washington. By eight o'clock in the morning, when she could stand conditions no longer, she remembered "one man there, who would set it right, if he knew it, who possessed the power, and who would believe me if I told him." She demanded conveyance back to Belle Plain. By using all the pressure she could, she rounded up four fast horses and a light army wagon that took her ten miles at an unbroken clip "through field and swamp and stumps and mud." A steam tug took her back to Washington. She got home at dusk and at once sent a messenger for Henry Wilson. He arrived at eight o'clock, "saddened and appalled, like every other patriot, in that fearful hour by the weight of woe under which the nation staggered, groaned and wept."

He listened attentively to her story of suffering and faithlessness, said Clara, then hurried away "with lips compressed and face like ashes." By ten o'clock he was in touch with the War Department, summarizing what she had told him. The story was received with skepticism, since no requisitions had come from the military authorities commanding Fredericksburg. But Wilson held his ground. As Clara describes the incident:

It was then that he proved that my confidence in his firmness was not misplaced, as facing his doubters he replied: "One of two things will have to be done—either you will send some one to-night with the power to investigate and correct the abuses of our wounded men at Fredericksburg, or the Senate will send some one tomorrow."

This threat recalled their scattered senses.

At two o'clock in the morning the Quartermaster General and staff galloped to the 6th Street wharf under orders; at ten they were in Fredericksburg. At noon the wounded men were fed from the food of the city and the houses were opened to the "dirty, lousy soldiers" of the Union Army.

Both railroad and canal were opened. In three days I returned with carloads of supplies.

No more jolting in army wagons! And every man who left Fredericksburg by boat or by car owes it to the firm decision of one man that his grating bones were not dragged ten miles across the country or left to bleach in the sands of that traitorous city.

Whether or not Clara was solely responsible for this amelioration, the fact remains that the deadlock was broken, the wounded were rescued from their terrible plight, and one of the most inhuman chapters of the Civil War was ended.

For the rest of the month she worked in the field with intense concentration. Returning to Fredericksburg with a wealth of supplies she was held up at the wharf by minor officials, who questioned her papers. She flashed a letter from Henry Wilson and arrived triumphantly at the base with all her treasures. She doled out beef tea, eggnogs, and her famous gruel to the shattered men of the Wilderness campaign.

Clara had excellent relations with the surgeons and often gave practical suggestions for the soldiers' comfort as she assisted them. But while working in this area she exploded one day over an instance of "medical imbecility" when an army post doctor prescribed treatment for one of her patients that she believed to be responsible for his death. She protested the hourly combined dosage of whiskey, quinine, ammonia, and opium, when she saw the man become "crazy as a bear and all exhausted . . . full of dreadful dreams, thought he was dead and lost."

She consulted Dr. Henry G. Bates, a surgeon well known to

her. He concurred with her about the treatment but dared not interfere because of army regulations. "I begged that the dosing be
stopped for humanity's sake," Clara noted. "I knew he must die,
but could not tolerate that torture. I have seldom felt so indignant
as at the uncalled-for interference of the Post surgeon."

Drugs were used freely to deaden pain when they were available.
An opium pill or a quarter of a grain of morphine was standard
treatment and liquor was favored to rally patients in shock. After
surgery, it was customary to use opiates, liquor, and quinine, with
cold fomentations. Clara watched surgeons rub morphine into
wounds in the early days of the war, but by this time the medical
facilities of the battlefield had improved and the hypodermic syringe
was in use.

Since she rarely worked in the city hospitals and was often close
to the front, she was familiar with the grossest aspects of Civil War
medicine. In the course of three years she had hardened herself to
the sight of piles of severed arms and legs in the vicinity of operating
tents. She was used to seeing surgeons looking like brigands with
scalpels held between their teeth while they worked over bleeding
soldiers or probed for bullets with porcelain-tipped instruments. She
frequently applied chloroform by cone or napkin in a moment of
crisis, or tied a clean apron around the waist of a blood-smeared
surgeon.

Clara assisted at operations in hospitals, tents, churches, barns,
farmhouses, and out in the open, where the surgeons preferred to
work because of the light and the good air. She was handy with
sponge and basin and, like a girl of fifteen rather than a woman in
her forties, she would run fleetly across fields to streams for water
when there was any to be had. She would husband this precious
commodity, which often was lacking when it was most needed.
Sometimes she and the surgeons would go for two or three days
without washing their hands. Her ubiquitous hot coffee must have
saved many a soldier from dysentery, since it was often the substitute for tainted water. The Sanitary Commission urged the distillation or boiling of water and, in some instances, the military
hospitals were supplied with filters. Although there was no sound
conception of asepsis at the time, Clara put much faith in hot coffee
and strong toddy. No such refinements as distillation were possible

close to the battlefield and she came to view every trickle of water or a good downpour of rain as true manna from heaven.

Almost fanatical on cleanliness and order in her private life, Clara suffered over the dirty instruments pulled from plush-lined cases and used over and over again without proper cleansing; the sponges that fell on the floor, were rinsed in dirty water, and re-applied; the smeared aprons of the surgeons, and the filthy bandages which often were hard to remove. Pyemia, erysipelas, gangrene, typhoid, and dysentery were all too familiar to her, but her most lasting memories were of men lying bedded on straw while she tried to make them comfortable as they waited their turn on the operating tables. More often than not amputation lay ahead of them.

She became expert at helping to rig up emergency operating tables—a door torn from its hinges, a kitchen table in a farmhouse, three wooden chairs lined up in a Negro cabin, a wide shelf in a colonial manor, a bed of heated bricks covered with a rubber sheet, a cot with a pallet of straw, or whatever came to hand. She made ingenious use of tarpaulins and blankets, put warm socks on dying men, banked heated bricks around them, and fed them the wine, gruel, and eggnogs they so desperately needed.

Chloroform was used in 76 per cent of the Civil War surgical cases. It was less bulky than ether, worked fast, and was non-inflammable. But Clara had been on the scene more than once when neither anesthesia nor bandages were available, and she knew the horror of this situation. She was well schooled in the treatment of simple gunshot wounds. They were covered with wet or oiled linen, held fast by sticking plaster. She understood the importance of keeping all dressings wet by the drip method when there was water to be had. She was expert at applying poultices, could handle a tourniquet, and sometimes stemmed a spurting artery by holding tight with her thumb until help arrived. There were few emergencies she did not meet at one time or another. But her special gift lay in nourishing the men and helping their morale.

Remembering the leeches that had all but drained the life out of her ruddy brother David, she watched with dismay the blood-letting by lancet or leech sometimes prescribed in the early days of the war when there was massive internal hemorrhage. But this practice was abandoned as medical techniques improved in the field. Minor hemorrhages were usually treated with persulphate of iron, per-chloride of iron, tannic acid, turpentine, alum, or nitrate of silver, standard equipment in every medical knapsack.

Clara's ministrations extended to the personal comfort of the surgeons, too. She often prepared meals for them, setting up tables where they could pause for a few minutes and refresh themselves. She would use a sheet for a tablecloth, bringing a touch of civiliza-tion into a wilderness of death and suffering. She wrote down her own view of this on a May day in 1864 when Grant's campaign was swelling the casualty lists to mammoth proportions:

Got supper of boiled eggs, crackers, toast and tea for the men. Set the table with a sheet for a tablecloth. Dr. Lamb at the head and how my little supper did seem of relish to them. My little stove is a jewel.

By the end of May, Clara was back in Washington, and on the last Sunday of the month noted in her diary: "Wilson called pleas-antly—spoke of his interview with the Sect. of War and his resist-ance to his request that some one be sent to Fredericksburg at my suggestion. Said that that move was the cause of opening the Aquia Creek R.R."

Thus Clara learned that Stanton had hesitated to act on her complaint, and that the matter had been pushed through only on Wilson's insistence. Now he was helping her again. On June 21 she set off with an introductory letter to General Benjamin F. Butler, who had relieved General Gillmore at Fortress Monroe. Her diary entry on her visit is cryptic: "Need not note the interview, for I shall never forget it. I am satisfied with my success with Genl. Butler."

He became one of Clara's most enthusiastic supporters from that time on. He appointed her superintendent of the Department of Nurses for the Army of the James and assigned her to Point of Rocks, Virginia. He gave her passes to go where she wished and ordered his medical officers to aid her in every way. But she had little need for such authorization now. "So little inclination do they display to thwart me that I have *never* shown my 'pass and order' to an officer since I have been in the department," she noted.

Clara was informed that General Butler had said: "Honor any

request that Miss Barton makes without question. She out-ranks me." Again she flourished after the lean days of dissension and medical bickering in the Charleston area. She had more or less of a free hand, which always made her a more effective worker. She was "well received and nobly sustained" while with the Army of the James. Her old friend, Dr. Kittinger, was on the scene again. "In all my trials for the past two years he has stood faithfully by me, endorsing every act, willing to cover and forget every fault, and resent every injury," wrote Clara. "Others may be all that could be expected under the circumstances, but he has been more."

The patients changed constantly as boatloads left for Fortress Monroe. In the middle of July she accompanied one of these contingents and then went on to Washington for fresh supplies. She was back at her base in time to catch the repercussions from the explosion of the mined fort in front of Petersburg. She got off from City Point with her supplies *just in time* to avoid that terrible catastrophe." She was not "blown to atoms, but might have been and no one the wiser," she wrote to Frances Childs.

Once the flag of truce was flown and identification of the dead began, Clara worked over some of the wounded who had lain "perishing in the blistering sun—with no mortal power on earth great enough to reach them with a cup of water or a crust of bread." She was to see some of them die when they were brought in to her new base, for at the end of August Clara had moved up with the Tenth Corps close to Petersburg. She was stationed at the "Flying Hospital" immediately behind the front lines. The men injured in the explosion were among the first patients she encountered in this area. Most of their wounds were mortal and by request of the surgeons Clara made thick eggnogs and chicken broth for these desperately injured men. She had twelve hundred soldiers to feed at this point, for the cook and his assistant both had fever and she stepped into the breach and became a large-scale provider. It was all in the day's work. "We keep cheerful and toil on," commented Clara.

Her family in North Oxford read with interest of their battle prima donna, in striped print dresses and kerchiefs, dealing in such large scale operations as 700 loaves of bread for breakfast, 170 gallons of coffee, tea in wash boilers, 200 gallons of soup, 500 slices of buttered toast, 100 slices of broiled steak, and a wash boiler full of whiskey sauce for puddings. She made bread pudding and ginger-bread in quantity and as many as ninety pies at a time. She had a washtub full of codfish which she treated in the "old home way," so that the "Yankee soldiers cry when they taste it." But she was never too busy to stop and meet the whim of a pain-stricken soldier. Summing up one day's labor in this area Clara wrote:

I have had a barrel of apple sauce made today and given out every spoonful of it with my own hands. I have cooked ten dozen eggs, made cracker toast, cornstarch blanc mange, milk punch, arrow-root, washed hands and faces, put ice on hot heads, mustard on cold feet, written six soldiers' letters home, stood beside three death beds. . . .

Clara's powers of organization at last had official recognition. The army commissary was now in better order, too. The lean days when she did not have a cracker to pass around, or a cup from which to drink, were over. Her supplies were plentiful, her equipment good, and she did mass-scale cooking, ordering, and housekeeping with a masterly touch. "I begin to think I can 'keep a hotel,'" she boasted.

Again she found men from the 21st Massachusetts, her most be-loved regiment. "I would divide the last half of my last loaf with any soldier in that regiment, though I had never seen him," she noted. This warmth of feeling on Clara's part was returned by the men of the 21st. Their historian, Charles F. Walcott, wrote of her:

Our true friend, Miss Clara Barton, however, a 21st woman to the backbone, was now permanently associated with the regiment, and, with two four-mule covered wagons, which by her untiring efforts she kept well supplied with delicacies in the way of food and articles of clothing, was a ministering angel to our sick. General Sturgis kindly ordered a detail from the regiment of drivers and assistants about her wagons. And this true, noble woman, never sparing herself or failing in her devotion to our suffering men, always maintained her womanly dignity, and won the lasting respect and love of our officers and men.

It was in this area that Clara first came across a wounded Swiss youth, Jules Golay, who was to figure later in her Red Cross work. She nursed him tenderly, wrote to his family, and, after the war, was to have her first spark of interest in the Red Cross lighted in his Geneva home.

During this emergency Clara was quartered in a tent "bare as a cuckoo's nest." It had a dirt floor, a narrow straw bed, a three-legged stand made of old cracker boxes, and a wash dish. But it was not Clara's custom to cavil at field accommodations; only to remember them later as picturesque details. She fell ill, however, and afterward was moved into a log cabin, one of a row of Negro houses flanking the old stone mansion that served as hospital. The Tenth Corps had taken up quarters on a deserted plantation. Soldiers built her an arbor of cedar "so close and green that a cat couldn't look in." New floors were laid and carpeted, and the walls were papered. She had two floors and often brought in a badly wounded patient for special care. This was the most sumptuous home in all Clara's battlefield experience.

She had ready access to General Butler, quartered only a short distance away. She pictured him in his tent, "shaded by a few dried bushes and marked by a flag, dignified, wise and princely, and still, perhaps, the most kindly and approachable personage on the grounds."

He was never "Beast Butler" to Clara, who continued to view him as a benign and tolerant man. He was responsible at this time for reuniting her with her brother Stephen, who had stubbornly held his ground at Bartonville, although he had long since sent his helpers North. Clara had aided them in Washington, and some, including her nephew Sam, had at once entered the Union Army. When their father died Stephen was still incommunicado in Confederate territory, a grief to the entire family.

But he had stubbornly refused all of Clara's pleas to move North, even when she sent him a letter by Commander C. W. Flusser, of the North Carolina Fleet, who sailed up the River Chowan with gunboats to Bartonville and offered to take him away. Stephen insisted on staying to protect his property. Clara later read in the New York *Tribune* that he had been ordered to leave North Carolina for having sent his helpers North, and had then got into trouble for fighting the men who had come to challenge him. Now General Butler's men had picked him up forty miles from his home, where he had gone for medical supplies, and had thrown him into prison in Norfolk. All his possessions had been seized, including his papers and $1,000 in cash.

The news reached Clara on a chilly autumn day as the wounded were being brought in on stretchers and she was having "unusually sharp work." She had just sprung to the aid of a lieutenant, shot in the lungs. She was seated on a coil of rope, holding him in her arms until a surgeon could reach him, when an orderly rode up and handed her a letter.

Clara, with only one hand free, tore open the envelope with her teeth. It was from Sam, enclosing a letter from his father, Stephen, telling of his imprisonment. Clara read it with indignation. As soon as a surgeon took charge of her patient she stepped into an ambulance and was driven direct to General Butler's quarters. She showed him Stephen's letter. The General knew her brother of old.

"This is hard," he said. "What can I do for you?"

She begged to have him in her cabin. General Butler cautioned her to keep silent on the matter and he would have Stephen brought in. It was a delicate situation all round, since the suspicion of disloyalty clung to him because of his stubborn stand. When he arrived several nights later at her cabin door Clara could scarcely believe the evidence of her eyes. She remembered Stephen as a man of magnificent build and healthy countenance. Now he weighed 130 pounds. Thin white locks hung to his shoulders. He walked feebly with a cane. His face was ravaged and almost unrecognizable.

Clara was deeply moved and took him to General Butler, to whom he swore that he had never been a Rebel. The men who arrested him were called in and were thoroughly tongue-lashed by the General. For the moment Clara saw where Butler had earned his reputation as a tough man. "Then for once," she wrote, "I had the satisfaction of seeing and hearing General Butler try a case, and learned how more than hard must be the way of the transgressor who should fall into his hands."

Stephen's papers and money were promptly restored. He was given a pass to go anywhere within the Army of the James or to travel North, which he eventually did. But first he was nursed by Clara for six weeks until he had picked up strength. Together they knelt by his cot and prayed for Abraham Lincoln and his armies. Clara saw the drama of this:

And there, under the guns of Richmond, amid the groans of the dying, in the darkling shadows of the smoky rafters of an old Negro hut, by the rude chimney where the dusky form of the bondsman had crouched for years, on the ground trodden hard by the foot of the slave, I knelt beside that rough couch of boards, and sobbed "Amen" to the patriot prayer that rose above me.

The cannonading was continuous while Stephen rested in her cabin. When he went with her to her cooking tent, he marveled to see Clarissa the teacher, Clarissa the daredevil rider, turning out mammoth quantities of custard and applesauce while the guns roared. His little sister had traveled a long way from her early days of fear. He watched her closely and wrote home that she rose at half past six in the morning, spent most of the day superintending the cooking, took her meals at the surgeons' table, and rode on horseback once a week to the base hospital to receive the boxes and barrels of food and raiment constantly arriving from "the charitable people of our yet great nation." Stephen saw that Clara was an effective commissariat in herself.

Early in January, 1865, with the war in its closing phase, Clara left the base and returned to Washington to see Stephen, by that time a dying man. She attended a reception given by Mrs. Lincoln and had a long talk with Henry Wilson about army surgeons, commenting afterward: "I think their rank will be raised." Few knew more about them than Clara.

On February 10, a diary entry fixes the only recorded instance of Miss Barton and Miss Dix encountering each other head on. "Met Miss Dix at Junction, exchanged cards, promised to call. She went to Annapolis. I went to Washington."

These two notable Civil War figures must have studied each other with some degree of interest. Clara had had plenty of trouble with Miss Dix's nurses, and had learned to avoid areas where her command was supreme. Miss Dix, in turn, must have had her own opinion of Clara's solitary operations and dauntless ways. But Clara was large minded and nowhere do her papers suggest ill-will or a vindictive spirit. She was a diplomat in many respects and displayed surprising tact for one so matter of fact and forthright. However gloomy her diary references to Miss Dix's operations, they were always tinged with courtesy and respect. Years after the war she named her among the eight great women of her time. Dorothea's sphere was primarily that of the hospital. Clara always viewed herself against the larger canvas of the battlefield.

## CHAPTER VII

## MISSING MEN

A MONTH before his death Abraham Lincoln sent Clara Barton a letter that left historic echoes. It cleared the way for her to pursue her search for the missing men of the Union Army; to give recognition to the Unknown Soldier; and to establish a national cemetery at Andersonville, Georgia.

He wrote it on March 11, 1865, the day after her brother Stephen died. It gave her the sponsorship she needed for a plan that had grown out of her correspondence with soldiers' families. It was circulated all over the country and evoked thousands of letters.

So many inquiries about missing men had reached Clara as a result of her unique work on the battlefields that by this time she had decided the best service she could render her "country and humanity would be to collect and impart information respecting the lost." But the demands were overwhelming. "Ask Miss Barton" had become a routine phrase when someone from New England was reported missing. She felt that her plan should have government backing and that something so close to the welfare of his army would appeal to tender-hearted Abraham Lincoln. She was right. It did, when finally the matter was brought to his attention. But Clara had some hurdles to overcome first.

She went three times to the White House to talk to him about her plan, taking with her a petition in her finest copperplate script. On the first occasion he had already left for his afternoon drive and she turned away, bitterly disappointed. A friend had lent her furs and a becoming bonnet for her visit, since Clara was "in some anxiety about my dress in which to appear at the President's."

As she was leaving, Henry Wilson drove up by chance and he took the petition, saying he would give it personally to Mr. Lincoln at the first opportunity. Clara had a sleepless night, thinking that her good friend might be too busy to bother about such minor business, with the cataclysmic events gathering around him.

First thing in the morning she went to his hotel, took back her petition, and asked for a note to President Lincoln. Wilson promptly scribbled off a few lines: "Miss Barton calls on you for a humane object and I hope you will grant her request. It will cost nothing. She has given three years to the cause of our soldiers and is worthy of *entire* confidence."

She got as far as the East Room by ten o'clock that morning, only to find that Mr. Lincoln was engaged in a Cabinet meeting. In quick succession she saw General E. A. Hitchcock, head of the Volunteers, who found her plan both "humane and interesting," and General W. Hoffman, Commissioner General of Prisoners. Both urged her to go full steam ahead. "But I dare not," Clara wrote in a moment of panic. "I do not feel it my duty to bring myself to public mortification in order to do a public charity. I am certain that if I publish my intention Secty. Stanton will follow it with a card to the effect that I am acting without authority."

Clara was never quite sure of her ground with Stanton, but she knew that if Abraham Lincoln gave her his blessing, all would be well. For the third time she set off for the White House, on this occasion in the pouring rain. She watched Stanton walk in without a glance in her direction, as she stood outside dripping wet, her new veil plastered to her face, the fingertips of her too-large gloves soggy and crinkled. Finally she went home and wept. "Could not reconcile my poor success," she wrote. "I feel that some hand above mine rules and is staying my progress. I cannot understand but try to be patient. Still it is hard. I was never more tempted to break down with disappointment."

The war was nearly over and Abraham Lincoln's own end was at hand. His days were filled with colossal effort and he may not even have known of Clara's visits. She was invited to the Inauguration Ball and attended a White House reception, observing that the President kissed a baby, which she thought "the most attractive feature of the levee." She could not very well approach him in the receiving line nor could she get anywhere near him at the ball. This time her friends had dressed her in a green silk skirt and white lace waist and "after much rigging" she had set off for the ball with a well-known escort, John Bigelow. It scarcely mattered to Clara that she could not dance. It would just be the usual crowded rout. She noticed that General Nathaniel P. Banks of Massachusetts, Admiral David G. Farragut, and Henry Wilson were there, three gentlemen well known to her. The crush was dense and no one paid much attention to Clara. She observed "a great crowd and rush for supper, of which I saw only the crowd. No supper for any of us."

Next day Henry Wilson called to see her and stayed only a few moments. He was tired after the previous night's function. Clara was aloof. "I cool and he left soon," she noted. "I have accomplished little or nothing today."

As usual, when consumed with fervor for some cause, Clara could find neither peace nor satisfaction until she had had her way. She knew that Henry Wilson was seeing the President all the time. Why were things not moving for her? But two days later, on March 10, all other worries were forgotten in her grief over the death of Stephen.

Wilson called on her as soon as the news reached him. He knew Stephen well. "Was kind and gentle," Clara observed. "Asked to take the place as nearly as possible of the dear brother I had lost. Said he should be proud to do so and have me for a real sister, so I adopted another brother."

Wilson may well have jogged the President at this point, for the letter Clara wanted was written next day:

To the Friends of Missing Persons: Miss Clara Barton has kindly offered to search for the missing prisoners of war. Please address her at Annapolis, giving her name, regiment, and company of any missing prisoner.

[Signed] A. Lincoln.

The President referred her to General Hitchcock, who told her first "to go bury my dead and then care for others." She traveled to Worcester for Stephen's funeral and was in deep personal woe when the news reached her that Lee had surrendered to Grant at Appomattox Court House. The same front page of the Boston *Daily Journal* that gave her the details of this historic event also carried the obituary notice of her nephew, Irving S. Vassall, who had suffered for years from tuberculosis. Clara had seen hundreds die in the field. These two were her own.

Within the month she was back in Washington and was returning home from a late evening call when she heard a rumor in the street that Abraham Lincoln had been assassinated. Her diary entry on this memorable event was brief: "President Lincoln died at 7 o'clock this morning. The whole city in gloom. No one knows what to do." The following day she noted: "Assassins not detected. . . . I was quiet all day."

For a time a sentry was posted at her own door. She was a popular wartime figure and panic had spread in the capital. Clara stared out at the dripping street. She listened to the bells toll. Her own personal melancholy mingled with the sense of national mourning. On the day of Lincoln's funeral she remained indoors but later, at General Grant's request, she went to Philadelphia for the ceremonies there.

She wrote one hundred letters bearing on missing soldiers while Lincoln lay in state in the Capitol. It took the War Department some weeks to establish her at Annapolis as the "General Correspondent for the Friends of Paroled Prisoners." Inquiries greatly outbalanced information on missing prisoners. These arrived, in response to Abraham Lincoln's note, faster than Clara could handle them.

The official rolls of prisoners proved to be so unrewarding that she enlarged her plan to include all men who had disappeared in the national service during the war. This covered much territory, including the unidentified dead—the unknown soldiers buried without recognition. Only 172,400 of the Union dead were identified at the end of the war, although there were 315,555 graves. In addition there were 43,973 recorded deaths in excess of the known number of graves. The dead numbered 359,528 in all. This left a large margin of homes where the fate of sons, husbands, and fathers was unknown, a situation that appealed deeply to Clara's sympathies.

She organized her forces and set her usual assistants to work— Sally, "half a mile away by horse car"; Jules Golay, whom she had rescued close to Richmond; her old friend Samuel Ramsey; and Edward Shaw, who had shared her copying fee at the Patent

Office and lived "one and a half minutes' away on foot." By May her first rolls of missing men were ready and she faced a new problem. No private printer in Washington had large enough forms or sufficient capital letters to print her lists.

On May 31, 1865, Clara wrote to President Andrew Johnson, asking that he authorize the Government Printing Office to do the work. She enclosed a circular, on the insistence of her friends, asking for financial aid. She was already much out of pocket on the project. "The work is indeed a large one; but I have settled confidence that I shall be able to accomplish it," Clara wrote to Andrew Johnson.

He moved fast on her behalf. On June 3 he wrote to John Defrees, Superintendent of Public Printing: "Let this printing be done as speedily as possible consistently with the public interest."

General Grant, who was always cordial to the woman his soldiers revered, promptly commended her to all his officers for aid in her quest, and authorized free transportation for Clara and two assistants. She was allowed a small fund for stamps, stationery, and other office supplies, and was assigned tent quarters at Annapolis. She now had the full endorsement of two Presidents and the top army commanders, and felt encouraged to go on with her work. The names of the missing men were arranged according to states, and regional papers published them. Soon an edition of twenty thousand copies was in circulation. The response was overwhelming. Her information came from many sources. Men still presumably "lost" in prison camps found their names in Clara's lists. Not all were gratified. Soldiers who had seen comrades die helped her to place the date and occasion. Families that had sheltered and buried wounded soldiers volunteered information. Her correspondence at this time was charged with human drama. It went on for years, in dwindling ratio, but her name was linked as long as she lived with the missing men of the Civil War.

An impressive roster of prisoners' names was brought suddenly to her attention by Dorence Atwater, a young soldier who had been incarcerated in the notorious Confederate prison supervised by Captain Henry Wirz at Andersonville in Georgia. Atwater was an orphan from Terryville, Connecticut, who enlisted at the age of sixteen and was taken prisoner at the beginning of the war. Early in 1864 he was transferred from Richmond to Andersonville with the first detachment of soldiers sent there. For a time he was in the stockades but was removed to the hospital when he became ill.

Working for a time as a clerk at a desk close to Captain Wirz, he was assigned to keep the death roll of his comrades, who for one period were succumbing to dysentery, scurvy, gangrene, and starvation at the rate of 127 men a day. More than 10,000 died in seven months. Many were shot as they tried to escape. All were buried side by side in the shelterless stockades.

Atwater recorded the company, regiment, the soldier's home state, the date, and cause of death. These were vital statistics of great value. Horrified by what went on around him, he secretly made duplicate lists which he took out with him concealed in the lining of his coat. He was removed to Columbia, South Carolina, in February, 1865, and a month later was a paroled prisoner at Annapolis with the record of approximately 13,000 dead at Andersonville. He offered his list to the War Department but no action was taken on it.

Reading about Miss Barton's work, he decided to get in touch with her. She was much impressed when he told her that he believed he could identify almost every grave at Andersonville. She instantly saw the importance of his list and approached General Hoffman with a plan to go South with Atwater, mark the graves, and have the burial grounds enclosed. This seemed to Clara to be a logical development of the work she had undertaken. General Hoffman thought well of the plan and submitted it to Stanton, who immediately sent for Clara.

Her relations with the Secretary of War had been fleeting up to this time, and she had sometimes thought that she felt the chill of his displeasure, but on this occasion he greeted her with voluble cordiality, meeting her halfway across the room with extended hand and "thanking her handsomely" for the work she had done in the past. He told her that if he had known more about her efforts he might have aided her from time to time. "Now he desired to thank me for helping him *to think*," Clara reported, "and for suggesting one good, sensible, practical, unselfish idea that he could take up and act upon with safety and credit." The upshot was that Stanton told Clara he had appointed Captain James M. Moore, Assistant

Quartermaster, to head an expedition to Andersonville. He asked her, since he could not "order her," if she and Atwater would accompany him, taking the register.

They all sailed for the South on July 8 on board the *Virginia*, taking with them a strange cargo of headboards, with fencing, nails, paint, axes, spades, and a staff of clerks and workmen. After a long delay at Savannah, where they awaited rail transportation, they traveled slowly South, Clara observing the invaded country with the closest attention. She found Augusta "uninjured by the war," Atlanta "torn in fragments, a shocking place," and Macon showing the signs of "sudden surprise and capture, as its partially finished immense public buildings testify."

At Andersonville they settled into tents. Clara was no stranger to emergency quarters. "My little tent does well," she wrote, "have table, my trunk and big chest, but no chair. I sit on the floor to write, setting my desk upon the lounge of my trunk."

This was Clara's unique trunk bed, and the field desk which she used in conjunction with it. Squatted Indian fashion on the floor she wrote at once to Stanton, reporting that the identification of the graves could be carried out "to the letter" and that the field was "wide and ample" for much in the future. She suggested that the grounds of Andersonville could be made "a National Cemetery of great beauty and interest," and that the American people would bless his name in the future for his "prompt and humane action" in making it so.

Clara anticipated twentieth-century recognition of the Unknown Soldier when she informed Stanton:

Interspersed throughout the death register were 440 numbers against which stood only the dark word "Unknown," so scattered among the thickly designated graves stand 440 tablets bearing only the number, and the touching description "Unknown U.S. Soldier."

The other graves were readily identified, partly from original records captured by General James H. Wilson from the Confederates and partly from Atwater's list. The area covered nine acres. The grounds were enclosed. Biblical texts were posted at the gates and along the areas marked out for walks. "A uniform and comely tablet" took the place of the starkly numbered boards, until 12,920 graves in all had been decorously marked.

But trouble was brewing in the little group. Clara and Captain Moore had regarded each other with mutual suspicion from the start. He had been heard to curse her and to remark: "What in Hell does she want to go for?" Clara, in turn, resented his authority and was unsure of her own status with the War Department. She later reported to Stanton and Wilson that Captain Moore had failed to show her consideration and respect; that she was not consulted on any question of taste or fitness; and that she was not fully informed of what was being done, although it was her understanding that she had inspired the entire expedition. The situation with Atwater was even worse. He and Captain Moore rowed openly.

Stirred up over the situation, Clara and Dorence went to the cemetery together, spotted "hosts of errors" made by Moore's staff, and had headboards pulled up and reset. Consulting lists, they found that many of the dates were wrong, and promptly had them corrected. Nor were the texts letter-perfect. Clara knew her Scriptures.

On August 17 she ran up the Stars and Stripes at the dedication ceremonies of the National Cemetery at Andersonville. "My own hands have helped to run up the old flag on our great and holy ground and I ought to be satisfied," she wrote. "I believe I am."

Before leaving she and Atwater went carefully over the prison site, while her new protégé recounted the horrors of Andersonville to Clara. She found the stockade a "terrible place, beyond description of wretchedness." In her report to Stanton on her return she told of the wells dug by the prisoners in their frantic efforts to escape, of the tunnels they had made that had sometimes fallen in and killed them, of the crude utensils they had fashioned—drinking cups made from horns; cups and bowls scooped from gourd vines; platters and spoons wrought from old canteens; kettles and pans made with solder from pieces of tin or sheet iron.

On her return to Washington Henry Wilson hurried to Clara's rooms to try to mollify her about Moore, but the feud between them now blazed in the open and the Captain was making serious trouble for her at the War Department. Wilson assured her that "no man could do that without striking through him, that he should see the Sect. and set the matter straight."

Clara was determined to publish the Andersonville list under Atwater's name. Captain Moore accused Atwater of having stolen it from the Government when Dorence refused to turn over the list on his return from the South. He was ordered to restore it at once to the War Department. His rooms were searched. Nothing was found. He was suddenly arrested and court-martialed for larceny and conduct prejudicial to good military discipline. He was convicted, fined $300, and sentenced to eighteen months' hard labor, along with dishonorable discharge from the Army.

"Beautiful state of affairs," commented Clara. "I cannot believe that Mr. Stanton will tolerate it."

She worked hard for Atwater and somehow obtained the secret minutes of his court-martial proceedings for Joe Sheldon and Robert Hale to use in preparing his legal defense. She followed Stanton to West Point to plead his cause, but the Secretary of War advised her not to get into a controversy. He refused to interfere with the finding of the military court and Clara was balked in that quarter.

Next she turned to General Butler, who thought the list the best means of detecting fraud in the settlement of claims that the Government could possibly possess. He promised to see both the President and Stanton about it. But the official swing seemed to be all in the other direction. Early in December, Moore's rank was raised to lieutenant colonel and he was appointed chief of the U.S. Burial Bureau, which Clara insisted was created by the Government directly from her plan. He would thus have control of the Andersonville records and much else of her carefully amassed material.

This was a severe blow to her. General Butler had led her to believe that she would be put in charge of this work, with full government status. Now she wrote to him firmly saying that she would never hand over her papers and become a clerk, a "mere tool" in a work she had originated. Instead, she would bow out. "You have comprehended me when others could not," she added, "and professed me aid and sympathy when others would not, and I only know that when my arms grow weak, and my eyes dim, the mention of your name must recall momentary strength to the one, and kindle the fading light in the other."

But Butler's star was in decline. At that moment he was under heavy censure from General Grant. "It is pitiful to see how mercilessly he deals with him," commented Clara, who liked both men. "It will tickle his enemies but on the whole Grant will not gain by it, I think. . . ."

Henry Wilson understood the matter, too, wrote Clara, but he was busy with other affairs. His relations with Andrew Johnson were not what they had been with Abraham Lincoln. Neither of her supporters was in the saddle at the moment. Wilson showed traces of impatience with Clara at this point and when he found her in a state of deep depression he tried to shake her out of it. Her diary entry on this visit is illuminating:

And today my good master and friend comes and finds me crouched meekly in my bare little nest, and asks me briskly, but kindly, "What I am lying there in idleness for, & why I don't go into the great stone house and work and eat?" He forgets that I have neither been called to labor, nor bidden to the feast.

Again I am not slothful, and would work if I might. But my wants like my strength are full grown, and in the daily sight of four years of deadly strife, I have learned to stand upon rights, and could no longer consent to nibble the chaff from which others, well fed and housed the while, had extracted the grain.

Clara had lost some of her earlier humility. Obviously she now demanded more of life, and was outraged by the treatment she had received. She found it easier to get to the President than to Stanton at this point. She believed she "had acted nobly for her country and humanity," she wrote to Henry Wilson, and why the jealousy of a "little *worthless* petty officer should be allowed to trample me *speechless* in the dust, I *cannot* understand."

This was a most unusual outburst for Clara, who was not given to vituperation. Henry Wilson had to bear the brunt of it. He also had to tell her just before Christmas that all hope of Government backing seemed to be over for her. He was "very troubled and thrust $20 upon me, fearing that I lacked necessities." Wilson called this a Christmas gift, but Clara proudly rejected it, and told him not to distress himself about her—it was no more than she had expected. Crisp confirmation of her defeat reached her a few days later from General E. D. Townsend. She had hoped for a separate bureau of her own, but was informed that this would merely overlap on the newly created Burial Bureau of the War Department. "Thus ends the chapter of government aid," Clara commented. "I shall never hear more of it and I trust never say more."

Her birthday reflections that year were morbid. She was now forty-four, and wrote with sadness of the loss of Stephen and Irving: "I have never felt the partition so thin between the two worlds as since they left us. . . . It has grown to be only a veil, a gauze, and I can almost feel them through it." Haunted by her old sense of frustration, Clara added: "How time flies and how little I do accomplish. I must believe my life an entire failure. I am not able to do anything of worth to any person and am growing no better myself."

But Dorr, as she now called Atwater, was released unexpectedly at Christmas under a general Presidential pardon for all persons convicted by court-martial of crimes less than murder. Clara sent him word at once to stay away from Washington, "not to say a word, but play possum, act dead," prepare the roll for publication and give it to any newspaper that would publish it. She warned him not to take a cent for it but to make a gift of his list to the country and "give the lie to their shameful suspicions that he wanted to make money out of it."

Clara, who had stayed in the background even through strong suggestions that she had spirited the Andersonville record to safety, told Dorr that he could now use her name in his statements if it made them "any more plain or strong." She met the New Year with spirit, for she still had another ace in the hole. "If there is any luck in my hand I shall win," she wrote, "for I have played it well, and I know it has been closely watched." She now appealed to Horace Greeley to publish the controversial list under Dorr's name. "If Atwater is ever set right before the country, then God be praised," she added.

Finally, the *Tribune* appeared on February 14, 1866, with a two-column article by Clara bringing the full story into the open. The word *Andersonville* was sprinkled all through the issue as a filler. Atwater's list was too long for a newspaper to print, but Greeley published an eighty-page pamphlet with all the names and it was sold at news dealers' for twenty-five cents. Dorr got full credit, and Clara was satisfied. The entire matter took on fresh proportions with this publicity. The families of missing men clamored for the pamphlet, and Clara was deluged afresh with mail. It brought peace to many families. Moreover, the idea of national war cemeteries by this time was taking root in the public consciousness. So was the image of the Unknown Soldier. Gettysburg and Andersonville represented two different aspects of the ultimate toll of human life in the Civil War.

In the beginning, Clara's work was done without any compensation, except for the small allowance for office supplies. Finally, Mrs. Frances Gage submitted a financial statement of her operations for consideration by the Committee on Military Affairs. She claimed that Clara had spent $1,000 a year of her own money for her work on the battlefields, and $7,533 more on the quest for missing men. Senator Wilson moved for an appropriation of $15,000 to cover her outlay and provide for the continuation of her work. This was passed in 1866.

Three years later Clara submitted an accounting to Congress of her stewardship, showing that by that time she had expended $16,759 in all. "My own time and services have been cheerfully given," she noted. She had distributed 99,057 printed rolls of names and 58,693 circulars of advice. She had supervised 41,855 letters sent to individuals, and 63,182 exchanges of information. In the final analysis she was responsible for more than 20,000 soldiers being entered on the rolls who otherwise might never have been identified.

Dorr's fate became a matter of much concern to her after this. Feeling that she was largely responsible for his imprisonment, she tried to help him in every way she could. She argued that the greater good had been served by the dissemination of his list. For a time he traveled with her as secretary and business manager on her lecture tours. The Andersonville relics were exhibited, sometimes with the added flourish of a brass band, and in 1868 he gave her legal possession of his original lists and all of his interest in the souvenirs of that haunted site. Clara's description of Andersonville was always one of the climactic points in her talks:

I have looked over its twenty-five acres of pitiless stockade, its burrows in the earth, its stinted stream, its turfless hillsides, shadeless in summer and shelterless in winter, its wells and tunnels and graves, its seven forts of death, its ball and chains, its stocks for torture, its kennels for blood-hounds, its sentry boxes, and its deadline . . . surely, this was not the gate of hell, but hell itself, and for comfort, I turned away to the nine acres of crowded graves and I said, here at last was rest, and this to them was the gate of heaven.

Through her political influence Clara later had Dorr assigned to foreign consulates. The first was the lonely Seychelles in the Indian Ocean. The next was Tahiti. From time to time he returned to the United States and shared briefly in her ventures. Before her death his dishonorable discharge from the Army was canceled and he received the recognition that she had long sought for him. Clara always told her audiences that Dorence Atwater had done a work which "God approved and angels smiled on." A monument recalling his war service marks his grave in Papeete.

## CHAPTER VIII

## SOUTH BEND TO CORSICA

CLARA TRAVELED through floods and snows to keep her lecture appointments in 1866, 1867 and 1868. She had become a well-known figure on the lyceum circuit. Trains broke down. She forded rivers. On a March night in 1868 she found the Illinois River so high at Lincoln that she could not cross, until she had commandeered a "skiff" to take her over. At South Bend, she noted: "Dreadful rain—bridge again off at S.B. where great accident was some years ago. Walked over."

She took an open wagon to Morrison's Hotel in Des Moines and "froze without a fire, cold, could not sleep." While riding in a stage-coach from Wayland to Dansville in New York State, a wheel came off a mile out of town and Clara tramped through the snow into the hilly little spa where she was to recover her health after the Franco-Prussian War and found the first American Red Cross chapter in 1881.

Clara was still so fresh from the fields of war, and so many of her hearers were in mourning, that the response to her lectures was warm and immediate. She was a natural subject for publicity. Generals beamed on her and bowed over her hand. Old patients showed up to call her blessed. Mothers with whom she had corresponded turned out to view the now well-publicized Angel of the Battlefield. A surgeon jumped up to identify himself as a participant in one of the incidents she was describing. Children gazed at her with wonder. Her name became a household word. A national heroine was in the making.

Clara's own view of life broadened as she met the more prominent citizens of each community and felt the pulsing growth of the country. She traveled through Illinois, Iowa, Wisconsin, Michigan, Ohio, Indiana, and Pennsylvania, as well as the New England states. Her fees ranged from $50 to $125 a lecture, but she cut them obligingly for an army organization, for a small hall, or where funds were tight. G.A.R. gatherings were her special interest. "I am not naturally I think ambitious of gain and mere money never parts me from my friends," she wrote to one supplicant who begged for a cut in fees.

Clara was apologetic for charging anything, and for the fact that she repeated the same lecture. When she spoke in Brooklyn she dreaded a full report of the text lest it be recognized when she repeated it in Manhattan. On this occasion Theodore Tilton introduced her as the American Florence Nightingale when she spoke at the Lee Avenue Baptist Church in Williamsburg. The day was to come when her admirers would refuse to concede that Clara was a carbon copy of any other well-known figure, but her reputation was still in the making.

She was alert to regional interests in all her lectures, remembered the home regiments, and usually recalled some appropriate incident. Intermittently she was billed as the "Heroine of Andersonville" and the "Soldier's Friend." When Dorence Atwater was with her, she drew attention to him as one of the heroes of the war. On the third anniversary of the fall of Richmond, crowds flocked into Steinway Hall in New York to hear the "Florence Nightingale of America" speak for the benefit of soldiers' families.

The horror and heroism of battle were recalled by Clara with the same quiet emphasis she applied to the manifestations of nature. She revived every battleground with reminiscent personal touches— the long, exciting march down the mountain passes in the autumn of 1864, Fredericksburg with its "pontoon bridge, sharp-shooters, deserted streets, its rocky brow of frowning forts . . . the falling back, the night retreat across the Rappahannock." . . . South Mountain with its "stubble hillside and burning September sun." . . . Antietam, "a chain of Etnas," and afterward the "pale moonlight on its cooling guns . . . the dying and the dead. . . ."

Clara had seen "bright days, bright uniforms, bright hopes and bright blossoms all pass into limbo" and she never forgot it. She told the same story over and over again in "Work and Incidents of Army Life," an intimate account of her personal experiences on the battlefields—a thrilling tale at many points. Finally she worked up two other lectures: "The Moral and Religious Effect of the War Upon the Soldier and the Country" and "How the Republic Was Saved, or War Without the Tinsel."

These had less impact than her original lecture, but her confidence grew as the months went on, and she found crowded halls and responsive audiences wherever she appeared. Toward the end she was slightly more at ease, and in spite of clammy hands and trembling knees would occasionally extemporize and let her natural wit flash out. But oratory was not one of her many gifts and it put a great strain on her as she traveled from state to state, her notes in half-inch letters propped before her, with exclamation marks as thick as clusters of matches. On one occasion she confessed: "I am the most timid person on earth. All speech-making terrifies me. First, I have no taste for it, and lastly I hate it."

Studied today, Clara's lectures seem flamboyant in text, but the contemporary newspaper reports suggest that they were delivered so calmly and quietly that their effect was not melodramatic. Her low-pitched voice was always remembered by those who knew her. It took on a deeper note on the rare occasions on which she was angered, and the many occasions on which she was moved. It was frequently hoarse from repeated colds while journeying through the West. Clara always had outward serenity; none suspected the turmoil revealed in her diaries. Her air on the platform was so stately in the Victorian manner that in spite of her meager inches she was remembered by some reporters as being of impressive stature. This was not the Clara Barton in striped prints who hopped nimbly on top of packing cases. It was the Clara Barton in brown silk and ruffles who spoke in slow and throaty accents of that other and more adventurous self.

The souvenirs of Clara's lecture tours abound in her papers today. Pressed flowers and leaves crumble between the pages of her diaries. Notebooks and wallets are stuffed with railway stubs, hotel bills, calling cards, and receipts; with clippings, notes, and reminders; with livery bills evoking the coaches and pioneering exigencies of the 1860's. She made quick shifts in temperature and conveyance. Trains rattled along on erratic schedules. After her lectures she sat up until five in the morning, bundled in shawls, filling in her diary, writing letters, planning her days. She slept fitfully in cat naps as she traveled. The varying food, the odd hours, the local hospitality were upsetting to her always-delicate gastric system, but the compensatory excitement of her days kept the indefatigable Miss Barton going.

Her most startling adventure befell her in a train between Chicago and Toledo. At midnight, while asleep in her berth, she was wakened by a man searching through her pockets. "He flew back to his own bed and as no one came through the car I sat bolt upright all night and watched him and he watched me," she wrote.

This duel of wits ended at five in the morning when the Negro attendant arrived to build the fire in the car. Clara then left her berth and indicated the man who had molested her. He was taken off and the incident ended for her with the brief diary note: "I then retired and slept till 9 at Toledo."

Clara avoided sleeping berths after that. She invariably sat upright in day coaches, or dozed against her shawl. She dined largely on crackers and apples, which she usually carried with her on her journeys in brown-paper bags. Her fare was always frugal and austere. She avoided meat at different times in her life and periodically, if not consistently, was a vegetarian. After the Civil War her gastric troubles drove her from one experiment to another. Later, when she traveled abroad, her food vagaries created serious problems for her, since she was unable to cope with table-d'hôte meals and recoiled from oil and pasta. Her interest even in Vesuvius was tempered by her inability to eat a Neapolitan dinner. Clara readily became bilious and dosed herself with the nostrums of the day.

She consulted many doctors, both men and women, in the course of her life but had periods when she avoided them altogether and threw out all her remedies. She got her best results from physiotherapy and the self-application of mental control. When whipped up by excitement, hard work, or applause, Clara had the bearing of a woman of immense endurance and robust health. When dissatisfaction ate at her vitals, and her days drifted by without form or purpose, she became ill and deeply neurotic. But common sense usually prevailed in the long run, and the uncertainties and gloom revealed in her diaries had small reflection in the active, cheerful life she lived.

At this point, however, she was heading into a long-drawn-out collapse. Setting forth on her third season, with more than two hundred lectures behind her, Clara noted dismally on an October day in 1868 that "by some unaccountable means" her health had begun to fail her. But she pulled herself together for a gathering in Boston in November at which she met Henry Wilson, and talked to Thomas W. S. Higginson, whom she found "stiff as steel." She was much taken by Julia Ward Howe and exchanged Civil War experiences with Louisa May Alcott. On this occasion she met both Lucy Stone and her exuberant husband, Henry B. Blackwell.

While in Boston Clara bought herself a velvet hat costing $10.75 and had her hair "put up on form for evening dressing," an indulgence costing her $2.25. (She always jotted down her expenditures, even to the last cent.) She bought point lace for a collar for her brown traveling dress, and fringe for the brown silk in which she customarily lectured. These bursts of interest in her apparel usually beset her when she was thrust into public notice, or had important interviews pending. She considered New England home territory, and was conscious there of the critical scrutiny of friends and family. In the course of her lifetime Clara traveled all the way from incipient Bloomerism to plush trains and ruffles of point lace, but her striped prints and battle jackets were undoubtedly her most memorable attire.

Once she had broken ground as a public speaker, Susan B. Anthony and the other suffragists sought her support. Miss Anthony made the practical and indisputable point that Clara could draw men to an audience, a state of affairs novel in suffrage ranks. Later, when Clara had become internationally known for her Red Cross work and owned a string of foreign decorations, Susan always urged her to wear her medals.

"We want to *exhibit all the good-looking of the strong minded*," she wrote to Clara on April 29, 1869, inviting her to the meeting in New York of the American Equal Rights Association. "Would like you to make woman's plea for the right to a voice in government from the standpoint of what *she risks* in *war* in *which* she has no voice in making."

This was the official beginning of Clara's long association with the suffrage movement, and her personal friendship with such women as Miss Anthony, Mrs. Howe, Lucy Stone, and Frances Willard. She was never wholly committed to all their theories and methods, but was solidly with them in principle. Clara had worked too long and too closely with men under stress to feel that they were her natural enemies. In fact, she sought their favor and always began her lectures: *"Gentlemen and Ladies."*

But she let no one extol her at the expense of her sex. When advertised in an Iowa town as one who would not lecture on women's rights "after the style of Susan B. Anthony and her clique— Miss Barton does not belong to that class of women," Clara delivered her usual lecture with equanimity, then finished with a stinging reproach:

That paragraph, my comrades, does worse than to misrepresent me as a woman; it maligns my friend. It abuses the highest and bravest work ever done in this land for either you or me. You glorify the women who made their way to the front to reach you in your misery, and nurse you back to life. You called us angels. Who opened the way for women to go and make it possible? . . .

For every woman's hand that ever cooled your fevered brows, staunched your bleeding wounds, gave food to your famishing bodies, or water to your parching lips, and called back life to your perishing bodies, you should bless God for Susan B. Anthony, Elizabeth Cady Stanton, Frances D. Gage and their followers. . . .

No one, said Clara, had stood so unhelped, unprotected, and maligned as Miss Anthony, and none deserved so well. "I would have the first monument that is ever erected to any woman in this country reared to her," she added, proposing three cheers for Miss Anthony. The hall was swept with applause. None could rouse a battle cheer like Clara when she raised her arm and led it.

But there were other occasions when the single-minded Lucy Stone felt that she could have struck more effective blows for suffrage than she did. Clara was slow to go to extremes on public issues. When she established the Red Cross in America she was anxious to keep it clear of the harsh winds of prevailing controversies. She believed in adhering to the broad plane of human succor.

Her own affairs were going badly in the winter of 1868–1869. Recurrent sore throats, earaches, and bronchial distress were overwhelming her. She was also plagued by neuralgia and rheumatism. The grueling pace of the lecture circuit, following her years on the battlefield, proved to be too much for her. One winter night she stood on a platform in Portland, Maine, staring out over rows of friendly faces, and could not utter a word. She was midway through her lecture and had been describing Lacy House.

Her audience waited politely. Clara showed distress, then rustled off the platform. The major collapse of her life was upon her. For the next decade she moved in and out of the shadows, a nervous wreck, until by rest and will power she fought her way out of it and climbed to fresh heights. But for the time being she returned to Washington and faced the spring of 1869 in a mood of deepest depression.

Her doctor ordered total rest for Clara and a clean break with all the distractions of her postwar life. Friends, relatives, office seekers would not let her alone. He suggested that she go abroad and live in a bland climate. In May she gave Jules Golay $420 in gold to buy her passage to Europe. In August she made her will, bequeathing $5,000 to her sister Sally, leaving money for the family burial plot in North Oxford, and for the care of all books and papers relating to Andersonville, ever a deep-rooted interest with Clara. The residue of her estate was to be divided among her numerous nephews and nieces.

Clara had handled her finances with care. She now had the $15,000 voted her by Congress, and had earned almost an equal amount by her lectures. She had land in Iowa, which she would later sell at a substantial profit. She had invested most of her income in railroad bonds, a promising field with the West opening up rapidly. Judge Hale handled her finances. She banked with Brown Brothers on Wall Street. She was now a woman of property and independence.

But the strings that Clara had sent out still bound her to a desk. Letters continued to reach her from all parts of the country. There was no end to the claims made upon her energy. At last she realized that the time had come to loosen her hold and let go. She was nearing forty-eight when she sailed with Sally on the *Caledonia* in August, 1869. The freshness and sparkle had gone from her face. She looked the tired, middle-aged woman she was, and saw little ahead of her. Her passport on this occasion described her, with one glaring inaccuracy, as being five feet five in height, with broad forehead, brown eyes, prominent nose, large mouth, broad chin, dark brown hair, sallow complexion, and oval face. Clara had little idea when she sailed that she was heading for more battlefields and the most important work of her life—the Red Cross.

Sally went with her only as far as Scotland, for her family feared to let Clara cross the Atlantic alone. She had a "brief and unrewarding view" of Glasgow, Edinburgh, Stirling Castle and London before hurrying on to the Geneva home of Isaac and Eliza Golay, parents of Jules, who had persuaded her that the Swiss climate would do her good.

But the wintry skies, the snow, ice, and searing winds only aggravated her bronchial condition. Soon she was considering Algiers, Madagascar, or the Seychelles, where Dorr was stationed. Finally she settled on "little sea-girt Corsica" which she found "weird, wild, soft and bewitching." But the wind blew fresh and cold off the Mediterranean, too. She was bitten by fleas at Madame Paradis' pension. The table d'hôte disturbed her digestion, so that she lived wholly on olives, cheese, bread, and wine. The chimneys smoked. There was no water for bathing. She could not see to read or write by taper and her eyes became inflamed. Her bed was icy cold. A thief entered her room on her arrival and searched her trunks. She challenged him boldly, and he bolted, cursing her in Corsican. She skidded the length of a tiled floor but her "marvellously good joints" which had survived so many slips in the mud of the Civil War upheld her again and she was "no sooner down than up and standing upon my feet again."

She moved to the Hotel Suisse, where the English snubbed her because she was not a Rebel, Clara thought. But when John Hitz, Swiss Consul to the United States, and his wife Kate arrived and introduced her to the Corsican Prefect, she was taken into the official set. Clara's diary written in Ajaccio is filled with lively impressions of the Corsican scene: of shifting clouds, sails, and aquamarine waters; of the violets and geraniums that grew in abundance; of women walking to the well, like Rebecca, with terracotta pitchers balanced on their heads.

The peasant life warmed and cheered her. She found the children gay and sturdy as they tossed their multicolored balloons in the air or carried wiry loads of brush for kindling. The mules and donkeys struck her as being a wretched lot, lacking bridles, halters, or the touch of a curry comb. But Clara had an eye for the picturesque effect of their loads—the jugs, casks, tanned hides, brush, vegetables, and human beings.

On Christmas Day, her forty-eighth birthday, she stood under a spreading tree at Milelli, Napoleon's favorite haunt when he visited Corsica in his adult years. She speculated on his thoughts eighty years earlier. "He *might* have dreamed of the crown of France . . . but did he dream of Waterloo and St. Helena?" She visited his birthplace, pored over his battle trophies, took away two tiles with her for souvenirs. "Poor Bona," wrote Clara, "it was the sweetest of all your little islands, and had no fetters."

Was it perhaps the thought of Napoleon that had drawn Captain Barton's daughter to the isle of Corsica in the first place?

## CHAPTER IX

## THE FRANCO-PRUSSIAN WAR

A GROUP of Swiss dignitaries, headed by Dr. Louis Appia, stopped at the Golay home to talk to Miss Barton, of Civil War fame, before she left for Corsica. The elder Golays had told stirring tales of her work for the wounded, and how Jules had been saved from death while under General Butler's command close to Richmond.

It was a crisp October day in 1869 and Clara was far from home when she first heard of the Convention of Geneva from its functioning committee. It surprised her to learn that twenty-two nations and the Papal State had signed the Treaty while the United States stood aloof. Clara was shocked, when its purposes were explained to her, although she had never before heard of the movement and was quite unconscious of the symbol of the Red Cross—the colors of the Swiss flag reversed.

But she listened, absorbed. The wounded were her natural interest. She knew all aspects of their care on the battlefield and the deadly cost of faulty arrangements. She had no answer for Dr. Appia when he asked her why a great and humanitarian nation like America withheld its interest and support.

"Our position was incomprehensible to them," Clara commented. And the more she heard about their work, the more incomprehensible it became to her. She was deeply impressed with "the wisdom of its principles, the good practical sense of its details, and its extreme usefulness in practice." Clara assessed its roll of nations and commented:

Not a civilized people in the world but ourselves missing, and saw Greece, Spain, and Turkey there. I began to fear that in the eyes of the rest of mankind we could not be far from barbarians. This reflection did not furnish a stimulating food for national pride. I grew more and more ashamed.

Dr. Appia told Clara of various attempts made to draw in the United States, but William H. Seward, Secretary of State, had stood like a rock against it, resting his arguments on the Monroe Doctrine. As Seward saw it, a modification of the international laws of war was involved, suggesting political complications contrary to national policy. When Charles S. P. Bowles, working on behalf of the United States Sanitary Commission, first brought up the matter officially in 1864, Seward ruled that while the government was ready "to forward all humanitarian action" it had a well-understood policy "of holding itself aloof from all European congresses, or compacts of a *political* nature."

At the last moment George C. Fogg, American Consul at Berne, was asked to attend the Geneva Convention of 1864 in an unofficial capacity. By this time the United States Sanitary Commission was well established and had done impressive work in the Civil War. Both Bowles and Fogg were associated with it, and they used their influence again with Seward in 1865, strongly urging adherence. This was followed by the powerful advocacy of Dr. Bellows, who asked Seward if the cessation of hostilities had not altered the case. Dr. Bellows' petition was turned over to Stanton. But feeling was cool between the Secretary of War and the Sanitary Commission.

In May, 1866, the President of the Swiss Federal Council made a formal plea for acceptance. The Marquis de Montholon, French Minister in Washington, pressed the point hard. Several of the diplomats prodded Seward. But the issue went dead until Grant became President and Dr. Bellows raised the question again, this time with Hamilton Fish. The new Secretary of State sustained the stand of his predecessor. He referred Dr. Bellows to the earlier correspondence, with which he was all too familiar. Again the door was closed firmly.

At this point Dr. Bellows gave up hope on the international front, but continued his work at home until 1872 with the American Association for the Relief of the Misery of Battle Fields, which had developed from the Sanitary Commission. He hoped that it might serve eventually as a connecting link with the Convention of Geneva. The Sanitary Commission and the Swiss organization had evolved almost simultaneously, with closely allied aims. In the long run the Geneva group profited by the organizational strength of the

Sanitary Commission. Dr. Bellows and his colleagues shared full information on their methods with Jean Henri Dunant, the man who gave the world its first conception of the Red Cross.

Clara's interest was captured at once as she listened to Dr. Appia talk. She told him she was sure her fellow countrymen were as ignorant of the matter as she. It had simply never been brought before them in popular form. She thought that language might well have been one of the stumbling blocks. At Dr. Appia's request she agreed to take up the cause on her return. He promptly supplied her with books and pamphlets.

Clara caught the drama of the movement more fully from Dunant's own story. He was a Geneva youth who had worked his way to affluence and now was a well-known banker and philanthropist. While traveling in Italy on business in June, 1859, he chanced to be in Castiglione della Pieve, close to the battlefield of Solferino, the horrors of which have lived in history.

He went to work personally on the battlefield where thousands of the dead and wounded lay untended in the blazing sun. He bathed and dressed wounds, and gave drinks to men burned up with fever. He enlisted the medical services of near-by towns and villages and sent his coachman into Brescia for supplies. He rounded up groups of local women to act as volunteer nurses and used a local church to shelter some of the wounded. Victor and vanquished were treated impartially. *Tutti fratelli* (all are brothers) was the rule he spontaneously applied.

The whole experience preyed on his sensitive nature afterward. He was shattered nervously and brooded over the callous treatment of the wounded. He felt that much of the suffering was needless, and that the simplest kind of preparation for care and nursing would have made all the difference. His memories haunted him for the next three years, until in 1862 he wrote *Un Souvenir de Solferino*, a brief book of real significance to mankind, since it held the germ of the Red Cross in its pages. Just as the Sanitary Commission was getting under way in America, Dunant's book was being quietly circulated in Europe among public figures, men of cabinet rank, editors, and the heads of welfare societies. It was promptly translated into German, Spanish, Russian, Swedish, Dutch, and English. One edition followed another and Victor Hugo wrote: "You armed humanity and served liberty." Joseph Ernest Renan, French historian, called it "the greatest work of the century." In its way, it was a historic tract, and Dunant became known as the "Samaritan of Solferino."

Clara now read it with the keenest interest and understanding. There was much about Florence Nightingale in its pages, and he wrote most movingly of the horrors of the battlefield. Dunant advocated an international principle to apply to the wounded of all belligerent countries. He proposed relief societies to be sustained in times of peace with "zealous, devoted and thoroughly qualified volunteers" who would aid the wounded in time of war. He urged a neutrality clause, to protect the work of these societies. In other words, he forged a stout shield for the protection of all men caught in the tide of battle. The symbol of the Red Cross, one day to blanket the earth, was used officially as early as 1866, and first flashed into prominence during the Franco-Prussian War.

Clara familiarized herself with the headway already made by the small group of humanitarians in Switzerland who had taken up Dunant's dream and given it practical application. He was visionary and an effective propagandist rather than an organizer. He traveled across Europe, approaching men of influence everywhere. National volunteer committees were appointed. Sixteen nations were represented at the first conference in the autumn of 1863. A year later, on August 22, 1864, the Treaty of Geneva, otherwise known as the Geneva Convention, was signed with ten articles. Clara would live to see two important additions made to the constitution in 1899. The Hague Convention at that time ruled that national Red Cross societies should be officially recognized by international law, and the provisions for neutral relief were extended to cover naval warfare.

The movement was already spreading in Europe when Clara stepped into the picture. The Franco-Prussian War opened her eyes to its practical application. News of battle stirred her to the core as she rested in a chalet near Berne with the Sheldons and Minna Kupfer, a new friend introduced to her by Mrs. Hitz. She had returned from Corsica with a touch of malaria, and after a brief stay with the Golays in Geneva had proceeded to Berne "in quest of strength among its mountain views and baths."

Joe Sheldon had a factory in England, and usually passed part of each year abroad. He and Abby were shocked to find Clara so apathetic on her return from Corsica. She did not care whether she "lived or died across the sea." But she was stirred to action with the announcement of war. In her own words:

The bugle-call to arms again sounded in my war-trained ear, the bayonets gleamed, the sabres clashed, and the Prussian helmets and the eagles of France stood face to face on the borders of the Rhine. . . . I remembered our own armies, my own war-stricken country and its dead, its widows and its orphans, and it nerved me to action for which the physical strength had long ceased to exist, and on the borrowed force of love and memory, I strove with might and main.

When Dr. Appia and his group came to the door of her chalet in July "inviting me to go with them and take such part as I had taken in our own war" Clara longed to accompany them but was so uncertain of her strength that she feared she might be a drag on their party. She told them she would follow in a week. She then proceeded to the International Committee's headquarters in Basle, where all supplies were sent for distribution. The storehouses were filling up fast. Boxes and barrels were arriving from "every city, town and hamlet in Switzerland, even from Austria, and Northern Italy."

Clara took note of the nurses, ready for action, Red Cross brassards on their sleeves and the same symbol on every box and barrel, "rendering it as safe and sacred from molestation as the bread and wine before the altar." She stayed in Basle for a week to study the system, but soon felt the urge to get out in the field. The other was a "fudge," not close enough to the wounded. The tide of battle influenced her at this point, for a summons arrived from Mülhausen. "Dr. Appia and his noble band of pioneers had evidently passed that way," she observed.

She set forth with a young companion, Antoinette Margot, who was to figure in her life for years to come. Swiss by birth, French by education, Antoinette had reached Basle from Lyons, where her father was a silk manufacturer. She was intent on doing war work and had papers from the International Committee. She was a slim, fair-haired girl of melancholy appearance, an artist of some reputation, who was to attach herself to Clara and become the first of her volunteers. Clara found Antoinette "lovely, gentle and mild." She was also useful as a translator, since Clara was not yet fluent in French and German.

They were soon breasting the fleeing tide of refugees, traveling by train, by coach, and by road. Germany was armed to the hilt. France was already losing ground. The Prussians were crossing the Rhine and Clara was warned repeatedly to turn back, but she was determined to get "to the front," wherever it happened to be. "That expression was very strange after a lapse of five years, and I had thought never to hear it again in connection with myself," she wrote.

They were not needed at Mülhausen, and pushed on determinedly toward Strassburg. No one wanted them; no one heeded them. They were all part of the general confusion until they reached Strassburg, not yet under siege, and found that the American consul there was a veteran surgeon of the Civil War named Felix C. M. Petard, and the vice-consul had served as an army chaplain.

This put Miss Barton at once where she belonged. Dr. Petard was about to dispatch a busload of tourists who were fleeing from Alsace. Clara was intent on getting to Haguenau. He put her in charge of the expedition for part of the way and they passed sentinel after sentinel under the shelter of the American flag, until one doubter demanded something more. In their haste getting off, they had left the International Red Cross flag and their insignia behind them.

Clara vanished from view, took the bow of red ribbon she habitually wore at her throat, fashioned it into a red cross, and sewed the symbol on her sleeve with the thread and needle she always carried with her. This is the first known instance of Clara Barton wearing the red cross with which her name was ever afterward identified. It was a makeshift device but it served its purpose.

The tourists got away and Clara and Antoinette pursued their uncertain course. When they arrived at Brumath, where the casualties from Haguenau were being taken, they were not allowed to get anywhere near the wounded. On August 26, 1870, frustrated and impatient, Clara wrote in her diary:

These days wear very hard. It is not like me, nor like my past, to be sitting quietly where I can just watch the sky reddening with the fires of a bombarded city, and neither have anything to do in or with it, nor be able to go near enough to see the shells which set the fires.

At this point she and Antoinette stuffed their satchels with cold meat, bread, and boiled eggs, and set out again on foot, with shawls and waterproofs, determined to find the battlefield for themselves. Clara had visions of a miracle opening the way for her, as had so often happened during the Civil War. But they were soon discouraged by an eerie night passed in Vandenheim, where four thousand soldiers were billeted. Clara found that she had more trouble in one night with these men than in all her combined operations in the Civil War.

Her motives were misunderstood when she sought shelter during a downpour in the only place she could find—a tumble-down, disreputable house. When she and Antoinette arrived late at night, footsore, weary, and desperate for shelter, a German woman reached down a wooden stool from a high window. Clara leaped up with all her old agility and landed on the window sill. She pulled in the youthful Antoinette after her. They were glad to find cover of any kind but Clara soon decided that "robbery, if not murder, was abroad."

They were suspected of being spies until the spread eagle on Clara's passport carried conviction. Next a six-foot soldier, roaring drunk, pinioned Clara to a wall in a mock gesture with his sword. She had met emergencies before. She rose to this one with her own commanding presence: "I made no motion whatever, did not raise a hand but . . . I looked him directly in the eye. He returned my look, still keeping the sword against my heart. No one in the room appeared to breathe. . . ."

Stared down by small Miss Barton, the Prussian officer dropped his sword and clanked off, flinging his cloak across his shoulder as he left. Clara could see the humor of all this swashbuckling later, but not at the moment. When a second soldier invaded their tiny chamber that night, on the pretext of protecting them, Clara announced in her deepest tones: "If you enter, I will kill you—if I can."

In the morning they drove back to the comparative safety of Brumath and their distant view of battle fires. At this juncture Clara received a summons from the Grand Duchess Louise of Baden to visit her at Carlsruhe. She had wavered between helping the French and the Germans. She knew that the French were in greater need of aid, and she had written to the American Minister in Paris, Elihu B. Washburne, whom she knew, offering her services. But her visit to the Grand Duchess swung her into the German ranks for the time being, although she viewed her work on a strictly neutral basis and, in the long run, helped both sides, giving aid where it was needed by the very nature of the Geneva tradition.

The two women surveyed each other with interest. The Grand Duchess had heard of Clara's work through Dr. Appia. She had also just finished reading a magazine article about her. Clara, on the other hand, knew that Louise was the daughter of Emperor William I and that her mother, the Empress Augusta, headed the Red Cross in Germany and was a noted philanthropist, fostering hospitals and schools.

Clara observed that the Grand Duchess, rustling toward her in black silk, was small, delicate in build but regal in bearing. Her complexion was pale, her mouth of generous proportions. Her hair was severely dressed, but for one ringlet dangling down on her neck in the prevailing fashion. Clara decided that she was in the "full bloom of grace and power . . . at once modest and assured." She thought that her face reflected devoutness and intelligence.

The two women became lifelong friends and their correspondence testifies to their shared interest in Red Cross matters and other philanthropic causes. Clara always wore an amethyst brooch, fashioned like the petals of a pansy, given her by Louise after an all-night vigil at the bedside of her son, whom she thought to be dying at the time.

On this occasion the Grand Duchess invited her to tour the military hospitals. The royal residences of Baden, which had been turned into hospitals, were well organized in Clara's opinion and efficiently run. Her developing interest in the Red Cross was further stirred by what she saw, and she and the Grand Duchess had long discussions on the subject. They were sitting chatting on a balcony of the palace late in September when a courier rode up with the news that Strassburg had surrendered to the Duke of Baden's siege. Clara decided to leave at once and do what she could for the inhabitants.

Two days later she crossed the Rhine in a small boat and entered the city through one of its wrecked gates. It was still a smoking shambles as the slim woman, nearing forty-nine, climbed over the dismantled ramparts and picked her way through barricaded streets. She went at once to the Civil Hospital and took notes to submit to the Grand Duchess on the most pressing needs. Clara was struck by the fact that more than half of the wounded were women—"a phase in military observation new, even to me." However, with her strong sense of equality in all things, she wrote that women had the same privilege to be shot at as they had to be protected, the same right to danger as to safety. "No one will take occasion to complain of this view from me," she commented, "for all know too well that I have personally illustrated and *lived* my opinion."

The misery and bereavement on all sides were overwhelming. Thousands of the inhabitants had been stripped of their homes and all their possessions. Half-naked children whimpered for food in damp cellars. Fear, shock, hunger were the dominant characteristics of the stricken city, aggravated by the terrible wounds that had torn the bodies of men, women, and children.

Within forty days Clara had dispensed a surprising amount of bounty. Supplies poured into the city from the International Committee. The Grand Duchess gave lavishly, always specifying that Miss Barton should be the distributor. Well aware of the bitterness felt by the Alsatians toward their conquerors, Clara "deemed it wise" to have some of the supplies reach them direct from German sources. No doubt Louise saw the advantage of having a neutral agent in an area so bitterly hostile. She found Clara a mediating power "who volunteered her cooperation as well as her mediation, and adjusted our relations with the city authorities."

But the indiscriminate distribution troubled Clara. She felt it might prove demoralizing and urged the city authorities to restore the people to the status of workers, instead of making them beggars. Taking the initiative herself she organized workrooms, first in the shelter of a rock, later in a suitable hall. Materials, patterns, expert cutting, and guidance were supplied. Soon three hundred women were turning out fifteen hundred garments a week. They were paid for their work at the rate of two francs a day. The finished garments were arranged in sizes, tied in dozen lots, and sent to the Strassburg committee for distribution by voucher.

Clara was still working under her rock and was presiding over a strange assortment of chemises, pantaloons, and baby sacques when Count Bismarck, Governor General of Alsace at that time, came clanking in. The Grand Duchess had told him about Miss Barton and she already had a pass to work with the army volunteers. She found him genial—"gentle and good at heart"—a tall man with a kind face. She told him at once that she needed better quarters for her work, and Gustav Bergmann, of the Strassburg relief committee, stepped forward to say that he would help.

Clara had written to Bismarck in rather meek tones on December 9, 1870: "I am neither a diplomatist nor political counselor; I am only a maker of garments for the poor." [1] Nevertheless she made her point and showed a dash of her old political prescience when she reminded him:

This population must always be the neighbors, if not a part of, the German people; it will be most desirable that they should be also friends; they are in distress—their hearts can never be better reached than now; the little seeds of today may have in it the germs of future peace or war.

Clara made headway with the hostile Bergmann until he was her friend. In a small way she played her role as mediator with considerable skill, kept supplies flowing without rancor, and finally arranged the "first social meeting between a leading French officer, M. Bergmann, and the German Court since the war." The Grand Duchess visited her workrooms on different occasions and approved her arrangements. The nobles of Baden fell into line, taking their cue from Louise. Soon Countess Bismarck was taking her for drives and she and Antoinette visited the Chancellor's family at Neuhofen.

By this time Clara had a new helper named Anna Zimmermann, a governess from the court. She was a clergyman's daughter from Carlsruhe, independent, ambitious, "with all the fire of Anna Dickinson, with twice her ready knowledge and ten times her scholar-

---

[1] Superior figures refer to the numbered sections in the Appendix, beginning p. 271.

ship," according to Clara. The families of Antoinette and Anna had trouble reconciling themselves to the thought of their sheltered young daughters following Miss Barton wherever her daring footsteps led her. There were many scenes before they finally broke loose. In the end Anna married a clergyman and died of consumption. Antoinette accompanied Clara to Paris and London, entered a convent in France for a time, then visited her in America in the late 1880's.

Clara needed helpers and translators. Antoinette was an expert needlewoman who kept close check on the sewing operations. Anna was a link with the court and an intelligent worker. Clara kept a weather eye on all the practical arrangements, and in the midst of her paper patterns took time to write a humorous letter to Annie Childs in Worcester:

Now wasn't that the last thing you would have thought of, that I should come to Europe and set up dressmaking, and French dressmaking at that? Well, you should have seen the patterns! And didn't I cut them myself? And didn't I direct all the making until I had imparted my wonderful art to others? . . . How rich I should have been with you at my side. . . .

A glimpse into the future at this point might have surprised Clara and Annie. The modest Production Service at Strassburg, with its 1,200 garments a week, was the forerunner to 160,000,000 knitted and sewn garments, and 3,000,000,000 surgical dressings, produced by Red Cross volunteers in America between 1919 and 1955.

Toward the end of 1870 the House of Baden feared it might lose Miss Barton's services when she went to Geneva to talk to her old friend, General Burnside, and the American consuls in Brussels and Antwerp, about establishing headquarters in Brussels for the distribution of American funds and supplies for Alsatian relief. Clara was convinced that American aid was going astray for lack of organization. Burnside was cordial, as of old, but she was surprised to find her countrymen so cool to her plan. She noted indignantly:

But I was only one woman alone, and had no power to move to action full-fed, sleek-coated, ease-loving, pleasure-seeking, well-paid, and well-

Clara Barton

Clara Barton at the age of eighteen
(Library of Congress)

Miss Barton's birthplace in North
Oxford, Massachusetts

One of the first free public schools in New Jersey, established by Clara
Barton at Bordentown

Grand Duchess Louise          Count Bismarck

Sponsors of Clara Barton's Red Cross Work During the Franco-Prussian War

Antoinette Margot          Anna Zimmermann

Early Red Cross Volunteers in Franco-Prussian War

General Ambrose E. Burnside, under whose command Clara Barton functioned in the early days of the Civil War

General Benjamin F. Butler, who gave Miss Barton carte blanche in her operations under his command

Senator Henry Wilson, Miss Barton's most influential friend and supporter

Dorence Atwater, who helped Miss Barton identify the dead at Andersonville and establish the national cemetery there

Clara Barton at the time of the Civil War

Clara Barton raising the national flag at the Andersonville cemetery

[ Facsimile ]

Washington
Feb. 28th 1865.

To President Lincoln
Dear Sir,
Miss Barton calls on you for a humane object and I hope you will grant her request. It will cost nothing. She has given three years to the cause of our soldiers and is worthy of entire confidence.

Very truly
H. Wilson

SENATOR HENRY WILSON'S LETTER TO PRESIDENT LINCOLN

THE SOLDIERS' TRIBUTE TO THEIR DISABLED COMRADES.

# LECTURE,

## Work & Incidents of Army Life,

BY

### Miss CLARA BARTON,

The Florence Nightingale of America,

GIVEN UNDER THE AUSPICES OF

POST No. 24, GRAND ARMY OF THE REPUBLIC,

IN AID OF OUR DISABLED VETERANS,

### Cooper Institute, Wed. Eve, Feb. 26,

At 8 O'clock.

#### TICKETS, 50 CENTS,

For Sale at the Principal Music Stores, Theatre Ticket Agencies, and at all the Booths of the Soldiers' Business Messenger and Despatch Company, and at the Door.

EXECUTIVE MANSION,
WASHINGTON.

Will the Secy of State please hear Miss Barton on the subject herein referred to.
J A Garfield
Nich 30, 1881.

President Garfield's letter to his Secretary of State requesting he see Miss Barton about establishing the Red Cross in America

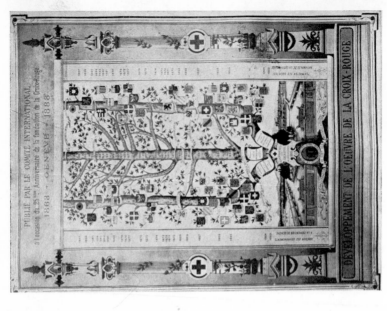

The Red Cross Tree shows the growth of the international organization from 1863 to 1888

J. Henri Dunant, founder of the International Red Cross (Library of Congress)

## APPEAL TO THE AMERICAN PEOPLE.

The President having signed the Treaty of the Geneva Conference, and the Senate having, on the 16th instant, ratified the President's action, the American Association of the Red Cross, organized under provisions of said treaty, purposes to send its agents at once among the sufferers by the recent floods, with a view to the ameliorating of their condition so far as can be done by human aid and the means at hand will permit.

Contributions are urgently solicited. Remittances in money may be made to Hon. Charles J. Folger, Secretary of the Treasury, chairman of the board of trustees, or to his associates, Hon. Robert T. Lincoln, Sec'y of War, and Hon. George B. Loring, Commissioner of Agriculture. Contributions of wearing apparel, bedding, and provisions should be addressed to "The Red Cross Agent," at Memphis, Tenn.; Vicksburg, Miss., and Helena, Ark.

CLARA BARTON,  
J. C. BANCROFT DAVIS,  
FREDERICK DOUGLASS,  
ALEX. Y. P. GARNETT,

MRS. OMAR D. CONGER,  
A. S. SOLOMONS,  
MRS. S. A. MARTHA CANFIELD,  
R. D. MUSSEY,  

*Committee.*

WASHINGTON, D. C., *March 23, 1882.*

The first Red Cross appeal

Clara Barton in 1882, when the American National Red Cross was established (Library of Congress)

George Kennan, newspaper correspondent and officer of the Red Cross (Library of Congress)

Dr. Julian B. Hubbell, Field Agent for the Red Cross and Miss Barton's chief aid (Library of Congress)

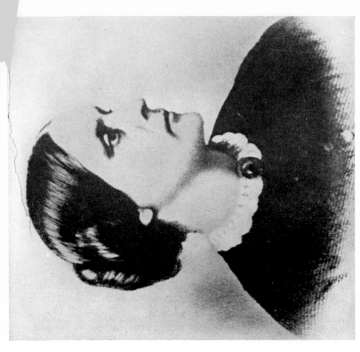

Susan B. Anthony

The charcoal portrait of Clara Barton by S. L. Phelps which hangs in the Red Cross headquarters in Washington

Trunk, holding clothing and opening as a cot, used by Clara Barton

Clara Barton's room in the Red Cross headquarters in Beaufort, South Carolina

American Red Cross corps waiting at Tampa, Florida, to go to Cuba during the Spanish-American War

Clara Barton's relief ship, *State of Texas*, which led the U.S. Navy into Santiago after the defeat of the Spaniards (Library of Congress)

Window in St. Thomas Church in
New York in which Clara Barton is
memorialized (Library of Congress)

Red Cross headquarters in Galveston, Texas, during the 1900
disaster (Library of Congress)

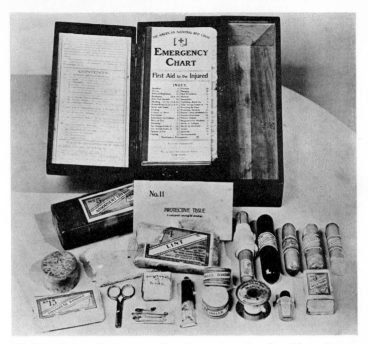

Earliest first aid kit, introduced in America by Clara Barton (Library of Congress)

Clara Barton's home at Glen Echo, Maryland; headquarters of the Red Cross from 1897 until 1904 (Library of Congress)

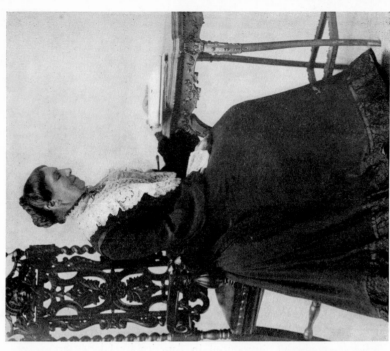

Miss Barton in her seventies (Library of Congress)

Miss Barton in her eighties

placed countrymen in this war-trampled, dead, old land, each one afraid that he should be called upon to do something.

Clara headed next for Metz, which had just been reduced by siege, and worked briefly among its "famishing, fevered population" before returning to Strassburg for a winter of strenuous effort. Dorr joined her in the spring. The consulate in the Seychelles had been abolished. Paris was in chaos when they journeyed north in June to see what aid they could give the French. The city had survived surrender to the Prussians in January and the Commune that followed. Clara felt she was more needed there than in Strassburg, where her work was now well organized and capably run.

She arrived with forty thousand garments and other supplies, leaving them seven miles outside the city, which she entered on foot, since most of the horses had been eaten by the starving population. The Mayor of Villette gave her quarters to distribute her bounty. She worked through the Protestant churches in Paris and concentrated on three groups—the families of the prisoners of Versailles, of the ship crews of the Manche, and of the Alsatians who had chosen France as their refuge. She thought it unwise of the Alsatians to flock into France, but since they did she tried to promote the idea of a colony in the South of France, a scheme that came to nothing.

Clara walked through the shuttered streets of Paris with observant eyes. She saw the column in the Place Vendôme lying in the mud. Political prisoners languished in jail, waiting to be shot. Business was at a standstill. The hungry population drifted around in spectral groups. The city was strewn with filth. The echoes of horror were all around her, and she noted that "it was reserved for Paris, alone, to show the world the refinement of cruelty and madness."

By degrees she came to the conclusion that she felt more kinship for the German nature. She decided she had no natural affinity for the French, and did not "feel at home with their customs and characteristics." On the other hand, "Germany is more like us," she commented. "There is a fixedness of purpose in her people, her anchor goes to the bottom. France swings in the water, and changes with every whipping wind."

But Clara felt well that summer. To be useful gave her the usual upsurge of mood and she was not so overworked as at Strassburg. She slept longer hours, and her digestion was excellent. "It has refused nothing of late but lobster and that it always did." She felt equal to beefsteak and potatoes for breakfast. She found a good deal of American life in the French capital and went to Sunday-night parlor gatherings where they all sang hymns and native tunes.

In August she visited the Margots in Lyons and continued her relief work there, meeting the refugees at the trains and giving them food and clothing as they passed through. Antoinette and she wrote letters for the American press, describing conditions and inviting help for the Alsatians. Clara appealed specifically to Horace Greeley, who was never indifferent to her projects. At this time Antoinette painted her portrait, showing a child kissing the hem of her garment in the workroom at Strassburg. She wrote of her dispensing charity in France, "standing from morning till night, smiling and graceful as always, receiving family after family," while she listened to their stories, appraised their needs, and met them accordingly. Some of her Strassburg families followed Clara all the way to Paris.

Henry Wilson, visiting the war area, joined her in Lyons. His sturdy presence was so reassuring that Antoinette's parents, who had been withholding permission for their daughter to accompany Clara any further on her relief missions, now gave her permission to go to Dijon. They had been wrangling determinedly with their rebellious daughter. Finally they set off for Switzerland and left her to continue as a protégée of Clara's.

She was famishing for news from home and as she and Henry Wilson drove through the gardens and visited the conservatory, they discussed politics and the course of reconstruction. Wilson listened with absorbed interest while Clara told him of her war experiences and her meeting with Bismarck. Soon Wilson would be Vice-President. In five years he would be dead. But to Clara he was at all times the most sympathetic of friends and supporters.

Help was now reaching her from America. The women of New England had not forgotten Clara Barton. Edmund Dwight, a Boston lawyer, sent money through the London office of the New York French Relief Fund. Clara appointed Dorr her agent in the British capital, and he received funds from Benjamin Moran, the American Chargé d'Affaires. In the autumn of 1871 Clara toured the warstricken areas, using Antoinette as interpreter. They spread American bounty in Besançon, Belfort, Mülhausen, and Montbéliard, Clara distributing money and supplies personally under the aegis of the town officials. In Belfort policemen were assigned to keep the hungry mob from rushing her, but when the crowds and gendarmes clashed Clara was the one who restored order. In Montbéliard she gave the women vouchers for wood and rent. "It was Boston that did this good little thing," she wrote to Sally.

Clara had done her best to fulfill Dwight's wishes for the distribution of New England funds, but she was far from satisfied with the handling of American relief operations in France, and felt that they had suffered through lack of a central organization like the Red Cross. Supplies arriving from the United States were not under the regulations of the Geneva Treaty, and baffled agents moved about in confusion, not knowing how to apply them. Although the Red Cross symbol had covered Clara's own operations time and again, and she had taken careful note of its uses in the battlefields, her link was still a loose one, and she worked with the Red Cross much as she had functioned with the Sanitary Commission. But she was never able to get to the core of relief operations in France and was glad to return to the more sympathetic air of Carlsruhe, where the Red Cross was strongly entrenched.

She passed her fiftieth birthday with the Zimmermanns. With Anna she gave a Christmas fete for the women who had used her workrooms in Strassburg. Three hundred gathered around two splendid pine trees brought in from the Black Forest. Wax candles flickered among the branches. Morocco purses with silver coins dangled from the trees, along with gay baubles for the children. Gustav Bergmann was present to do Clara honor with a bust of herself, hung with Christmas greens. It still stands in her home at Glen Echo, a souvenir of her second war.

That winter Clara attended the opening of the Badish Parliament with the Grand Duchess Louise. The peal of bells, the crimson throne, the gold lace, the three Imperial shouts, the Grand Duke's polished speech, all were pungently described by Clara, who drew from the occasion food for political thought. "The empire gives far more liberty to the masses than they had before," she commented. "The tendency of all Europe is towards more liberal government. Step by step it is demanded and yielded."

Now that she had passed the peak of her service, reaction set in with Clara, and the usual signs of nervous prostration developed. During most of 1872 she was all but blind, although she still insisted on writing letters in a large, sprawling script, even though her eyes were bandaged. Joe and Abby Sheldon, realizing that Clara was close to collapse, arrived suddenly from London to take her home. They found her almost too weak to walk. She no longer had any zest for the social life of the court, nor could she function in the relief field. The Grand Duchess sent her the Cross of Baden and bade her a loving farewell. Antoinette gave her a locket, with twists of her own and Anna's hair.

But instead of returning to London with the Sheldons, Clara soon found herself listening to a "deluge of opera" in Milan, viewing Napoleon's sword at Marengo, floating along the Grand Canal in a gondola and climbing the one thing before which her "soul stood in awe in Europe"—Vesuvius.

Passing through Paris they had encountered Joseph E. Holmes, American Commissioner of International Exhibitions, who was starting off for the grand tour of Europe with his family. Seeing the wretched condition Clara was in, and dreading the effects of a London winter for her, they asked her to join their party.

She stored her trunks in Paris, "took a little hand satchel with one single change, a shawl and waterproof," as if she were going on a scout, and soon found herself traveling close to the battlefield of Solferino. Clara in her diaries gave all the traditional sights along the route their full pictorial value, adding her own pointed comments.

Mr. and Mrs. Holmes, with their daughter and son-in-law, Mr. and Mrs. F. B. Taylor, followed the accepted route, neglecting nothing from Elizabeth Barrett Browning's tomb to the Tower of Pisa. Clara preferred the plain grave of Theodore Parker in Florence to the "gilded tombs of the Medicis." Rome tired her profoundly. She decided that Venice lived solely on its glorious past. Bellagio on Lake Como interested her as a favorite haunt of the Prince and Princess of Wales.

The Sheldons awaited her in Paris to take her back to America. She had been receiving invitations from the G.A.R. to return home and lecture, "but I think this would be harder than working in Europe," she wrote to Edmund Dwight, and decided to accompany the Taylors to London instead. Until the fogs and damp set in, she felt reasonably well and entered on a brisk round of visits. Her eyes seemed better. She had the inclination to keep her diary and make notes. With her Bradshaw and a Reynolds colored shilling map she roamed around London with a satisfying sense of freedom. She went to the theater and to vaudeville. She visited the Crystal Palace as well as Windsor Castle. She explored charitable institutions and sampled the various churches. The famous preacher Charles H. Spurgeon struck her as being "good but very orthodox." When she found her old friend Fowler the phrenologist, she wrote joyfully: "He is the same gentle, kind man he used to be so many years ago, gray now, stoops a little, but is wise, considerate, as he always must be."

Clara's correspondence flourished. She replenished her wardrobe and attended small social gatherings held by a few American families, who met once a week at the Taylors' for tea and talk. Clara surprised them all with one of her spontaneous poems, indicating her mood at the time. She visited Kate Field in Half Moon Street and talked to Ida Greeley about her father, Horace. She followed Julia Ward Howe's activities with interest and her first visit to the British Museum was to copy the text of the "Battle Hymn of the Republic."

But she deplored her brief association with a Prison Conference in London attended by Mrs. Howe and other American feminists. She had been persuaded to serve on a committee, but she did not function well in harness and was bored eventually with the issues involved. "They have no confidence in their own success and fear a failure," she wrote. "I am miserable with all these people. Cannot come near them. Don't want to go live near them. They are all good, but I am not at home with them. . . . I have about determined not to go to America. I don't know if ever I want to go any more," she finished in a burst of discouragement.

For a time Clara lodged at the home of John Chapman, editor of the *Westminster Review*. He forewarned her about the importance of *Middlemarch* and urged her to watch for its publication. She enjoyed the flavor of these associations, and at this time her strongest instinct was to write. Over the years Clara repeatedly showed a genuine yearning in this direction. Her monumental correspondence and diaries suggest that she was not wholly misled in her ambition, although her other exploits quite overshadowed this capacity. Her favorite newspaper interview, written by Mrs. Walter P. Phillips when she had already turned eighty, drew attention to Clara's literary style. This pleased her greatly. She said that no one had ever noticed it before. However, President William McKinley remarked that Clara's were the finest letters he received. She was particularly versatile in this form of communication, usually writing in pungent and lucid style, with characteristic flashes of humor and an agile descriptive sense. Even when her work became international in scope Clara took time to write to all members of the abundant Barton clan, showing the most minute concern for their affairs. Her letters to her small nieces and nephews illustrate the special grace and understanding with which she approached the very young.

But the stream was slowly dammed during her wretched year in England, because of the condition of her eyes. A month on the Isle of Wight with Antoinette and Mrs. Taylor did little to restore either her health or her spirits. Except that she learned to row and feather her oar on the anniversary of Antietam, a day always noted in her calendar, the month seemed wasted. She could find no time for herself. "Nothing makes me so sick of life as to feel I am sacrificing it," she complained.

Worse was to come. The winter in London that followed was one of the most wretched of her life. She suffered from the cold, the damp, the fog, the darkness, the discomfort of her surroundings. Her bronchitis was rending her apart. Her eyes were bandaged most of the time. As she was unable to use her arms, her room at 13 Beacon Hill was in confusion, a severe trial for orderly Clara. Her spirits sank lower and lower, until she felt as if she were already in a "metallic coffin, only waiting to be closed in a little snugger, and have the screws turned down." She found the English skies "a sheet of zinc."

Late in November she wept over the death of Horace Greeley.

She now had Mamie Barton, David's daughter, staying with her along with Antoinette. All three were depressed, for Clara's groans filled the little household. The capable aunt, who stood like a beacon to all the Barton descendants in New England, was a broken wreck, unable to cope with the simplest aspects of living. She could not bear to be touched or even to comb her hair. She had never felt her "nervous system more broken," she wrote on Christmas Day, 1872, her fifty-first birthday.

Indignant with herself, she bought a concertina to cheer up the girls, and had a dancing teacher come to her rooms to instruct them. Knowing she was not being fair to their youth, she wrote Mamie a letter signed *Old Dolorous,* urging her to laugh with Antoinette, to sing and go in for nonsense, to throw away the "dim tapers" with which they surrounded her, to ignore her tears and lamentations, and move about in the normal way, instead of humoring her in her misery.

When word of Clara's melancholy condition spread among her American and German friends, they wrote to English acquaintances, who soon came calling on Clara or otherwise offering her aid. Florence Nightingale and Clara Barton were never to meet, but at this juncture a link was established, and Clara wrote:

Among others, very early, came a message from Florence Nightingale, expressing her deep regret at my illness and also that she herself was far too ill to come to me—but begging me to accept any rooms and service and comfort that could be obtained in her magnificent St. Thomas' Hospital and the hospital authorities were directed by her to extend the same invitation to me, which was beautifully done. But I, alas! was too ill to be removed and remained in my so-called lodgings—comfortable apartments—through all the long Winter and Spring, with never a ray of sunshine, until at length at the last of May I was able to be helped out and to a train for France, where during the Summer my strength came back sufficiently to allow me to reach home; but not sufficient to keep me up. . . .

This was the closest contact that the Lady of the Lamp and the Angel of the Battlefield ever had with each other. In 1901 Clara wrote to a Baltimore friend, Janet Richards: "Friendly messages have always passed between us; but we have never met." Clara was to outlive Florence Nightingale by two years, and to survey her field of operations at Scutari.

Again the Sheldons came to Clara's rescue. This time they took her back to America on the *Parthia* in October, 1873. Her horizons had widened in spite of her ill-health. She had new and powerful friends. She had moved in court and military circles, in London's literary set, in humanitarian groups. She had survived another war, but three years of constant illness had worn her out. "I returned home worse broken than I had left," she confessed. But she had not forgotten about the Red Cross. In retrospect she wrote:

When in 1873, after four years of exile, I left old Europe for my own land, it was with the firm pledge to the members of that convention, that I would present it to our government in its true significance, ask its consideration and signature, if approved, or learn its reasons for withholding, and that I would do everything possible to make the American people understand it. . . .

In spite of her good intentions, several years passed before Clara was able to function effectively. She went straight to Washington on her return, full of plans, but was ill most of the winter, and when word reached her late in May that Sally was dying she rushed north to Worcester, found her already gone, and collapsed in nervous prostration herself. She divided the next few months between the family homes in North Oxford and Worcester. Then Minna Kupfer, hearing in Germany of her illness, joined her in America, kept house for Clara, and nursed her through the months of illness that followed.

# Part Two

✳

Part Two

## CHAPTER X

# THE RED CROSS REACHES AMERICA

AS HENRY WILSON lay dying in November, 1875, his thoughts turned to his old Civil War friend. "Do you know anything of Clara?" he kept repeating as he clung to J. W. Westfall, a member of the Capitol police guarding his room. "I haven't seen her for so long a time."

On hearing this from Westfall, an old ally of hers, Clara wrote at once to the Vice-President but he was dead when her letter arrived. She wept over the final details that reached her in a letter written on November 23. "His last words to me when told I should hear from you in a few days were: 'When you hear from her you will let me know, won't you?' And it seemed to give him so much pleasure to know I had kept you advised of his sickness."

Wilson had insisted on carrying on his work, even in his dying hours. Visitors came in. Letters were delivered to him. Westfall wrote that he had longed for Clara to be there "to direct what must be done, and what left undone." In the end he went "without a struggle."

Clara was just recovering from the shock of Sally's death when the news about Henry Wilson unbalanced her again, and she sank deeper into the shadows of complete nervous prostration. "I have no idea what went past me in those strange silent months," she wrote as her strength revived and she worked with all her old resolution to have America enter the Convention of Geneva. No doubt she had counted on his aid in the Senate. He had backed every cause she had ever put up to him.

Now she could not stand, or read or write, or have any contact with the outside world. Her letters were not given to her; all links with her old friends were severed. Her rich brown hair turned silvery gray and thinned during these months of extinction. Clara Barton was lost in the nebulous mists of unreality, but slowly she found herself again and started on a life of greater scope and usefulness. Help came through the simple regime of a sanitarium in Dansville, New York, known as "Our Home on the Hillside," and patterned after the establishment run in Austria by Vincenz Priessnitz, father of hydropathy.

The cure was a "wonder," Clara wrote. It was a back-to-nature movement, relying on therapeutic baths, fresh air, sunshine, natural foods, and abundant rest. Those too ill to move, as she was in the beginning, were carried out to the broad piazzas, or lay in hammocks under the trees. For patients who could participate there were picnics, musicales, sermons, stereopticon viewings, sleigh rides, dances, lectures, and poetry readings. Clara found the company stimulating and intelligent.

The sanitarium was run by Dr. James H. Jackson and his chief of staff was Dr. Harriet N. Austin, a gentle and intelligent woman who, however, had succumbed to the fad of Bloomerism. Turkish pantalettes hugged the insteps of her closely fitted boots. Long brown ringlets dangled over her shoulders. Clara respected Harriet, and grieved when boys shouted after her in the streets, men stared, and the "good dames gathered in their parlors disapprovingly." She became a mild disciple herself for a time, finding comfort in an unbound tunic dress with voluminous pockets, high boots, and short stockings. But when Dorr came to visit her he laughed at Miss Barton in these habiliments and she thought them rather comical herself. Clara's sense of humor had not deserted her during her illness.

At Dansville she abandoned nostrums and cultivated spiritual repose. It was one of the most significant moves of her life, for her entire philosophy of living underwent a change in this environment. She began to take a new view of her own life, to have some insight into her self-demanding nature. Clara ceased to strain for perfection and drifted a little in this relaxed atmosphere. Her rigorous Calvinist conscience was stilled. She was content to idle, and she grew to love the little town nestled in the shelter of the Genesee Valley. Its invigorating air, its orchards, lakes, glens, and waterfalls, appealed to country-bred Clara. In time she was to have homes of her own in Dansville, to found the first Red Cross chapter there, to become one of its most honored citizens.

When she took up her correspondence again in 1876 she was well on the way to recovery. There had been no diary entries for years. Her handwriting had become grotesque—sprawling and erratic. But the day came when Abby Sheldon was delighted to get a letter from Clara "looking as of old." And Joseph wrote: "I am glad to see your handwriting clear and large—and hope the water cure is doing you essential service."

In the spring of 1877 she wrote one of the most revealing letters of her life—her own estimate of herself as a woman, and her analysis of her recurrent breakdowns. Curiously, it was addressed to Professor Theodore Pfau, a German scholar whom she had never seen but who was meditating a trip to the United States and expected to meet Miss Barton. Clara dreaded his coming. She did not wish to meet him, lest she disappoint him. He had asked her for a photograph. She declined and wrote of herself scathingly as being "uncomely":

I was *never* what the world calls even "good looking," leaving out of the case all such terms as "handsome" and "pretty." My features were strong and square, cheek-bones high, mouth large, complexion dark; my best feature was perhaps a luxuriant growth of glossy dark hair shading to blackness, but that is comparatively thin now, and silver gray, all within the last three years. It changed from its original blackness to its present shade in the first six weeks of this present illness in 1874. I never cared for dress, and have no accomplishments, so you will find me plain and prosy both in representation and reality if ever you should chance to meet either." . . .

Clara then gave her own shrewd appraisal of her breakdown to the professor whom she had never met. She called it "complete prostration of the nervous system." She was not aware of any organic disease, except in so far as all her organs were affected by "this great letting down of nerve power and force." She suffered from a *"hot sore* spot in the spine, high up between the shoulders, leading up to the base of the brain, bursting into flame at every over-taxation of mental energy." It was an illness that had become her master and would one day be her conqueror, she predicted.

This was how Clara viewed herself when she left the sanitarium and established herself in a home near by, still keeping her associations with the institution. In the winter of 1877 she moved into a "snug brick city-built house" in Dansville. Then in the spring she settled in a much older and "country-like wood house, which has some trees, grass, and shade, a garden, and *perhaps* some flowers." Not strong enough yet to garden, Clara wrote that she relied on that "good sturdy old dame, mother earth, to dress herself without the aid of a *fille de chambre*."

Although she was nearing sixty and her friends considered her public life at an end, actually she was moving toward her most significant achievement. Teacher, government clerk, veteran of two wars, lecturer, finder of missing soldiers, Clara was at last ready to engage in the work for which she would be best remembered—the Red Cross. She was emerging from a decade of ill-health wiser, more tolerant, more sympathetic, more determined than ever. She was sleeping after years of insomnia, she wrote to the Grand Duchess Louise, explaining her long silence. She was putting on weight and was getting back her endurance. She could no longer sleep on the ground, as in her battle days, but she liked to lie on her stretcher "like a soldier under the trees."

The threat of war between Russia and Turkey was stirring long-dormant instincts in Clara. She wrote to Dr. Appia from Dansville on May 17, 1877, acknowledging that for four years she had been "powerless to strike a blow on the great anvil of humanity," and too weak even to hear of those who did. But now she saw again the "flash of the bayonet, the march of armies trampling down the harvests," and the Red Cross rising over the scene "like the bow of promise." Clara was her true self again when she wrote: "Like the old war horse that has rested long in quiet pastures I recognize the bugle-note that calls me to my place, and, though I may not do what I once could, I am come to offer what I may."

She pointed unerringly to the weak spot in the national picture. Not one person in a hundred in America had ever heard of the Red Cross. Not one in five hundred had any clear conception of its purpose. The country did not know that "this holy child was ever an applicant for her adoption." She proposed a committee to publicize the movement, and an organization with national headquarters sanctioned by the Government where the Red Cross flag would float day and night, in war and peace. She suggested state organizations and smaller relief societies, all working under its insignia. Finally, Clara asked for an official letter from headquarters to submit to the President and Cabinet officers. She proposed a head for the organization—preferably not herself, since "I have little ambition at best and none now."

Dr. Appia replied enthusiastically, urging Clara to become the active working head of the order. He suggested that she surround herself with a small group of persons full of good-will and capacity, either women or young men, and especially doctors. The roll of civilized states in the Convention of Geneva was now virtually complete except for the United States, he said. Montenegro had just come in. He told her what to do. She must see and interest the President. She must publicize the movement, and raise money for it. She must create a skeleton organization into which life could be breathed when the need arose. She must have documents and pamphlets translated into English. He would send her a batch of printed material covering all aspects of the rapidly growing movement. He pointed out at the same time that the Red Cross had given birth "to an entire new literature," creating a library of its own, in many different tongues.

"And now, my worthy friend, go on courageously with faith and hope," wrote Dr. Appia. "The cause is good; let us defend it everywhere and let us be firm in upholding the banner of charity. It will be ever the surest means of combating the principle of war."

Gustave Moynier, president of the International Committee, promptly sent Clara a letter dated August 19, 1877, to be delivered to the President of the United States, in which once again he urged participation in the Treaty of Geneva and recommended Government sympathy and protection for a National Society of the Red Cross. "We have already an able and devoted assistant in Miss Clara Barton, to whom we confide the care of handing to you this present request," added M. Moynier.[2]

He and Dr. Appia had clearly chosen Clara as their favored representative and sent all their communications directly through her. Both men had responded with such wholehearted confidence in her ability to push the matter through that she journeyed to Washington that autumn, her first trip in four years. Clara was expert at strategy, and understood every move in the political game. She was not a green hand at moving the immovable, or applying pressure to Government officials. She was convinced that the whole project had fallen flat in earlier years because the groundwork had not been properly prepared. She decided "to guard the outposts" (Clara instinctively used military phraseology), and have everyone concerned well informed on the purposes of the Red Cross before she approached President Rutherford B. Hayes. She brought her cousin, Judge Hale, into the picture to protect her in all legal aspects of the undertaking.

At this point she embarked on a steady campaign of mounting intensity, pursuing her course with single-minded purpose at the Capitol, where her plumed bonnet, her dark silk suits and laces, reminded veterans that Miss Barton was on the warpath again. Her worn, earnest face had aged in two decades. Her skin was sallow, but the humorous glint was still alive in her eyes, and her perceptions were as keen as ever.

She prepared and circulated a brochure: *The Red Cross of the Geneva Convention: What It Is.*[3] She flitted in and out of offices, seeking interviews, leaving her tract. Carl Schurz was sympathetic. Ben Butler gave her his "old kind smile," the "*grim* all fled from his face," and urged her to call on him at any time. Richard W. Thompson, Secretary of the Navy, was genuinely interested, listened attentively to Clara at her most eloquent, and carefully studied her documents. In fact, she had him in tears.

John Sherman, Secretary of the Treasury, wished to be informed. He was "bluff but not unkind." Postmaster David McKendree Key listened closely to Clara but did not commit himself. Judge Omar D. Conger, of Michigan, was cold to her until he learned that she had nursed his brother during the Civil War. After that he became one of her most ardent friends and helpers. Bob Hale, who was close to W. M. Evarts, infuriated her by not pushing the matter when he had such easy access to the Secretary of State. Hitz had specifically warned her to watch out for the State Department— that efforts would be made to block her there.

Clara was in fine fettle at the New Year's Day reception given in 1878 by John and Kate Hitz at the Swiss Consulate. Wearing a green velvet dress with bustle and long plush train, in which she had her portrait made, she seemed to her old friend, John Defrees, of the Government Printing Bureau, to be the Clara Barton of long ago. He promised to take her to the White House three days later for an interview with President Hayes. Clara felt she had done the preliminary spadework. She was back in the national picture and finding her bearings again.

She was charmed by Mrs. Hayes—commenting on her bright and lovely face, her abundance of rich black hair, her sprightly manner, her clear voice and melodious laugh. She observed that her "deep-set, dark-brown eyes spoke to one continually, and always pleasant things." In short, she found her the "superior of her husband, who seems to be an experienced business man of mild, affable manners." Mrs. Hayes gave Clara a bouquet, which was pressed, and became another one of her numerous souvenirs.

President Hayes accepted M. Moynier's letter from Clara with "great respect" and promptly gave her a note to Evarts, since the matter fell within his province. The President, evidently not deeply moved, wrote to his Secretary of State on January 4, 1878: "Miss Clara Barton of New York State has some plans regarding the mitigation of the cruelties of war which she wishes to present to you. Please give her a hearing and such aid and encouragement as may be deemed by you fit."

Evarts took the matter so lightly that he did not even see her but turned her over to his assistant, Frederick W. Seward, son of the famous William Seward who had coldly turned his face against the Treaty of Geneva as an "entangling alliance." The younger Seward studied his father's comments and those of Hamilton Fish and with the same glacial exterior told her: "It is all settled; the question will never again be considered." She reminded him that Charles Devens, the Attorney General, had assured her that no serious legal obstacle stood in the way.

This made no difference. Clara saw that she had come to a dead end and must wait for another administration. "I saw that it was all made to depend on one man," she wrote on a little scratch pad, "and that man regarded it as settled. I had nothing to hope for then, but did not press the matter for a third refusal. It waited and so did I."

Clara had lost the first round but she knew how to wait. Things lagged after this and she paid some summer visits, but in the late autumn she was back in Washington and going the rounds again, encountering nothing but apathy. She was briefly cheered by an affectionate letter from Colonel Elwell, who was living in Cleveland and had not forgotten the halcyon days at Hilton Head:

My acquaintance with you came at a time when . . . I was almost overwhelmed with care and trouble and can never make known to you how much your woman's love did for me. In your own language, written at Port Royal, "some of those hours and words were to be in after life *golden threads* woven into the web of life; there to shine for ever and ever." They do shine and grow brighter as the years glide over them. How I would love to meet my dear one again.

But discouragement again brought ill-health and Clara was back in Dansville during 1879 and most of 1880. As the months passed she came to the conclusion that she must found a national society first; then work for its ultimate tie-up with the international body. Her correspondence picked up rapidly in 1880, and she restored the links with some of her old protégées. She wrote to Anna Zimmermann a week before her fifty-ninth birthday, telling her she had heard that she was a happy wife and mother, living a full life, but that she had never received a line from Antoinette since her return to America. However, she had learned from Antoinette's father that she was back in Lyons and teaching, after some years passed in a convent followed by a breakdown. Clara did not know it but Anna at this time was in the last stages of consumption.

Jules Golay died that summer from blood poisoning after an arm amputation. And Clara heard from Dorr, who was now making a "capital consul" in Tahiti. He had married Princess Moetia, of the reigning family, but he found life somewhat boring on his tropical island. He had asthma. He could not stand the food. Tahiti was dull. Moetia's hair was falling out and she weighed 195 pounds. She constantly nagged him for a trip to the United States. "If it had not been for the Queen's child 'Boots' I don't know what I should have done to kill time," wrote Dorr.

Clara's comment on this communication was as optimistic as she could make it: "I tried to bring my boy up sensibly—and I trust he will not disappoint me, but he was a stubborn fellow and required a strong rein—but a sterling piece of material."

With James A. Garfield now looming on the horizon as a Presidential candidate, she took a lively interest in politics again. He was an old battlefield friend of seventeen years' standing, and she felt that she could go to him with the Red Cross cause. She campaigned on his behalf and urged the Republicans of Dansville to vote, not for a "dead but a living leader."

She wrote to her old friend, Gustav Bergmann of Strassburg, on December 26, 1880, praising both Grant and Hayes as Presidents but saying of the President-elect: "We know we have a statesman, a man of firmness, culture, courage, physical and moral—just, humane, and of unimpeachable integrity of character. He is revered and beloved by the people and we are hopeful for the results of his administration."

In this same letter Clara showed pride in the Presidential wives, except for "poor Mrs. Lincoln who was no doubt insane and naturally a source of grief and often deep mortification." Clara Barton appraised the others for Bergmann. She knew them all.

Mrs. Grant was a good, kind, sensible calm lady, not brilliant, but always correct and her influence was wide and valuable. Mrs. Hayes is the peer of a princess, beautiful in person and mind, graceful, accomplished, gentle and intellectually and morally is considered to be one of the strongest women in the country. And Mrs. Garfield is held her equal, even more scholarly than Mrs. Hayes—has herself fitted her sons for college. . . . We have something to hope, I think, from the rule of men with such wives. They cannot act very badly with this home check on them, even if disposed. For the outcome of our "New Government" you and I, with all the world, must wait.

Clara sent Garfield a photograph of herself and a letter of congratulation on his election. She watched the inauguration procession on a snowy March day and promptly urged her old friend, E. B. Washburne, long familiar with the workings of the Red Cross in Europe, to lay before the President a simple plan for bringing the United States into the Geneva Convention. Within the month Clara herself called on Mr. Garfield with her four-year-old letter from M. Moynier.

"We fought together in the Civil War, didn't we?" he commented as the worn but spirited Miss Barton walked into his presence. He had seen her without her plumed bonnet and her tidy polonaise, up to her calves in mud, the mush ladle waving through a haze of smoke.

They had a good conversation. Then he referred her to his Secretary of State, James G. Blaine, who warmed Clara with his interest and sympathy. She gave him her ablest presentation of her cause. He confessed total ignorance of the plan. When he heard of the rock on which it had foundered he remarked that the "Monroe Doctrine was not made to ward off humanity." He did not feel that the new administration would be influenced by what had gone before. But catching the international implications of the treaty he urged her to see Robert T. Lincoln, the Secretary of War. He promised to study her pamphlet and inform himself on all the international aspects of the Treaty of Geneva.

Clara left his presence elated, feeling that she had made more headway in these two weeks than in the previous four years. With her nephew Stevé she visited Lincoln and recalled his father's kindness to her. The younger Lincoln was "very genial and promised kind consideration." He said he would support adhesion to the Treaty of Geneva if the administration backed it up.

Things slowed up after this. Blaine was much preoccupied with affairs of state. Roscoe Conkling had erupted and resigned his Senate seat. Finally on May 17 a resolution drawn up by Senator Conger was submitted to the Senate asking the Secretary of State to submit translated copies of the Articles of the Convention signed at Geneva in 1864, along with the forms of ratification used by the other signatories. This was a concrete step, welcomed by Clara. They had all been bothered by the stumbling block of the need for Congressional action on the articles of war.

Three days later, since Clara was still the vibrant link between them, Blaine wrote asking her to assure M. Moynier that the President and his Cabinet were in sympathy "with any wise measures tending toward the amelioration of the suffering incident to warfare." He added that should the President approve—and he did not doubt he would—the new administration would recommend to Congress the adoption of the international treaty.

Clara wrote at once to M. Moynier, for the bridge seemed to have been crossed at last.

Back came his answer: "I await with complete confidence the result of your sympathetic endeavors. . . ." [4]

On May 21, 1881, Clara held a meeting at 1326 I Street, sending out her invitations on a letterhead inscribed "The Red Cross of the International Convention of Geneva" and listing herself as "American Representative." Her role had now become official. A group of her friends gathered in her plain parlor and as Mrs. Peter V. DeGraw, wife of one of Clara's newspaper friends who was also a founder of the Gridiron Club, later recalled the scene:

The chairs were pushed back against the wall in a square. At the end of the room stood Miss Barton. She spoke of the horrors of war and of the need for an impartial society to treat the wounds of the injured, friend and foe. Men who had fallen on the battlefield had little chance of recovery, Miss Barton told us, emphasizing the need for emergency treatment of the wounded to bridge the gap between the time of injury and arrival at the field hospital.

All present pledged their support. There had been earlier meetings at the Hitz and Conger homes, but they had been inconclusive. This was the starting point of organization. Clara read her brochure on the Red Cross and a constitution was adopted which laid stress on peacetime activities as an important *raison d'être* for a national relief society.

This was of the greatest significance to the future of the Red Cross in America, a peace-loving nation not often embroiled in war but frequently visited by the major catastrophes of nature. In the next seventy-five years the Red Cross was to participate in four major wars, but it was to serve in upward of six thousand disaster relief operations. Its expenditure for disaster preparedness and relief would total $242,000,000, of which $203,000,000 would be spent in the United States.

Clara foresaw that the organization would need a sustained functioning base; that yellow fever was a recurrent plague in the South; that the Mississippi periodically overflowed its banks; that tornadoes and hurricanes were of fairly frequent occurrence; that droughts plagued the farmers; and that forest fires were a constant hazard.

She put so much emphasis on this aspect of the work that she profoundly influenced peacetime Red Cross activities around the world. Actually the original idea was Dunant's. In the third edition of *Un Souvenir de Solferino,* published in 1863, he enlarged his conception of the functions of the Convention of Geneva to cover "the incessant war with the elements, certain dangerous works, and the accidents that fall to man." He proposed that Red Cross workers be posted at stations, mines, fire stations, industrial plants, and where large crowds gathered. The Treaty of Geneva in itself did not provide for disaster relief.

The brochure that Clara had been circulating among the legislators emphasized the peacetime possibilities of the organization she proposed. In time she dramatized for the world this aspect of the Red Cross through the magnitude of the catastrophes that struck the United States in the late nineteenth century and the original measures she used to meet them. Even at Galveston in 1900, her last major venture into the field, she could scarcely have dreamed how imposing this aspect of Red Cross work would become, right down to the floods of 1955, when some $27,000,000 was spent for emergency and rehabilitation aid.

The little group gathered in Clara's Victorian parlor had no grandiose objectives in mind. They were concerned chiefly with seeing the United States take its rightful place in the Convention of Geneva. Neither Mr. nor Mrs. Garfield would accept the presidency offered them in turn by Clara, who argued that in other countries kings and emperors headed this important body. Garfield nominated Clara Barton for the honor. He was dead when the group was chartered by the District of Columbia in October, 1881. It was reincorporated in 1893 as the American National Red Cross.

Judge William Lawrence of Ohio drafted the constitution in close collaboration with Clara.[5] Her publicity sense was well developed from her Civil War and Andersonville days, when she dealt with such men as Horace Greeley and Charles A. Dana. Three of her earliest officers were writers. Walter P. Phillips and George Kennan were newspaper correspondents of national reputation. English-born Colonel Richard J. Hinton was known in the writing field from Boston to San Francisco. They were to support Clara on a volunteer basis through many difficult years. When she had anything to communicate to the American public, the press-service wires were always open to her, giving her a great advantage from the start.

Few aspects of Clara's career show more ingenuity than the way in which by gradual stages and clever publicity she made the Red Cross a familiar symbol to Americans. She herself was always the pivot, because of the picturesque character she was, and the strong way in which she functioned. Until the turn of the century she and the Red Cross were one. It was good strategy at the start, but as the organization grew, it became a major weakness.

As usual, in the moment of triumph her spirits drooped. "Still, I am so sad," she wrote. "I dread the future, not knowing it well." Yet everything at this point was set for climactic action by Congress. She had full Presidential and Cabinet support. She had a functioning organization. On July 2 she was about to leave Washington for the summer when hurrying crowds in the streets brought the well-remembered suggestion of something gone wrong. She was on her way with Stevé to visit Dr. George B. Loring, but they stopped in the street, stunned by the news that President Garfield had been shot. First they went to the station, then back to the Treasury, and finally to the Capitol gate, which was closed. Here Clara ran into Kennan, from whom she picked up the details of the attempted assassination by the fanatical Charles J. Guiteau. She went home, sorrowing, then decided to continue on her way to Dansville.

Heavy hearted, Clara thought of Abraham Lincoln. She was beset, not only by her personal sorrow, but by the implications of this new turn of events for her nearly consummated plans. She wrote urgently to Moynier on July 28, saying she feared that if the outcome were fatal, the work would have to be done all over again. But if the President recovered "there is nothing to fear for our cause until it come to a vote in Congress."

A month later she was writing to Walker Blaine that the "end seemed to draw certainly near, the dark curtain about to fall. . . . Never perhaps in the annals of the world has a nation clung with such tenderness to the bedside of a chief Magistrate." But not forgetting the Red Cross she added: "My concern lies in the possible beyond; when, if it must be, he shall have gone, what then?"

She put in a busy summer propagandizing her cause from the Dansville area. Phillips worked from Washington, trying to stir up interest in the New York papers. "Mr. Blaine can, if he will, induce Whitelaw Reid to do something," he wrote to Clara. Meanwhile A. O. Bunnell, of the Dansville *Advertiser*, joined with Dr. Jackson in helping Clara draw up a plan for a local unit. It was first drafted in the apothecary shop run by G. Bastian.

A meeting was held at the First Presbyterian Church early in August to whip up interest. This was followed on August 22, 1881, by the organization in St. Paul's Lutheran Church of the first local Red Cross unit in the United States. Clara, who had come to Dansville a total invalid four years earlier, read the constitution in her deep, soft voice to fellow townsmen who knew her well and had much faith in her.

The newly founded society went into action quickly when the Michigan forest fire broke out that autumn, sending the first Red Cross relief supplies into an American field. Near-by Rochester and Syracuse quickly founded units and helped in this emergency, leading the long parade of chapters which totaled 3,713 three-quarters of a century later.

After President Garfield's death in September Clara went to New Haven to work with Joseph Sheldon on an extended pamphlet on the Red Cross, which she wished to have ready before Congress convened. She ordered 5,000 copies to be distributed gratuitously as she gathered up her forces for a new joust in Washington—this time with Chester A. Arthur and his administration. Sheldon helped her on legal points, or as Clara described it: "He fitted the entangling alliance argument and put in little joints where it did not connect well from my broken speeches." Together they devoted much concentrated thought to the Articles of War, the ticklish point at issue.

On October 20 Sheldon confronted her with a group of experts in his office and made Clara talk for their approval. This was quite an ordeal for her but Dr. Theodore D. Woolsey, ex-president of Yale University, applauded her exposition and "could see not the smallest shadow of reason in rejecting the treaty." The others who listened were the Rev. Dr. Edwin Harwood, H. B. Harrison, the Rev. John E. Todd and Professor Francis Wayland. They represented church, medicine, and education.

Clara and Sheldon were leaving no stone unturned to clear the way for their next move and together they decided that it might be diplomatic to call on Dr. Bellows in his New York home. It was an interesting encounter, since they had never met, although the Sanitary Commission and the Red Cross were indissolubly linked in purpose and practice. Clara knew its history well and its great contributions in the Civil War—its seven thousand aid societies and $15,000,000 worth of stores distributed. She was well aware that it had sprung up prior to and independently of the Convention of Geneva, and indeed had had its true genesis at a meeting of women called in the New York Infirmary by Dr. Elizabeth Blackwell.

Clara thought Dr. Bellows had a "pleasant kind face." He discussed his efforts to promote the Treaty of Geneva with the utmost frankness and said that Seward had "utterly disregarded it, had pooh-poohed at it; that every member of Congress and official he had ever spoken to of it had treated it as a delusion, a sentiment, but of no practical value—and that he had failed in every attempt, and had so written to Geneva."

Clara then told him where she stood. "He listened in apparent surprise," she reported. "He seemed also pleased, said I had done what he could not." He offered to go to Washington with her if she found herself in a difficult spot, and although he was not in accord with President Arthur and had never liked Blaine, if he "would not do the subject more harm than good he would act at any moment I desired and in any way."

Dr. Bellows' own organization had petered out in 1872, and he would die within the year, but his good wishes cheered Clara on her way. She was now assembling letters for her new campaign and by the end of October had at least fifty, including notes from her old Civil War friends, Grant, Sheridan, Burnside, Sherman, Butler, and Adjutant General Charles E. Townsend, as well as from Dr. Bellows.[6] She felt she had left no loopholes when she was smuggled into an anteroom for a third talk with Blaine on October 29, 1881. She found him as "genial and kind as a brother." He told her he felt that President Arthur would be on her side, and that he would prepare a clause for the Presidential message, "but I need not say so to the President."

Blaine proposed General John A. Logan, who would be his running mate on the Presidential ticket of 1884, as the best man to present the Treaty of Geneva to the Senate. He was interested to learn that Clara had the Iron Cross of Germany and other medals. He said he would like to see them. She promptly sent him a box with the Iron Cross of Merit, the Gold Cross of Remembrance, and the Red Cross of Geneva.

Next she went to call on President Arthur. He was just leaving for a ride but "did rush in a moment to say he regretted his inability to see me now but would I come again." He told her she need "not expect him to go back on humanity." Apparently he had been discussing the matter with Mr. Blaine. His private secretary suggested a letter setting forth her aims, which Clara promptly dispatched, along with a copy of her pamphlet.

She felt encouraged, and wrote: "I can go on confidently after this—men who would not *hear* before, will *listen* that they may hear now, and humanity will get its due." She no longer felt like an outcast, begging for a hearing. But that winter on the whole was a dreary one for Clara. Things did not move forward as fast as she had expected. She was depressed and lonely as she went home night after night to bleak, chilly rooms she had taken, with tall, rattling windows, a latrobe stove that failed to spread warmth, and secondhand furniture. Her diary entries on her sixtieth birthday suggest that she was again in a seriously depressed state of mind, although earlier in December the President had transmitted to the Senate Blaine's recommendation and the documents requested in the previous May. Three thousand copies were printed for official reading. Effective steps had been taken at last.

There was now a pause while the matter went into camera but Clara could not rest, and continued to visit men of influence in the Capitol. She was wracked by a more personal worry that threatened to swamp her at this juncture. In the moment of success a dark shadow had risen from the past, to threaten her prestige. Of various rival groups to the Red Cross that had been operating in the capital the Blue Anchor, or Woman's National Relief Association, had made the greatest inroad and had official backing that was proving hurtful to Clara's cause.

It was headed by Mrs. Hannah McLaren Shepard, one of her former helpers, and long known to her as "Shepherdess." They had been close friends and Mrs. Shepard, who wrote for years for the New York *Evening Mail* under the pen name "Scotch Granite," had helped to publicize Clara's movement through *Alpha* and other magazines catering to women's interests. She was the daughter of a minister from Auburn, New York. Clara had urged Charles A. Dana to consider her work, and had introduced her to Mrs. Hayes as a "woman of talent, culture and refinement," worthy of a post under government patronage. But with her inner knowledge of the workings of the Red Cross, Mrs. Shepard soon cut adrift, founded the Blue Anchor, and pushed it as the biggest thing women had been called to enlist in since the days of the Sanitary Commission. It sought Congressional support and represented itself as "an association of women, not an association of *one* woman." The wives of some of the most powerful Senators were behind Mrs. Shepard and Clara feared this might affect the outcome of her plans. The Blue Anchor helped to outfit United States Life Saving stations. It had worked for the victims of the Michigan forest fire.

But beyond all this, Mrs. Shepard was spreading calumny about Clara, who was slow to recognize betrayal in anyone she had befriended. In time the Blue Anchor was forgotten; the Red Cross lived on and flourished, but in 1882 it was a searing issue for Clara, who felt that Mrs. Shepard had used her program for her own ends.

In a state of great mental distress she reverted to her usual line of reasoning when in deep depression—flight from the country, or flight from life's ties. Time and again she was to ponder both possibilities, but while her diary revealed these dark shadows she went about Washington, functioning capably, and promoting her cause. Nothing showed on the surface. Clara's dual personality was rarely revealed to her friends.

She visited the newly appointed Secretary of the Navy, William E. Chandler, and was happy to find him a friend of General Butler. "I must make use of that fact to get the Navy all right with the Red Cross," commented Clara. She persuaded Ben Perley Poore to get her a Congressional Record and round up various documents she wanted at the Capitol. She attended some sessions of the Guiteau trial. "I was at a loss to decide if he were crazy or not," she commented. "His eye is his wisest feature and is decidedly bad." A few days later she called on the chairman of the Foreign Relations Committee, William Windom, a friend and supporter of the

Red Cross, but found him "half sad or as if something had come over the spirit of his dream." She fancied that some of her enemies had reached him. She wrote to Dr. George F. Shrady, editor of the *Medical Record,* which had taken friendly note of her pamphlet. She mourned the death of Dr. Bellows and her cousin, Judge Hale, who had died of Bright's disease.

On February 6, 1882, Clara prayed for guidance, a most uncommon act on her part. "I am so weary of this strife, this unrest, this doubt," she said. She was ready to retire, and let Mrs. Shepard have her way. But the following day she tramped through slush to round up General Sheridan at Wormleys. He was not in, so she left her card and a copy of her Red Cross pamphlet. Next she tackled General S. S. Burdette, one of her soldier friends, but he "pled great business," an excuse which caused Clara to note indignantly in her diary: "I cannot but think how much *more time* all these people would have if the Red Cross should fall heir to a few thousand dollars."

However, a long and entertaining talk with Phillips in the smoky offices of the Associated Press revived Clara's spirits. Here was an intelligent and charming man who understood what she was driving at and had choice means of conveying it to the world. It is also likely that he was aware of Clara's news value at this point. That night she noted in her diary: "The Associated Press is a power and Phillips is a power. I feel myself nothing and yet I suppose I have turned the crank that has set it all in motion. I wonder if I am not a *crank* myself."

After leaving Phillips she decided to go direct to the State Department and check up on what was going on. The new Secretary of State, Frederick T. Frelinghuysen, turned a "handsome beaming face" on her for a few moments, then sent out an aide named Brown with a bundle in his hand.

"Mr. Brown, I *would* like to know where the Red Cross hangs," said Clara humbly.

He handed her a document resembling an unbound book. He said it was not customary to let unsigned papers be seen, but "we *want* you to see if it suits you." He told her to sit down and read it at her leisure. Clara sank into a sofa and read, page after page, all that she had longed and hoped for, down to the final phrase—"that the United States of America Accede to this Treaty,"—with blanks for the signatures.

Then, as Clara herself recalled what happened next:

I had kept my eyes clear enough to read to the end, but then I could hold up no longer—and how long a cry I indulged in I do not know—but I know it rested me, and after some time—I was able to look up again—and good Mr. Brown came again, and said very gently—"does it suit you?" I said, "Oh yes, it is all it could be. I am only sorry I have done so badly myself, but I could do no better."

Brown laughed, and Clara asked him when it would be signed. He answered: "Any time now." She thanked him and left. "*At last* it was done," she observed. But Clara at this point could leave nothing to chance. She had been disappointed too often. She went straight to the White House and impressed on an ally there the importance of handing the document to the President for signature the moment it arrived. Actually he signed it on March 1, 1882, fifteen days before it was ratified by the Senate. Thus Clara followed each step behind the scenes.

The next official to befriend her was Senator E. S. Lapham. When she went to his home for news he slipped out of a stag gathering to whisper to her in the hall that the treaty had passed the Committee on Foreign Relations that day, and would be ratified within a few days. On March 16 he made this official with a note ending "Laus Deo." She could publish the glad news. The Senate had ratified the Geneva Treaty and there was no more need for secrecy.

"*Treaty Ratified*" Clara Barton wrote in purple ink in her otherwise penciled diary on March 16, 1882. The United States Government had at last become part of the congregation of nations that upheld the Red Cross. Working virtually singlehanded she had achieved a noble end. "So it was done," she wrote, as she used a wet towel "to wipe off the sadness and tears. . . . I had waited so long and got so weak and broken I could not even feel glad."

For years she had badgered politicians, diplomats, generals, professors, and editors with unflagging zeal to achieve her aim. She had approached three Presidents for support, and had traversed a long, rough road in reaching her goal. "Clara Barton has the brain of a statesman, the command of a general, and the heart and hand of a woman," Charles Sumner said of her after the Civil War. He might have added that she had the patience and persistence of a dedicated zealot. Years of illness had slowed her up. She had lost her strongest supporter in Henry Wilson. But in the end she had won.

Senator Lapham sent her a basket of flowers, and as the news was made public Mrs. Shepard wrote her an abusive letter that made Clara reel in the moment of triumph. "Of course it had its effect to stun and daze . . . she seems to be as wicked as a brigand." The Shepherdess was threatening legal action, charging that the head of the Red Cross had been reviling her organization. Clara went to General R. D. Mussey, newly appointed counsel to the Red Cross, and showed him the letter. "Do nothing," he advised her. "Never give her the scratch of a pen."

But this letter and the feeling behind it robbed Clara of much of her legitimate joy when the climax of all her efforts was reached. However, torrents of praise reached her from other quarters. Phillips helped her through the days that followed. She was weak, tearful, suffering acutely from reaction. He notified Moynier in Switzerland, who quickly acknowledged the "glorious telegram" and later wrote that "without the energy and perseverance of this remarkable woman we should probably not for a long time have had the pleasure of seeing the Red Cross arrive in the United States."

Phillips flashed out publicity over the press wires. The United States had taken a step forward in world affairs, but the national papers carried only quiet little paragraphs marking the event. On July 26 President Arthur issued a proclamation announcing America's adhesion to the Treaty of Geneva, the thirty-second nation to fly the Red Cross flag. By that time Clara was in Dansville, trimming her rose bushes, pruning shrubs, raking leaves. She had help for her haying, harvesting, and cleaning, and "was content." It was a rest to have her feet on the "soft green earth, the real gravel and the spring grass."

Clara's feet had always been planted with firmness and precision, whether on grass or city pavements. She walked like an Indian, with a straight, sure tread. Now, at the age of sixty, her gait had the calm deliberation that matched her habitual air of quiet courtesy and attention.

The heavy crop of rich brown hair of which she was so proud had thinned during her years of illness, and showed gray strands which she did not hesitate to treat with rinses and restoratives. Her strong features had taken on a rugged quality as she aged. The high planes of her cheekbones were more pronounced. Her sage brown eyes were still alight with humor but her mobile mouth had settled into a firm mold of determination. "No one who saw her shut her mouth when she made a decision could cherish any doubt of her tenacity of purpose; and her chin was anything but a weak one," commented the Rev. Dr. William E. Barton, her cousin and biographer. In her later years he viewed her thus:

Ladylike, sympathetic, energetic, and marvellously forceful . . . still patient, still persistent, rising at 4 or 5 o'clock in the morning and working until late at night, living with such simplicity of life that no soldier ever lived upon a smaller ration or slept upon a narrower or simpler bed than that upon which she slept night after night, always with a light at the head of her bed, where she might, as thoughts came to her in the night, write down those thoughts.

As Clara moved more prominently into the social world she became increasingly concerned with her attire, fussing about her laces, her hair, her train, and her published photographs. Her early instincts to appear "genteel" came well to the fore in the course of her Red Cross work. It had been difficult at times to sustain this tradition while jumping up on the wheels of army wagons and wading through the mud of the Civil War battlefields. Yet the soldiers always detected the "genteel" as well as the kindly in their battle-field angel. Her paradoxical nature encompassed a good sense of fun. She liked charades and card games in her later years, and never failed to crack a joke when she saw an opening. She had faced the grimmest realities of life and death, and this resulted in a deep co-mingling of earthy and puritan strains in the complex make-up of Clara Barton.

# CHAPTER XI

## A FOREST FIRE

THE RED CROSS had already begun to function on a local basis before the United States signed the Treaty of Geneva. Its flag for the first time signaled disaster relief in America when it flew over Clara Barton's quarters in Dansville after the Michigan forest fire of 1881. The pattern of the future was clearly outlined in this first operation.

The fire raged for days, sweeping everything before it—man, beast, forests, farms, or, as Clara put it: "There is no food left in its track for a rabbit to eat and, indeed, no rabbit to eat it, if there were." She was not at the immediate scene but she set up a solid barrage of aid through the three first units of the Red Cross—in Dansville, Rochester, and Syracuse.

The dazed survivors of the horrors of a forest fire were sustained and helped back into shelter. Food, clothing, medical and household supplies met their first needs. Then lumber and tools were provided to re-establish them. The field was held until the cold weather set in, and $80,000 was expended on the sufferers of the first catastrophe in which the Red Cross gave aid. This was part of a $900,000 program administered by Port Huron and Detroit local committees.

At this time Julian B. Hubbell moved into the foreground as Clara's chief field agent and helper. He was studying medicine at the University of Michigan when the fire broke out and, although he had not yet graduated, his proximity to the region of the fire suggested an appeal to him for aid. He was heading into Red Cross work in any event. Meeting Clara at Dansville in 1876, he was interested in joining her in the new organization. He was teaching chemistry at the time but Clara, remembering Dr. Appia's injunction to round up able young assistants, preferably doctors, persuaded him to take up medicine.

He came from a well-known Iowa family and Clara saw at once that he was well versed in agricultural matters, one of her own strong interests. She studied him carefully and thought him "humane in principle and practical in his outlook." He soon set off for the University of Michigan, writing frequently to his patroness "Mamie" of the progress he was making.

This was the beginning of Clara's most significant working partnership. As Field Agent for the Red Cross, Dr. Hubbell gave years of devoted service to her and her cause. He supported her in every move, went out to the field as her advance agent, and applied his specialized knowledge of agriculture to the various disaster areas. Dr. Hubbell grew old in Clara's service. His benign manner, his straggling Dundrearies, his scarlet scarf, his violin and kindly solicitude for Mamie all became an inseparable part of her ménage. Her own most revealing tribute to him was that he was "a patient man."

From this point on she deliberately built up a following of young men and women who could be useful to her in her work. As Dr. Appia had warned her—she would need "feet for running, to go, to come, to collect, to buy, to make multitudes of visits. . . ." Clara did a little of everything herself, and expected her helpers to do the same. But she always kept the reins firmly in her own hands and made the top decisions herself. When a real obstacle arose, Clara was the one who could surmount it. But as her organization grew her corps of workers increased. Some were brilliantly effective in the aid they gave her. Many were unselfish, industrious volunteers, but she was usually saddled with a few lame ducks and she made some disastrous choices. When her agents betrayed her and damaged her cause, Clara was reluctant to abandon them or think ill of their motives. Her volunteer service was an important part of her early work, and a basic principle of the Red Cross. The day would come when 1,650,000 volunteers would work the year around in the United States, and 8,200,000 would function in one year of the First World War.

Dr. Hubbell's work in Michigan pleased Clara so well that she arranged a college leave for him to send him down the Mississippi in the spring of 1882. He was then thirty-five and would graduate in the following year. There had been floods and she wished him to appraise the situation. He toured the Black River region and the plantations of Concordia through a "waste of waters," studying local rescue operations. He reported back to Clara that all necessary provision had been made by state and federal aid, and that the Red Cross, at this early stage of its development, would not be justified in entering the field. But he planned for the future and helped to organize Red Cross societies in Memphis, Vicksburg, and New Orleans. "A fine city for a society," he wrote of Natchez. "Many excellent people here. Have become acquainted with many." He found Louisiana state lottery tickets being sold at every street corner in New Orleans, and predicted in his report that the Red Cross might help to remedy the "unwise, and worse, the corrupt use of public bounty."

Clara was now established as a woman with a cause, and she had succeeded where others still were grappling with their problems. She often wrote to Frances Willard and had even considered asking the G.A.R. to establish a Temperance League. In one of her letters to Miss Willard she wrote of the Red Cross as a "little strange craft from a foreign land, bearing only the banner of peace and love, her messages of world wide mercy begging shelter and acceptance in our capacious harbour."

Susan B. Anthony and Lucy Stone were now hot on Clara's trail to make her an ally and advocate. Since she could always fill a hall with lusty, cheering crowds of masculine enthusiasts, both wanted from her an "appeal from the battlefield to the ballot box." But Clara would go so far with them and no further.

"We must have cordial championship volunteered to our cause by men," Lucy wrote Clara in the winter of 1881, adding:

They *must* feel and see that they will be *welcome* to the new sphere and to the duties and rights that belong to it. . . . You, being you, with the part you took in the war superadded, could write a letter that would be printed by every influential paper in the United States. We should thus reach an audience that would be moved and in turn move those who move our representatives and senators to enact justice to women.

Lucy took Clara to task after she spoke of her war experiences at the eleventh reunion of the First New York Dragoons in Dansville.

On this occasion Dr. Jackson hailed her as the Florence Nightingale of America. "Sherman's March to the Sea" was recited with flourishes. A section of the Confederate Flag from Richmond Capitol was handed to her. There were the usual bursts of wild applause for Clara.

"How *could* you have refrained from speaking for the enfranchisement of 30,000,000 women?" Lucy demanded.

"I do not know," Clara retorted crisply, "unless it was by the same discipline by which I could refrain from doing any other thing which seemed to me to be untimely or out of place."

However, she took the sting out of this by adding that the cause of woman's advancement was "dear and holy" to her and she would go many times the "breadth of the land, *unpaid*, to serve acceptably in such a cause." Lucy had proposed that she become a paid speaker for the suffrage cause, but Clara would not hear of this. However, she did send out a written appeal to her soldier friends to support woman suffrage.

Susan Anthony at this time was importuning Clara to do a graphic summing up of the work done by women in the "Hospital, Field, on the March" for her *History of Woman Suffrage*. Although she loved and admired Miss Barton she viewed her strictly as a heroine of the Civil War, and had no deep understanding at first of the cause she was nurturing so zealously. The Red Cross had no identity yet in America, while the powerful drive for woman suffrage and other reform movements was engaging all of Susan's energies. However, she was always willing to give countenance to a good woman fighter and she considered Clara the sturdiest of oaks.

But she would not accompany her to a social science convention held at Saratoga in the autumn of that year, as Clara wished, because she had to stay at home in Rochester and ride herd on the State Temperance Women's Christian Union meeting there—"for if we can get them lifted out of their narrowness they will be a splendid help to general suffrage."

On the other hand, in her own words, Susan "screeched" to have a woman appointed to a committee arranging a meeting in Rochester at which Clara hoped the Red Cross would be discussed. In 1888, addressing the International Council of Women in Washington, Clara made public acknowledgment of the fact that Miss

Anthony was the "first woman to lay her hand beside mine in the formation of a Red Cross Society in her native city of Rochester."

Although Clara was deaf to Lucy Stone's appeal to work for woman suffrage, she listened to General Butler, by this time Governor of Massachusetts, and went off at a strange tangent shortly after the Treaty of Geneva was ratified. For a period of eight months in 1883 she was the popular and extremely lenient superintendent of the Woman's Reformatory Prison at Sherborn, Massachusetts.

Different factors entered into her decision to take this step, but perhaps the strongest was Butler's persuasion. He had always had great influence with Clara and she felt she owed him something. In a sense she was also following the contemporary pattern of the women pioneers cutting fresh furrows in the late nineteenth century. Dorothea Dix was making the nation prison-conscious and Mrs. Howe and Elizabeth Chase had tried to interest Clara in the subject in England.

Nevertheless, she accepted the post with genuine misgiving, still holding firm her Red Cross link. Phillips functioned for her during her temporary leave. She had fought so long and determinedly for ratification that she was suffering from her usual extreme reaction —not collapse this time but chagrin over the opposition and calumny she had encountered. She had no need of a new cause or a new post. Generous in her public service, she had prospered herself, and now had three homes—one in Washington, one in Dansville, one in North Oxford. She had lived economically and her estate had grown by sound investments. She insisted on posting her own $10,000 bond when she accepted the Sherborn appointment. Her salary was $1,500, with living expenses.

But Clara gave the work her individualistic touch and tempered discipline with mercy. A batch of illiterate and tear-stained notes in her papers bespeak the impression she made on the alcoholics, prostitutes, petty thieves, vagrants, and near murderesses, ranging in age from fifteen to seventy-five, who were her charges. The most degraded could reach her. She had a complaint box for notes installed in the hall and she kept close track of certain cases where large families were involved.

Clara was depressed by the flood of human tragedy and disorder that she found at Sherborn. As she walked the corridors, hung with keys, she groped for basic causes and proposed more scientific search for mental aberration and the transference of mental cases to asylums. She attributed most of the errancy to drunkenness, and optimistically told a group of state legislators who visited the prison that if liquor were banned in Massachusetts, within six months they could "rent Sherborn for a shoe manufactory."

She was opposed to fixed prison terms and believed that severe punishment was worse than none at all. Not a single penalty was imposed during her own last month in office. "Cultivate the love of the convicts by all proper means—it is more potent than punishment," she argued. She did not plague the inmates with advice but talked to them in the chapel every day, telling them true-life stories of the reclaimed. Thus Clara applied her self-help theories to her sodden audience and hammered home the message of self-respect.

In retrospect she considered her acceptance of the Sherborn post the most foolish move of her life. It is hard to believe that in eight months she performed the miracles claimed for her by the press and General Butler. But aside from her leniency, her sense of system and her well-developed instinct for mass housekeeping were assets to the state. Clara served as treasurer and steward, as well as superintendent. She made better use of the newfangled sewing machines, kept the workrooms busy, and gave careful thought to the prisoners' fare. Here she was in her element. "I would have the food plentiful, but unstimulating, and the cooking wholesome," she ordered, recommending "more of grains, vegetables, and fruit, and less of meat." Sherborn was only six years old and represented the contemporary feeling for prison reform. In accepting the post for a limited period Clara no doubt felt that she was part of this movement.

By November, 1883, she was ready to break away. She had tackled the job with her customary drive but recognized her own unsuitability for this work. She knew that it needed the touch of a professional. Moreover, she felt the pressure of party politics, and the inner cliques in the institution. She had "waded waist deep . . . through spite, jealousy and detraction." She was also eager to get back to her Red Cross work, and wrote to her old friend Rucker, now a general: "My own work needs me and I want to be called back to it, to stand in national and not state matters. I have not the habit of states. I have been a national woman too long for this."

Clara was showered with compliments as she left. Governor Butler, his state appropriation assured, wrote her that her administration had shown that "fit women are the fittest to take care of women" and that she had proved that a prison could be administered "without blows, without harshness" and still be run with good discipline. She had made it an institution of which "the state may well be proud."

But Clara found it more intimidating than the battlefield, and shrank from the orgies of sentiment that shook the prisoners on her last night there. As she passed down the corridors and heard the women loud in their lamentations she sought her own room, shivering with emotion, and later wrote in her diary:

Had it not been all wrong? Was I far enough removed from them? Surely we must be too near alike, if not akin, or they would never have clung to me with that pitiful love. I went out from the prison walls next morning. I have never seen a face there since. I have never returned and I have no desire to.

On her return to Washington Clara found that Phillips had written to Congressman Perry Belmont urging government aid for the Red Cross in the form of an appropriation. Otherwise, the United States had simply built a "gigantic ship canal calculated to benefit all mankind and had neglected to turn on the water." He added that the Red Cross should have a hundred societies in America, and that those in New York, Boston, and Washington should be "stronger than any humane organizations in the world."

## CHAPTER XII

# DOWN THE MISSISSIPPI

CLARA TOOK to the field in a memorable way when the Ohio River washed over its banks with the melting snows of February, 1884, a prelude to the great Mississippi floods of that year. Millions of acres of cotton and sugar land were laid waste. Man and beast were swept to their death on roaring currents, or were rescued from the flotsam to which they clung.

This was the first major flood in which the Red Cross participated and Clara's arrival in Cincinnati was duly noted in the press. She was never to forget the scene she found. Entire streets were afloat, and houses sailed on the tide like ghostly ships. As she recalled it:

> The surging river had climbed up the bluffs like a devouring monster and possessed the town; large steamers could have plied along its business streets. . . . Bankers and merchants stood in its relief houses and fed the hungry populace, and men and women were out in boats passing baskets of food to pale, trembling hands stretched out to reach it from third story windows of the stately blocks and warehouses of that beautiful city. . . .

It was a scene that was to be repeated many times in the years to come, but Clara's participation on this occasion and the appearance of the Red Cross flag marked an epoch in disaster relief. No sooner had she arrived than a tornado near Evansville in Indiana spread further chaos and entire villages were swept away. Clara quickly decided to move her headquarters to this area of greater need. She found the survivors homeless and half clad. Freezing weather added to their misery. The coal mines were waterlogged. There was no way of reaching all the victims by land. Government boats had come in with tents, blankets, and army rations. Clara hoped to supplement these with fuel and clothing.

"We, too, must take to the water," she observed, and promptly chartered a ship, the *Josh V. Throop*, had it loaded to the water's edge with clothing and coal, and set forth on her pilgrimage of mercy. In her own words:

Good assistants, both men and women were taken on board; the Red Cross flag was hoisted and as night was setting in, after a day of intense cold—amid surging waters and crashing ice, the floating wrecks of towns and villages, great uprooted giants of the forest plunging madly to the sea, the suddenly unhoused people wandering about the river banks, or huddled in strange houses with fireless hearths—the clear-toned bell and shrill whistle of the *"Josh V. Throop"* announced to the generous inhabitants of a noble city that from the wharves of Evansville was putting out the first Red Cross relief boat that ever floated on American waters.

Sixty-two years old, keen, capable, and well muffled against the cold, Clara was her old self, responding briskly to a moment of crisis. A large iron cross, forged in Evansville and painted bright red, hung between the two smokestacks. As the boat zigzagged its way from landing to landing, people stared at the emblem of mercy still strange and unfamiliar to them. They quickly learned what it meant.

When the boat was wrecked some years later on a rock above Chattanooga, Captain John Throop saved this Red Cross and nothing else. "I had it fished out and I intend to keep it as long as I live, and if I am so fortunate to ever have another boat, that shall be her trade mark and Clara Barton will be her name," he wrote to Dr. Hubbell in 1888.

The captain went where Clara willed. Any little settlement that caught her eye might constitute a landing. As word spread through the backwoods many came, not only to get help, but to view the strange barge and the lady known as the Angel of the Battlefield. Wrecked villages sprawled on either bank. At each stop, Clara invited a group on board, made some appraisal of the local needs, appointed small committees to receive and distribute supplies, and then doled out the amounts she thought would suffice. She sailed off "quickly and quietly, leaving sometimes an astonished *few*, sometimes a *multitude* to gaze after and wonder who she was, whence she came, what that strange flag meant, and most of all, to thank God with tears and prayers for what she brought."

Clara and her helpers worked over their supplies between stops, sorting clothing, arranging items according to size, and keeping records. Outright gifts of $75 were given to many families for lumber to rebuild their homes. Clara worked in friendly concert with the government boats plying the same route. They reached Cairo in five days. Such was the national response that on her return to Evansville from Cairo, more supplies awaited her.

This was the first of four trips up and down the Ohio and Mississippi made by Clara and her band of helpers. As the waters of the Ohio subsided, the Mississippi broke loose, and cut a new and foaming channel thirty miles in width at some points. The animals in the fields were drowned or left to starve. Congress voted a new appropriation and the Government ships moved down the Mississippi. Discharging her Ohio River boat, Clara chartered the *Mattie Belle* at St. Louis.

True to form, she found General Amos Beckwith stationed at the dock to be her commissary. He had often superintended the dispatch of her wagons as she set off for the battlefields of Virginia. Now he boarded her ship and directed operations, as clothing, corn, oats, salt, and hay were stowed away. He had Clara's surplus stock transferred to a Government ship, since the *Mattie Belle* was so overladen with forage that she seemed to be in danger of sinking.

Fresh supplies were bought in the cities they passed, so that in the end "the hungry were fed, the naked clothed and the stock saved," Clara reported with Biblical simplicity. At times they plied a dangerous course, steering their way through shattered levees and roaring crevasses. Before they left St. Louis a stranger came on board who later seemed to have been heaven sent. The captain, pushing ahead through fog one night in his anxiety to make a headland a few miles away, was running into danger without knowing it. Tributaries pouring into the Mississippi were giving fresh impetus to the raging torrents. Suddenly the stranger approached Clara with the warning: "We are in a crevasse! We must pull out or we are lost! I have warned the engineer and captain."

Engines were reversed. The *Mattie Belle* went through a series of shuddering gyrations, then moved slowly backward, away from the deadly current. Next morning Clara saw that they had escaped a newly opened crevasse, with the water pouring in a torrent "down a depth of twelve or fifteen feet" into the current below, "and rolling off in a self-made track to some other stream or to the Gulf of Mexico."

The shoreless waste of waters, the roaring crevasse, the Negro faces and hungry animals they could not reach made Clara think of the ark. She suffered over the horses, mules, cows, sheep, and pigs that floated past on rafts and log platforms, or huddled on broken levees, with no food but leaves, and the tips of the willow branches and gray moss which the Negroes brought them by skiff. On more than one occasion she went with the men through bayous and slews in quest of isolated livestock. Her little group portaged their own boats over the levees from one tributary to another, Clara carrying soothing oils for the badly bitten livestock.

There was indeed something arklike about her progress down the Mississippi. Patriarch planters came aboard with troops of Negro followers. They welcomed the lamp chimneys, kegs of nails, salt, skillets, and feed she left them. At Gaines Landing Clara found a planter who still had three hundred Negroes in his employ. The freedmen took the meal, corn, and hay in skiffs to the storehouse and scurried away, waving good-by. Clara put Negro agents on some of the local committees to keep the balance steady. Blessings followed the boat as it moved away from tiny landings. At one Negro settlement, where supplies were left on the only sliver of land that could be reached, she noticed that their departure was marked by dead silence. By this time they were better used to cheers.

Looking back, she saw the Negroes on their knees praying. "The entire group had knelt beside the bags of grain and food and not a head or hand was raised to bid us speed," Clara commented. "A Greater than we had possessed them, and in tearful silence we bowed our heads as well and went our way."

Old songs still echoed along the river banks. As they traveled farther South the scent of flowers was sometimes strong in the air. Bouquets were brought aboard for Clara, who thought often of her army days. When they reached Vicksburg she took time for reflection and shed some tears in the cemetery there. Twenty hours later they arrived at Natchez on Easter Sunday and were welcomed with the most mellow Southern hospitality. Here was the Old South not yet wholly reconstructed. Clara and her companion, Octavia Dix of St. Louis, drove through the town, viewing the pillared homes of the plantation age, taking note particularly of the Dahlgren mansion. With her usual lively sense of her surroundings, she made pungent diary comments on what she saw. The moss-hung trees and flowering shrubs reminded her of the far-off days at Hilton Head, before she had ever heard of the Red Cross.

Among her helpers on her river trips, in addition to Dr. Hubbell and Octavia Dix, were John Hitz, who followed the growth of the Red Cross in America with the closest interest, and Miss Enola Lee of Evansville, who had become one of her permanent assistants.

Back in St. Louis again, Clara crossed over to Evansville, re-chartered the *Josh V. Throop,* and took on fresh supplies. St. Louis and Chicago both had formed Red Cross units by this time, and they kept her well stocked with materials. A carload of garden seeds had arrived from Watertown, New York. Clara now stocked up with lumber, arriving at landings with ready-made doors and windows for one-room shelters, household utensils, tools, and a group of carpenters. These emergency crews made trips in small boats, conveying all the parts of the shelter, putting them together, and by nightfall leaving a family under cover, a fire blazing, candles lit, bedding ready for the night, and food on the table.

Although the waters of the Ohio had subsided by this time the people, returning to their home sites, had found nothing but desolation. "We ask few questions," Clara commented. "They ask none. The whistle is as welcome to their ears as the flag to their eyes."

One of her most treasured stories of this river journeying concerned six boys and girls in Waterford, Pennsylvania, who raised $51.25 by giving a public entertainment for the flood sufferers. The money was forwarded by the Erie *Dispatch* to Clara, who made a special effort to find worthy recipients. When a gaunt and stricken woman named Mrs. Plew came aboard at a picturesque spot known as "Cave-in-Rock" on the Illinois side of the Ohio, Clara was sure that the occasion had come to use the children's money.

Mrs. Plew was living with her six children in a corncrib. She had survived three floods but had lost her husband and her home.

Clara waded over her shoe tops in mud to visit the little family and assure herself of their condition. "There was misfortune, poverty, sorrow, want, loneliness, dread of future, but fortitude, courage, integrity and honest thrift," she commented.

Clara told Mrs. Plew the history of the fund and said that the Red Cross would round it out to $100. The "Little Six" had wide publicity. When she revisited the Plew family a twenty-foot flagstaff was staked in the bank close to the spot where the new family home would rise. Its crossboard was lettered "Little Six Red Cross Landing." Bit by bit the symbol of Geneva was making its impression on the American consciousness, even in remote hamlets.

Newspapermen came on board to write about the floating ark of 1884. They were much impressed by Clara. Her looks, her manner, her kindly, practical ways were commented on in flattering terms. By this time she was expert at doing her own missionary work. She gave them all Red Cross pamphlets and interested them in her infant organization. An editorial in the Chicago *Inter-Ocean* of March 31, 1884, particularly pleased her.[7] It was one of the earliest tributes to the movement she was fostering in America, and it came from firsthand observation.

Clara was close to collapse on her return to Washington. She had traveled eight thousand miles and distributed money and supplies totaling $175,000. All donations had been acknowledged, a heavy task in itself. She was at once confronted with an invitation to send delegates to the Third International Conference of the Red Cross, meeting in Geneva that autumn.

She went to see Mr. Frelinghuysen and he promptly appointed her his representative.

Clara told him how tired and ill she was. She felt too exhausted even to prepare a report.

"That's because you have had too much fresh water, Miss Barton," jested the Secretary of State. "I recommend salt—and shall appoint you. . . . Our Government relief boats have reported you officially, and all the country knows what you have done and is more than satisfied."

Her fellow delegates were her old friend Judge Joseph Sheldon and Adolphus S. Solomons, vice-president of the American National Red Cross, and its first treasurer. This was the first official representation of the United States Government at an international conference held under the Treaty of Geneva, and Clara was the star of the occasion. She was the only woman delegate and the most honored. There was general knowledge of the feat she had performed in bringing the powerful United States into the Convention and she was studied with interest.

Judge Sheldon paid tribute to her on this occasion. "After our American war we used to call her our Florence Nightingale; but now we only need to call her our Clara Barton, and we consider that this name is enough," he observed. Then, paraphrasing Sumner's comment on Clara, he added: "She has done her work with the skill of a statesman, the heart of a woman, and the perseverence of the saints."

An Italian delegate jumped to the platform and proposed a vote of acclamation for Miss Barton, who "deserved well of humanity." Clara was used to the shouts and applause of soldier audiences, and was usually self-possessed in public, but she showed signs of being deeply moved on this occasion.

Both she and Judge Sheldon pushed hard for the extension of Red Cross work to cover disaster relief as well as the wounded. This was already an accepted factor in America and would become almost universal through the individual signatories of the Treaty of Geneva. Thus, although Dunant touched the trigger, Clara fired the gun and gave it impetus through her work on the Mississippi. The so-called "American amendment" was to have deep significance to the future of the Red Cross and the aid given to humanity. It was, in fact, to be a solid foundation stone.

Clara participated heartily in the demonstrations staged in Geneva. The public square was converted to represent a battlefield at night. Gymnasts impersonated the dead and dying. The old system of hand barrows, ambulances, and lanterns was demonstrated, alongside a portable engine with electric lights spotlighting the "dead and wounded." Different ways of rescuing the casualties were illustrated by a representative from London of the Society of St. John of Jerusalem, Clara's official introduction to "first aid for the wounded," which she was to bring to the United States.

At times Miss Barton was "perfectly besieged, and how she endured it at all is a wonder," wrote Antoinette Margot, who had rejoined her to serve as interpreter on this occasion. She also proved to be an effective publicist for her work. She had done some newspaper correspondence for the *Tribune* during the Franco-Prussian War. Now she sent items about Clara and the Red Cross both to the *Tribune* and the *Graphic* in New York. She pictured Clara seated in an assembly of gray-haired men "glittering with military decorations," looking calm, thoughtful, self-possessed, her vote eagerly watched for, grave questions referred to her, and all deference being paid to her judgment.

Clara, too, wore her decorations. She had done some worrying, as usual, about her attire, and Annie Childs had written from Worcester on August 9, 1884, that she had never seen Clara "look quite so genteely dressed as when she left." Pictures show her with muff, a fur piece, a bonnet with ribbon ties, and a long close-fitting wrap. A silver basque served her for evening wear, and a black satin dress with jet trimmings for semiformal occasions. Annie had made a garnet skirt which Clara liked. The polonaise came out a "botch," and an old green dress was freshened up with new velvet "to be respectable." Finally "a tight-fitting dress of silk" was submitted for visiting, street, and church.

She had made the swift transition from the muddy banks of the Mississippi to stiff officialdom at Geneva with the homely ease that was part of her adaptable nature. She now had strong and lasting links with Germany, as well as Switzerland, and before going home arranged for a showing of the handwork of German women, under the patronage of the Empress Augusta, at the New Orleans Cotton Centennial of 1885.

A Red Cross exhibit was a feature of the Centennial and on "Red Cross Day" a set of international flags assembled by Clara was on display. "I have the finest collection of International Flags you ever could find, some twenty in number," she rejoiced. After that she always showed her silken banners to visitors in her various homes. In 1884 she took up residence at 947 T Street, a house she had bought some time earlier. In 1892 she rented the house at Seventeenth and F Streets that General Grant had used as headquarters. Her third move was to Glen Echo in 1897. Dr. Hubbell was a member of her household from 1884 on. Antoinette joined them in 1885, but could not adapt herself to Clara's restless retinue of helpers, and their swift trips into the field. Eventually she broke away from the Red Cross ménage, going into lodgings for a time and teaching French. Her father left her his fortune when he died, and Antoinette then embarked on charitable work. She helped to found a new Catholic parish in Brookland, D.C., and to establish an Institute of Christian Oriental Research in connection with the Catholic University in Washington. She died in 1925.

Although her thoughts and interests often reverted to the place where she had recovered her own health, Clara severed her links officially with Dansville in 1885. The townspeople gave her a reception, and she stood before them in all the dignity of her sixty-three years, with her lengthening string of decorations pinned to her black silk dress. They told her publicly that she had given Dansville a "proud position among the villages of this country, for your world-wide fame has been shared by us."

Clara responded in kind: "To your soft breezes and your beautiful sunsets, winning me back to quiet sleep, I am grateful. To the rest of your valleys and the strength of your hills, I am grateful. . . ."

That summer Clara took note of the illness of General Grant. "He sees his last 4th of July," she wrote, "and fully realizes it." He had always been one of her friends. Her generals continued to interest her, long after her course had veered from wartime to peace-time work.

Her next call for service took her to Texas in the winter of 1886, where she found a "heaven of brass" and severe drought conditions. The Rev. John Brown, a Presbyterian minister, had whipped up agitation in Washington about conditions in his state and had sought Red Cross relief. Protests came in from Texas. At President Grover Cleveland's request Clara went South with Dr. Hubbell to study the situation at first hand.

The conflict lay between the Texas cattlemen and impoverished farmers who had moved in from other Southern states after the Civil War. They had expected a fine living but had found dust and aridity instead. Mr. Brown maintained that 100,000 families in northwestern Texas were destitute, but when he sought Congressional action he was cold-shouldered because of antagonistic interests in the state.

Clara and Dr. Hubbell traveled through dusty stretches by horse and buggy, studying the crops and weather conditions. They talked to scores of Texans. Grim as conditions were, Clara quickly saw that they could take care of the need themselves, and that it was clearly a case where state pride was involved. Although touched by what she saw, she was characteristically shrewd and reported back to the President that relief should come from within the state itself.

But she sparked up local feeling and set the machinery in motion. In Dallas she persuaded her old Civil War friend, Colonel A. H. Belo, to start a fund through his paper, the *Morning News*. He promptly headed a $5,000 subscription list for seed, to which Clara contributed. The Texas Legislature at this point appropriated $100,-000 to meet the emergency. Seed, fuel, clothing, livestock were forthcoming. Carloads of food and other necessities soon rolled into the stricken area.

The rains began to fall before Clara left Texas. The wheat crop would be saved. Having cleared up much of the misunderstanding that befogged the entire issue, "we concluded that our task was ended and that we could return to our home." It was one of her cardinal principles never to function in an area where the door was not wide open or local pride was involved.

Soon after her return from Texas Clara participated happily in the National Encampment at Washington, the first called since the Civil War. The Washington Monument grounds were ablaze with flags and uniforms, and she saw to it that the international flags of the Convention of Geneva were well in evidence, and that surgeons, stewards, nurses, and attendants of the medical and hospital department all wore the Red Cross brassard. Old soldiers gathered around Clara. Officers with whom she had worked paid her homage. Of all the functions she attended in the long years of her busy life, she drew most warmth from G.A.R. gatherings, and from the recurrent echoes of her life on the battlefields of the Civil War.

## CHAPTER XIII

## BISMARCK SALUTES THE RED CROSS

TWO WARRIORS who had done more than their share to fill the battlefields of Europe with wounded soldiers confronted Clara in the autumn of 1887. It might have interested Captain Barton of North Oxford to have seen his little Clarissa discussing battle casualties with Prince Bismarck and Count von Moltke at a court reception in Carlsruhe.

Clara had returned to Germany to attend the Fourth International Conference of the Red Cross, this time being held in the familiar stronghold of the House of Baden. She was accompanied by Dr. Hubbell and Dr. Lucy M. Hall, a young physician she had met at Sherborn who was now on the staff of Vassar College and had attached herself to Clara's Red Cross retinue. They were greeted with sumptuous hospitality. After a combined reception, banquet, and musicale Lucy exclaimed: "Ah me, will I ever see a reception again which will not appear tame after that *wünderschönes* one which was our last in Carlsruhe!"

The brilliant uniforms of a highly militarized state blazed with crosses, stars, ribbons, and decorations of one kind and another. The women in stiff brocades and ancestral jewels moved slowly in their ornate setting. Clara wore her silver basque and her sage, kindly face beamed on all this grandeur as she sat beside the Grand Duchess Louise.

But the day's sessions had more true significance for her as she sat brightly attentive in her scarlet ulster and scarlet jersey. She and Dr. Hall were the only women permitted on the floor while the conference was in progress. Germany's most distinguished physicians, nobles, officers lined the galleries, and the Grand Duke and Duchess of Baden and members of the court looked down from the royal box.

Two afternoons were devoted to the inspection of transportable hospital barracks, ambulance wagons, and cars, with practical demonstrations of the arrangement of straw couches for wounded soldiers. Clara was always full of strong opinions on practical ways of attending to wounded soldiers. But her chief interest at this particular conference was the misuse of the Red Cross insignia, which was already beginning to trouble her in America. She watched with concern the spread of such anomalies as cigars, brandy, whiskey, washing machines, playing cards, churns, soap, and dog collars, all using the Red Cross designation.

While staying at Baden-Baden late in October Clara had a special audience with the Emperor, who was visiting his daughter, the Grand Duchess, on the birthday of the Crown Prince. She wrote home to her family of being led through the great doors of the castle by attendants in scarlet-and-gold livery, the Baden colors; of warming herself at a baronial fire, since she had come in out of the rain; of surveying the reception and drawing rooms where the aged Emperor held court; and of watching him break away from a group to come over to greet her, leaning heavily on the arm of his daughter, Louise.

In spite of his great age she thought his tread even and steady. He greeted her in French, saying that in the name of humanity he was delighted to meet and welcome those who labored for it, as she had done. The Grand Duchess recalled Clara's work in Strassburg in 1870 and 1871, and indicated two of the cluster of decorations she wore. One was his own, given her on his seventy-fifth birthday. The other was from the Verein Deutscher Waffen-genossen of Milwaukee, German survivors of the Franco-Prussian War residing in Milwaukee. They had elected Clara a member of their society.

"And they make good citizens?" Emperor William I inquired.

"The best that could be desired," said Clara, "industrious, honest, and prosperous, and, sire, they are still yours in heart, still true to the Fatherland and its Emperor."

"I am glad to hear this; they were good soldiers, and thank God, true men everywhere," said the Emperor.

He spoke of America—its growth, its progress, its advances in science and humanitarian enterprise, its adoption of the Red Cross.

As he shook hands with Dr. Hubbell and Clara in parting, he turned back to say in French: "It is probably the last time," and, in English, "good-by." Clara found this "one of the most impressive and memorable" interviews of her lifetime.

Although simple in her own way of living, and direct in her outlook on life, Clara quite evidently enjoyed the pomp of European courts, and even regarded the smashing German effects with a touch of reverence. She was impressed, if not awed, by the gold-coach treatment she received from the House of Baden. But she was more her natural self steering Dr. Hall along the river embankments of Strassburg, showing her the spots "whence the poor wretches, all covered with ragged and festering wounds, crawled out after the terrible siege was over, to be cared for and succored by me."

Lucy detailed all this in the Vassar *Miscellany* on her return and later Clara was invited to speak at the college. She was not "to mind the clothes or the 'feathers' or anything else but the *coming*." She knew how Clara worried about her costume and she had assumed the task of keeping her reasonably modish. Clara also went to Wellesley that summer, and watched a "float" and the college crew doing their exercises.

But she was genuinely perplexed about what she should wear when asked to speak before the Sorosis Club at Delmonico's. Mrs. M. Louise Thomas, the president, had urged her to appear with her Red Cross insignia and all her decorations. "It is the only time in the year when gentlewomen are invited to Sorosis, and the things you will say about the Red Cross movement may be like seed sown on good ground and may bring forth fruit," wrote Mrs. Thomas. P. T. Barnum, Robert Collyer, Will Carleton, and many New York editors, judges, and literary men and women were to attend.

In response to Clara's naïve appeal about her attire, Mrs. Thomas said that she herself would wear black velvet, *en train*, with lace at the neck and sleeves, her Sorosis badge, and a fan and flowers at her waist. She did not "try to compete but just dressed as a well-bred, refined lady of common sense should." She was sure Clara would do likewise, and perhaps wear "a pretty lace" on her head, and fine ruching at neck and wrists. Mrs. Thomas did not doubt there would be many exquisite costumes in the room but "nothing will be so beautiful to me as your face, and your well earned decorations, all of which I want you to wear," she wrote.

But more serious matters claimed Clara's attention at once. On a quiet Sunday afternoon in February, 1888, a tornado whirled through Mount Vernon, Illinois, killing and injuring many, and wrecking 329 buildings. The small, prosperous town was thrown into chaos as the twisting cone ripped up trees, damaged brick houses, tossed light frame structures like chips before it, and cast its weird and murky light over everything. In a few minutes' time the atmosphere cleared. The sun shone brightly again on a scene of icy chaos. The town was unrecognizable. The wounded moaned in the wreckage. Fires broke out along the streets. A citizens' disaster committee was appointed and an appeal was made to the Red Cross for aid.

Clara responded at once. She arrived at three in the morning and tramped the sleety streets with a lantern, appraising the damage. A few hours later she talked to the homeless and distracted. The hospital was full. There were few nurses. Food was scarce and so was money. Clara found the relief committee but its members had little to distribute. She promptly sent out a simple message over the press-service wires: "The pitiless snow is falling on the heads of people who are without homes, without food or clothing and without money." She signed it *Clara Barton*.

By this time her name on any message brought an instantaneous response. Money rolled in for the Mount Vernon victims and Clara handed over $90,000 to the local disaster committee when she left at the end of two weeks. By that time the townspeople were beginning to dig themselves out, and supplies were arriving in abundance. Clara noted with satisfaction that "every man and boy was at work cleaning brick, repairing buildings, or building new structures."

It was while she was in Mount Vernon that Clara applied a much-quoted phrase to herself: "What is nobody's business is *my* business." She used it in writing a note to Robert G. Ingersoll, who had sat his bar examinations there. Urging him to use his oratorical gifts on behalf of the sufferers, she wrote on March 7, 1888:

Long ago I added to the true old adage of "What is everybody's busi-ness is nobody's business," another clause which, I think, more than

any other principle has served to influence my actions in life. That is,
What is nobody's business is my business. I act upon it in this matter.

While her thoughts were still full of the Mount Vernon disaster
Clara headed into a succession of personal sorrows. Her brother
David—daredevil friend of her youth—died on March 12 and in the
summer Annie Childs, who had faithfully dressed Clara all these
years and been one of her dearest friends, was the next to go. News
reached her, too, of the end of Emperor William I, to whom she
had recently said good-by.

But life moved on and Enola Lee, her prized helper, married Dr.
Joseph Gardner, another of Clara's workers. Both were to figure in
Red Cross affairs, although their home was in Bedford, Indiana.
They had been brought together working for Clara. Her retinue
was increasing. Dr. Hubbell was now closely identified with her
in all her work. He gave each of her campaigns the masculine support that Clara felt they needed. With his knowledge of medicine,
of farms and crops, and his mild approach to people, he was a
sagacious agent in the field. He felt that Phillips, who had done
much of the early publicity for the Red Cross, had grown *"rich,*
and *elegant* and *easy."* In actual fact, Phillips was busy with his
press-service work and although always willing to help Clara, whom
he truly admired, he had little time at his disposal.

With Phillips less active in the publicity field Dr. Hubbell became adept at arranging for translations, and placing news of Red
Cross events in the press. Clara had considerable skill at this herself, when she had a chance to use the personal touch, but now and
again she became impatient and bewildered by it all. She was somewhat dependent at this time on professional advice, for she was
flooded with requests for material on the Red Cross. During the
1880's, knowledge of the organization was gradually being dis-
seminated around the person of its founder. Magazines, from
*Demorest's* to *Scribner's,* solicited Clara's work. Henry O. Houghton, the publisher, whom she found "kind and noble," discussed
a Red Cross magazine with her.

She relied most heavily on Kennan and Phillips for the correct
newspaper touch. Sara A. Spencer, who turned against Clara in her
old age, and several other women acted on her behalf with the

magazines. The mysterious Samuel Ramsey, still in the background, helped her materially with charter forms for associate societies, and particularly aided her in her campaign against illicit use of the Red Cross symbol, which she considered the equivalent of "counterfeiting the current coin."

Another of her helpers at this time was Miss Mary Elizabeth Almon, a wealthy resident of Newport who had interested herself in the Red Cross and also in Dr. Hubbell, a romance quickly nipped in the bud by Clara. She designed an enamel Red Cross pin edged with a line of gold. Mea, as Clara called her, was to supply the insignia. Ramsey was to work on the charter for adequate protection of all Red Cross insignia. Then she would push the matter with Congress. This was one of Clara's hardest-fought battles. As an old expert on patents she maintained that the "emblem of a public institution of benevolence ought to receive as much protection as the trade names on common articles of merchandise."

The 1880's became a decade of great growth for the Red Cross, as Clara built up her dynasty and supplied the master touch herself on all matters of policy and procedure. She listened to her advisers but usually found the solution herself. By 1890 New York, Chicago, Philadelphia, San Francisco, Minneapolis, Milwaukee, Memphis, St. Louis, New Orleans, New Haven, and other towns had Red Cross units, somewhat loosely tied to the parent body. The strongest was the New York Red Cross Society, founded in 1888. Its plans were broader than anything Clara had envisioned. A Red Cross hospital and training school for volunteer nurses, known as Red Cross Sisters, was founded in New York by another committee made up of emigrants from Germany who belatedly sought Miss Barton's sponsorship.

By this time the suffrage women were claiming Clara as one of their own. Her rise in public affairs had been sharp and unmistakable. At the end of March, 1888, she addressed the International Council of Women, a gathering held in Washington under the auspices of the National Suffrage Association, celebrating its fortieth anniversary. Susan Anthony considered her the person best fitted to welcome the delegates from abroad, many of whom she knew.

On this occasion Clara reviewed the advances made by the Red

Cross in a quarter of a century. She cited four international conferences; the symbol of the Red Cross itself; the one military hospital flag for all nations; the insurance of supplies, both medical and nutritive, for all the needy who could be reached; and the best inventions for handling mutilated soldiers or civilians. She pointed out:

The most approved portable hospitals in the world are of the Red Cross. It has frowned upon all old-time modes of cruelty in destructive warfare; poisoned and explosive bullets are no longer popular. Antiseptic dressings and electric light at battlefields are established facts, and the ambulance and stretcher-bearers move in the rear ranks of every army.

Clara spoke effectively for her organization, describing the "clear, steady flame of the Red Cross, so broad that it reached the farthest bound of the horizon; so peaceful, wise, harmless, and fraternal, that all nations and sects, the Christian and the Jew, the Protestant and the Catholic, the soldier and the philanthropist, the warmaker and the peace-maker, could meet in its softened rays, and, by its calm, holy light, reveal to each other their difficulties, compare their views, study methods of humanity, and from time to time, learn from and teach to each other things better than they had known."

But these were the mountain peaks, Clara added. The "great Alpine range of humanity and activity below" could only be indicated. The Red Cross was a peace society that could not be sneered at in counsel, or ignored in war. It was the "bit in the mouth, the curb on the neck of the war horse."

Clara now needed all the support she could get, and she was glad to have the women's organizations interest themselves in the Red Cross, although she never obtruded on their own causes. That autumn she attended a reception given for Miss Willard. "Mamie went very plain," Dr. Hubbell commented. "Didn't decorate a *mite*—but gave all the 'glory' to Miss Willard, as she ought. . . . All the world was there. . . ."

Catastrophes came in a chain during this period and the Red Cross was drawn into new and unfamiliar situations, finding its own solutions with each emergency. Clara's first thought always was to get to the victims with lightning speed with whatever supplies she had on hand, and to avoid the smothering impediment of red tape. The simplicity of her organization favored this effect.

But the yellow-fever epidemic in Florida in the autumn of 1888 posed some new problems and brought harsh criticism of some of the nurses the Red Cross sent into the field. They were selected for their immunity and while some gave notable service, others incurred unfavorable newspaper publicity, causing Clara to hurry South to straighten matters out.

Jacksonville was the focal point of the epidemic, but Clara had called on Colonel F. R. Southmayd, secretary of the Red Cross in New Orleans, to recruit some of the Howard Association nurses, who were experienced and immune in this field. He was a Confederate officer who had lost his right arm at Shiloh. He set off for Jacksonville with thirty nurses, some Negro, some white. The plague had flashed up here and there along their route, and as they approached the little town of Macclenny he took the law into his own hands, had the conductor slow down the train, and asked for volunteers to drop off and nurse the fever-stricken. Macclenny was completely isolated and many were ill. Three men and seven women jumped off the moving train. For the next seven weeks they worked heroically under dismaying conditions and there were only nine deaths among the seventy-six patients at Macclenny.

But some of the nurses who proceeded to Jacksonville fared less well and Colonel Southmayd had to battle local opposition from the medical authorities. The Colonel was a loyal and able worker, but Clara learned on this occasion the importance of having the Red Cross enter a field where it was wholly welcome and could function harmoniously with the local authorities. Professional nursing was still an elementary art and some of its practitioners were intemperate in their habits, but one bright star, fresh from training school, had her baptism in this epidemic. Miss Jane A. Delano, who was to head the nursing service of the Red Cross after Clara's retirement, and to add distinction to her profession, did excellent work with the fever patients of Jacksonville.

## CHAPTER XIV

## JOHNSTOWN FLOOD

CLARA WADED in mud, climbed over broken engines and fallen timbers, past the bodies of the dead being borne away, past smoldering fires and the carcasses of animals, to establish the fact for the army that the Red Cross had arrived in Johnstown to help the victims of the flood of 1889, one of the major domestic catastrophes in American history.

Johnstown was under martial law on the June day on which she arrived in the stricken city. Although in a disaster area, she decided to report directly to the military officer in command as she would have been required to do in a theater of war. But headquarters was two miles from her hastily pitched camp. "Mountains of wreckage obstructed every passway," said Clara, finding it more difficult than making her entry into Strassburg after the siege.

General R. Hastings stared at her in perplexity when she walked in with her muddy boots and her amiable, competent air. He was much concerned to see a solitary female in such surroundings and wished to protect her. "It was with considerable difficulty that he could be convinced that the Red Cross had a way of taking care of itself at least," Clara noted. A week later the General was begging her for some of the lumber sent her in carloads from Iowa and Illinois. He wanted to run up suitable quarters in which to entertain the governor of the state on his first visit.

The waters of the flood had subsided by the time Clara arrived. The wastes remained. The dam over the Conemaugh River some miles from Johnstown had burst, and the waters had come roaring down, spreading death and devastation. For days after her arrival she was to hear of what followed and of those "gone down." Between three and four thousand of the city's population of thirty thousand were lost. Ninety-nine families of from four to ten persons were swept away. Millions of dollars' worth of damage was done. The entire region was laid waste. Villages broke up in sections. Houses floated along the waterways like teetering arks. Human beings clung to trees, to attics, to chimneys, to floating tables and chairs. The rushing waters picked up fresh debris, and swamped both the living and the dead, although their progress was slowed by the tightly packed mass of blockage.

Those who remained were in a dazed and battered state when Clara moved into action. Her working force increased to fifty, most of them medical men attached to the Red Cross unit in Philadelphia, which had built up a strong emergency service. She took up quarters in an abandoned railroad car until a small tent settlement was put together by her helpers. In all respects they had to start from scratch. As Clara described it, the banks had all gone downstream. The safes were at the bottom of the Conemaugh. Many of the businessmen of the city were dead, or unable to function. Western Union wires were so jammed with messages that dispatches were twenty-four hours late. Even before her tents were up, boxes, barrels, trunks, baskets, bundles, and carloads of supplies were arriving, addressed to the President of the Red Cross, Johnstown.

Her desk was a dry-goods box, and here in the weeks that followed she channeled the distribution of nearly half a million dollars' worth of money and materials. Some contributions came in without so much as a pencil mark to indicate their source, and her bookkeeping problems were overwhelming. Clara worked night and day. One large tent served as a warehouse where food and clothing were distributed in the beginning. "The people had come out of the wrecks with the clothing literally torn from their bodies," she commented. A committee of Johnstown women did a house-to-house canvass, drawing up lists of the most urgent needs. In the end more than twenty thousand persons were directly aided by the Red Cross.

One of her most effective measures was her use of the carloads of pine wood shipped by the lumbermen of Iowa and Illinois to put up emergency buildings. The first was a much-needed warehouse for supplies. This was followed by three apartment houses, roughly put together, for as many of the tent dwellers as they would accommodate. The Locust Street Red Cross Hotel was two stories high, was built of hemlock, and had a lantern roof. It was managed by a woman who had floated down the river in darkness for hours clinging to a tree, her clothing torn to shreds as she battled for her life.

Clara opened her floodtime hotel with a formal tea on July 27, 1889. Certain guests had keys beside their plates at the dinner that followed. Unknown to themselves, they were the lucky ones who had drawn the new apartments. There were thirty-four rooms in addition to the public quarters, and Clara used much ingenuity in having them furnished. In retrospect she was always greatly pleased with this little venture in rehabilitation. It worked so well that she then had the Kernville Red Cross Hotel built across the river, and finally Red Cross Block, arranged so that families could live as separate units. On top of this she organized the Johnstown Infirmary, composed of half a dozen portable houses known as Oklahomas set up beside the warehouse, fully equipped and well heated.

Two of her most interested helpers were Mr. and Mrs. John Tittle, who had held hands firmly for hours over the ridgepole of their house as they floated down the river, clinging to opposite sides of the roof. Each time his wife felt she must let go, John tightened his hold on her. Finally their house struck the bridge at Kernville, ending its long, careering voyage. Their rescuers found their Negro Mammy alive in the attic, as well as their setter Rob, and their parrot, its cage topsy-turvy, its squawks feeble but still denoting life.

Clara, in the midst of all her practical operations, took careful diary notes on the human-interest stories that reached her daily as she coped with the aftermath of the Johnstown flood. She stayed in the field for five months, perfecting one of her most competent operations, although it was only a small part of the general rehabilitation program. The Johnstown flood had aroused the whole country.

By October the shattered town had revived. "Enterprising, industrious, and hopeful, the new Johnstown, phoenix-like, rose from its ruins more beautiful than the old," wrote Clara. Schools were open again. Churches were reviving. Shops were doing business. Homes were being rebuilt. Business firms began to operate again. The time had come when outside bounty was no longer welcome. Clara decided to close up her operation, turning over the emergency buildings for winter use and leaving whatever supplies she had on hand.

Soon after she left there were demands that the Red Cross buildings be removed, to make the land available for other purposes. Her agent made quiet disposition of some of the materials to needy homes, and part of the lumber was shipped to Washington, where it was eventually used in the construction of the rambling building at Glen Echo, Maryland, which was to be the home of Clara and the Red Cross for a number of years. In the beginning it was used as a warehouse for supplies.

On her return to Washington a banquet was given for her in Willard's Hotel early in November, 1889. Tables were arranged in the form of a cross, and a bouquet of flowers from President and Mrs. Harrison lay in front of her. Clara had time only to open her house, get out of her field attire, and appear for this occasion. She was now quite celebrated, and had given life and substance to the Red Cross in America. Artists wished to paint her; magazines, to run her life story. Actually she was at the height of her career. As she neared the age of seventy her diaries grew less melancholy. The entries were full of affairs. Clara's fame had solid grounding, and a more authoritative note now crept into her writings and pronouncements. She knew that her opinions carried weight. She had crossed the continent several times to attend soldiers' and women's gatherings.

In November, 1890, she was the guest of the Johns Hopkins Medical School, which was opening its doors for the first time to women doctors. She attended the reception given for President Harrison by Miss Mary Garrett, whose beneficence had wrought this miracle in medical circles. Afterward Clara wrote enthusiastically of the "magnificence of the affair, the bright intelligence and vivacity of the audience, and the dress, and the diamonds, diamonds, diamonds!" Of greater interest to her, however, was the hospital itself. She eyed its appointments with admiration, noting the strides that medicine had made since the Civil War. The top men of Johns Hopkins welcomed her as a comrade and Clara basked in this approval.

Her honors were various and uncommon. She was fresh from

the G.A.R. Encampment at Detroit, where she was elected national chaplain for a year, thus becoming one of the national officers of the Woman's Relief Corps of the United States. "The Grand Army simply adore her," wrote Isabella Beecher Hooker, prominent suffrage worker, urging that she be appointed to the National Board of Commissioners. "She is the peer of any man on the Commission and has more foreign medals than any or all of them . . . every woman of us will work under her without a question."

But perhaps the most congenial occasion for Clara was a banquet held by the Ladies of the Potomac Corps at Willard's Hotel in 1892. In response to a toast to the women of the Civil War she read a lengthy poem she had put together at very short notice. She called it "The Women Who Went to the Field" and delivered it with much spirit.[8] On this occasion she was her more warlike self. Yet a writer in the *Outlook* of the same period viewed a different Clara: "The expression of her face, the quiet of her manner, and the exquisitely modulated voice are so harmonious, so restful, that the thought that this woman was born to command, to lead, to endure hardship, to witness suffering, seems past belief."

At the age of seventy Clara went on a camping trip in the West, sleeping under the stars, staging over the roughest roads, "gaming" along the way. She relished this life and slept deeply. In her own words:

You would think by the accoutrements, rods, lines, guns, revolvers, pouches and game bags that we might be anything from a troop of mountaineers to a band of brigands. Suffice it to say the table lacks nothing, and the green sweet scented firs a foot deep make a soft bed after a day's tramp. . . . The pines and firs are dense and green, the clear mountain stream falls in cascades at the very entrance of our camp. The lake and streams have plenty of fish, and the mountain plenty of game from the squirrel to the deer and bear. . . .

The trip was taken largely for Steve's health. His daughter Myrtis, his second wife, and Dr. Hubbell made up the party. Clara was used to tents, to floods, to physical hardship. At Yellowstone Park, instead of following the customary tourist pattern, they hired their own coach and four, with camping outfit, and spent eight days in the park. Clara thought it a miracle—"like the making of

Man: fearful and wonderful. . . . I gazed on geysers, walked fire, leaped rivers of boiling water, buried my scorched feet in seething lime and sulphur—and listened to the internal belching, thundering, the great God making a world," she wrote to Miss Leonora B. Halstead, a St. Louis friend, and sister-in-law of John W. Noble, Secretary of the Interior.

They proceeded to the Cascade Range and went into camp on the shores of Lake Chelan. This involved crossing the Coulee—"a gorge which would be a canyon if it were not too wide." They again took a stagecoach with four horses and journeyed through to the lake, fifty-five miles over the "barest road one could attempt to touch—and such dust as only the West can give." But Clara felt repaid, with "miles of water blue as the sky, clear as crystal, too deep for sounding, and winding like a great placid river between mountain cliffs of a most perpendicular rock, on either side, of less than a mile apart."

Soon after her return to Washington her attention was drawn to famine conditions in Russia. Both 1889 and 1890 had been poor crop years and by 1891 some thirty million persons were suffering from the great drought that had blighted nearly a million square miles of the best agricultural soil. Clara read that the peasants were burning their thatched roofs for fuel and exchanging their clothing for bread. Typhus, smallpox, and diphtheria raged in different parts of the country.

She communicated with James G. Blaine and Alexander Gregor, Russian Chargé d'Affaires at Washington, and learned that Russia would welcome aid from America. The farmers of Iowa threw themselves wholeheartedly into the campaign. Alice French, better known in literary circles as Octave Thanet, was a friend of Clara's, and she stirred up interest among the women of the Middle West. The governor gave his support and B. F. Tillinghast, editor of the Davenport *Democrat,* directed operations. Between them all, 225 carloads of Iowa corn, as well as wheat, rye, bacon, canned goods, and medical supplies, were shipped to the New York docks for handling by the Red Cross. A large contribution also came in from Johnstown.

The question of transportation then became the problem. The Society of Elks worked enthusiastically with the Washington group to get the grain shipped to Russia. Congress had turned down an appropriation to send aid on this occasion. Clara promptly wrote to her Boston friend of the Franco-Prussian War days, Edmund Dwight:

There seems to be such a muddle of ideas growing out of the mishaps in Congress that it was very apparent that somebody must say something, and that, you know, is the place where I always come in; the door that nobody else will go in at, seems always to swing open widely for me.

Clara was at the Astor House in New York early in February, 1892, hurrying around the city in snow and slush, bargaining for a ship. She wrote to Dr. Hubbell: "Fifty of the élite of the world of commerce meet tomorrow to decide what shall be done. I have been everywhere today, took a messenger boy and tramped. . . . I believe you can go to bed and sleep. By tomorrow night the battle will be won. I am glad I came."

Dr. Hubbell joined her in New York on his way to attend the Sixth International Conference of the Red Cross in Rome. Together they pushed through arrangements for the *Tynehead*, which sailed early in May bearing Iowa's contribution to Russia. Wearing a long cloak faced with scarlet, Clara boarded the ship before it left. She called it the Iowa-Washington ship, and in a farewell speech dwelt on the union of America, Britain, and Russia in this work. Supplies continued to pour in and another ship was chartered to convey them. Eventually there were mutterings of doubt about the ultimate fate of some of the cargo destined for Russia. Clara was beginning to feel the sting of criticism inevitably attaching to the purveyor of large bounty.

Dr. Hubbell, fresh from the conference in Rome, was at the wharf in Riga to receive the shipments, watch the unloading by Russian peasants, and direct the distribution. The total contributions sponsored by the Red Cross were valued at $125,000. This was a mere drop in the bucket in an area of such desperate need, but many lives were saved and the Red Cross had made its first venture into relief on an international scale. It was estimated that American contributions had supported 700,000 persons for a month.

The Iowa corn spread good will. Dr. Hubbell wrote glowingly

to Mamie of his tour of remote hamlets, and the distribution in eighty-two famine centers. Count Alexis Bobrinsky, Marshal of the Nobility of St. Petersburg, had ordered 320 freight cars to be used for conveying the cargo free of cost from Riga to any point desired. Some of it traveled almost to the foot of the Ural Mountains. The Red Cross symbol was painted on the cars. Russian and American colors hung at the hotel where Dr. Hubbell stayed. American sheet music was displayed in shop windows.

Dr. Hubbell visited the Bobrinsky family, large sugar millers in Moscow. He studied the homes of the peasants in surrounding villages, surveyed their needs, then visited Count Tolstoi at Yasnaya Polyana. He had organized his own relief, and was intensely critical of the political regime in St. Petersburg. Peasants streamed in and out of his house all day, discussing their problems with him.

Clara was deeply interested in Dr. Hubbell's letter about his stay in Tolstoi's home. He slept in the library and observed the substantial supply of books and magazines in English. The Russian author plied him with questions about his work, his thoughts and habits. He told Dr. Hubbell he had heard of Clara Barton, and felt that "she must be a very near relation." He sent her his affectionate regards.

Dr. Hubbell sailed down the Volga, visiting towns along the banks as he had once done on the Mississippi. "At each place the grain has been received and is being used," he reported back to Clara. Inland, he found American corn being ground in the windmills and baked in brick ovens. Since one of the leading businessmen in the United States had written that the Red Cross might as well ship a cargo of pebbles to Russia as a cargo of unground corn, this was gratifying news to Clara. There had been much pessimism about the fate of the shipments. Clouds of distrust surrounded the entire operation. It was suggested that the grain would spoil, that there were no mills in Russia to grind it, that the peasants knew nothing of corn and could not change their basic food habits.

Her first venture in the international field had caused Clara considerable anxiety, but all went well and in May, 1893, Dr. Hubbell received a gold cloisonné tea service from the Russian Imperial Legation in Washington, a souvenir of his distribution of American corn.

That same month she called a general meeting of her organization to reincorporate under the name of the American National Red Cross. She felt that this "would make an intelligent and needed distinction between the national body and the various societies which must eventually form to work in conjunction with it." Many new shoots were springing up at this time and Clara headed into a venture known as Red Cross Park which was to cause her endless heartache and embarrassment a decade later. Her friends, the Gardners, who held extensive property in Indiana, offered her 782 acres of their land, presumably for a token payment of one dollar, to be used as a center for Red Cross activities. They wrote that they wished to dedicate it as a thank offering to humanity.

Clara immediately viewed this property as having Utopian possibilities for the Red Cross. She accepted it with a letter of good faith on March 18, 1893, in which she wrote: "This land, as the property of the American National Red Cross, will be the one piece of neutral ground on the western hemisphere protected by international treaty against the tread of hostile feet."

While business headquarters would still be in Washington Clara foresaw the realization of an old hope of hers for an area where the Red Cross could "accumulate and produce material and stores for sudden emergencies and great calamities." She would have the boundaries of the domain defined, she wrote, and inscribed with the insignia of the Treaty of Geneva. Gardner became her adviser. John A. Morlan was appointed to run the farm, a disastrous choice.

He was one of her entourage who had first come into view as a rescue worker at Mount Vernon. Later he was one of her most enthusiastic helpers at Johnstown, and acted as agent in Washington in handling mail and checks involving the shipment of grain to Russia. Always trustful where her helpers were concerned, Clara by this time regarded him as one of her working family. "He had grown very dear to us, like a brother or a son," she wrote of the man who was to assail her financial probity at a crucial moment in her life.

At the time the transfer was made Red Cross Park was well publicized, with Colonel Hinton acting as promoter on this occasion. Clara gave a reception in her Washington home for the Gardners, and more than two thousand guests passed through her parlors before the night was over. She was decked out in white satin and Dr. Hubbell played host, "full of good will and good acts." A few days later Mrs. Grover Cleveland and Kate Field were present at a kindergarten meeting held in Clara's home. Every promising new cause affecting women and children claimed her interest.

By the middle of April she was grieving for Tommy, her Maltese cat, as if she had lost a child. He had lived for seventeen years and had traveled far with Clara. White-coated, green-eyed, he appears in a painting done by Antoinette Margot which hangs at Glen Echo today. "Poor little faithful friend, farewell," wrote Clara in her diary, after she had buried him beneath her window in a flannel-lined box. "He had given a great deal of happiness to us all, and had filled his place in life well."

In the middle of May she went West to survey her new acres and see what could be done with them. She was somewhat over-powered by the great quarries of fine gray stone, the mile of rail-road, the little white schoolhouse, some old log houses and barns, the wooded forests, valleys, and ravines, and a "big river for boats with the thick willows bending to the water on either side." In-stalled in a porticoed white house was John Morlan, who had moved his wife and three children from their home in Fairfield, Illinois.

Her spreading property was described by Clara in a letter to Steve's wife. She told of the livestock already installed—of chickens and turkeys, cows and pedigreed horses; of Prince Bob, a chestnut "weighing 1700 pounds, with tail to the ground, mane to his knees, and pantolets completely covering his smooth unshod hoofs"; and of Jefferson Clay in his padded stall, his coat so glossy "you could almost make a looking glass of him." In a moment of weariness, seventy-one-year-old Clara added:

Now I have only been there a part of two days and have seen *these* things, but the acres I have *not* seen tire me to think of, and it confuses me to know that I hold the deed to all this, and am expected to direct it, "during my natural life." It is new and crude as new land is, but its possibilities are immense, and one day—not in my day—they will develop into beauty and usefulness.

While in the West Clara put in a brief appearance at the World's Fair in Chicago and talked on the work of the Red Cross. In French

Lick, Indiana, speaking before a gathering of surgeons, she met James Whitcomb Riley. On her return to Washington she found demands from Morlan for a large sum of money for his operations in Indiana which she supplied out of her private funds. Clara was already becoming disillusioned with Red Cross Park. It developed that Morlan was gambling and using the land for racing horses. The noble purposes of the Utopian scheme were forgotten as he imported an "entire carload of elegant, costly race horses." The land deteriorated. No philanthropic purpose was being served and he and Dr. Gardner quarreled furiously. Clara implored them to make peace, telling them that she would rather give up the organization than that it "should come into rupture before the world, and disgrace itself."

Morlan vanished from the scene but Clara was to see him again. When he turned up in the next disaster area, the Sea Islands, South Carolina, she was shocked to observe the change in him. He was no longer the bright-faced young man she had known, but was "dark, troubled, irascible and quarrelsome." After that he plied an uncertain course and was variously reported working as a Pullman conductor, a patent inventor, and a detective. Most often he was out of work and appealing to Clara and her friends for loans. But in 1904 he was to revive Red Cross Park affairs with punishing effect for Clara.

She did her best to turn it into a productive venture. She sent Dr. Hubbell West for a time to apply his practical hand to her acres. He raised large crops and Clara hoped to build a home on the land for superannuated nurses or for orphans from her relief fields. But it was essentially an impractical scheme. In the end the title was allowed to lapse because of the accumulation of taxes and charges for maintenance. The property reverted to the Gardners and Red Cross Park became a painful memory.

## CHAPTER XV

## A HURRICANE SWEEPS SEA ISLANDS

CLARA'S FIRST hurricane expedition, involving the sustenance of thirty thousand stranded inhabitants on the Sea Islands, developed into an advanced experiment in rehabilitation. She practically made over the community, raised the standard of living, and left the people better off than they were before the storm. General William H. Sears described her work in this area as the "statesmanship of philanthropy."

The archipelago threaded with low-lying islands and inlets off the coast of South Carolina was highly vulnerable to the hurricane that roared up from the West Indies on a stifling August night in 1893. It was only a matter of minutes until the flatlands were awash. At least a thousand men, women, and children lost their lives. Thousands more were homeless and property damage exceeded $10,000,000.

Joel Chandler Harris, creator of Uncle Remus, who directed a small rescue expedition with tugboats and steam launches for *Scribner's Magazine,* reported that many were killed by the sheer pressure and fury of the wind on their bodies; that not a single child and few women survived in some of the settlements, and that most of those who lived were vigorous young men who could stand the buffeting.

Small homes on stilts sailed off from their moorings as wind and water battered them. Their occupants clung to the collapsing timbers until they were swept out to sea. Some scrambled up into the branches of the trees, many of which were uprooted, carrying their human freight with them into the turbulent waters, or lashing them to death. Survivors were bruised and battered, and their clothing was ripped from their bodies. Boats were sunk or wrecked, and all communication with the mainland was cut off.

A deluge of rain continued for two weeks and Clara and her working force found chaotic conditions when they arrived. The difficulties of communication hindered the work of rescue. Mule carts were driven around in quest of the dead, as bodies floated in from the sea. The wells were contaminated by the inflow of brackish salt water, and malarial fever, then of unknown origin, added to the general misery. Whenever possible the ill were taken to the mainland and were treated at a clinic and dispensary. Soon nurses and a physician worked on the islands, too, in tents carpeted with moss. Aside from the injuries sustained in the hurricane, dysentery spread rapidly from the contaminated water.

Clara knew the region well. Months passed in the Port Royal area during the Siege of Charleston had familiarized her with the terrain, the crops, and the nature of the people. Normally, the Sea Islanders lived on their fine silky cotton, their phosphate works and simple agriculture. The fishermen among them supplied the tables of Charleston with shrimps, prawns, and oysters from the sea, or terrapin from the marshes. The waterways ranged from mere threads of silver to the broader sweep of the Beaufort, Broad, and Coosaw rivers.

After Clara had made a personal inspection of the damage done, she hurried to Washington and urged a Congressional appropriation of $50,000, to be used for labor only. The petition was promptly shelved, but her trip served to draw attention to the plight of the people on the Sea Islands, and resulted in two ships being assigned to transport relief supplies from point to point.

Clara's own appeal for funds and supplies brought a fair response. For ten months she functioned on a budget of $30,000, first providing food, clothing, and medical attention; then repairing or replacing homes and draining the region with ditches; and finally restoring to the Sea Islanders their means of livelihood and showing them more enlightened ways of living and working. Supplies valued at $35,000 made a total relief operation of $65,000.

Harris reported that everywhere he went the Red Cross Society had been there before him. "There was no point so remote that its agents had not visited; there was not a case of sickness that had not received attention." He went to the Sea Islands without prejudice against the Red Cross, nor was he prepossessed in its favor, he said in an article published in the February, 1894, issue of *Scribner's Magazine*. He had pictured it as a "sort of fussy and contentious affair, running about with a tremendous amount of chatter and flourishing a great deal of red tape." To his surprise he found the opposite:

As a matter of fact, the Red Cross Society as I saw it at Beaufort is something entirely different from any other relief organization that has come under my observation. Its strongest and most admirable feature is its extreme simplicity. The perfection of its machinery is shown by the apparent absence of all machinery. There are no exhibitions of self-importance. There is no display—no torturous cross-examination of applicants—no needless delay. And yet nothing is done blindly, or hastily, or indifferently. . . . Miss Barton and her assistants adopted from the very first the most rigid system of economy—a system far more efficacious in the end than any lavish dispensation of charity could have been. . . .

Clara worked with her customary sense of order and system, channeling all aid from the warehouse she rented in Beaufort, her headquarters at first. Her own equipment was of the simplest—her bed a cot, her desk a dry-goods box. Furniture was made from packing cases "nicely upholstered with manila paper, or hung with tasty calico curtains."

Her work was highly personalized. When she toured the islands to appraise conditions for herself, she traveled the waterways by tug and skiff, and trudged along rough highways by foot or road cart. She drove over the rice fields in a lumbering cart, and walked five miles to talk to the phosphate workers whose dredges, lighters, and tugs had been wrecked or carried out to sea.

Clara visited the local stores that survived, followed the battered railroad tracks with a drove of dogs at her heels, and visited the Negro cabins by twilight and by the light of the moon, making diary entries that told their own story: "Julia Glover specially asks for seeds. She is a survivor of seventeen drowned at one place." . . . "On Middleton's Plantation found Elizabeth Prioleau, with sick husband and a half dozen children. She asked for a sack."

Clara spent one night in a cabin on Big State Plantation and held a midnight meeting to discuss the local supplies. "Not without some enjoyment of the melody of their songs," she commented. Although she was not musical, the spirituals penetrated her consciousness and in the moment of anguish, as in the moment of joy, the freedmen burst into song. The following morning she drove in a road cart across twelve miles of old plantation land, to find that one family needed seeds, another bedding, another saws and hatchets.

Bit by bit she found the way to supply all the pressing needs. Food was strictly rationed—one peck of hominy and a pound of pork to a family of seven for one week. This was doubled for men working to restore order. The ill were allowed some tea or coffee, sugar and bread. Small amounts of fish, fruits, and plants were still available locally.

Clara revived her Strassburg system. She formed local sewing circles and gave the women supplies with which to work, and direction in their operations. They enjoyed making over the tattered finery that came from the North, even though the local newspapers jested about the silks and satins, the bedraggled plumes and soiled laces that the Negro women suddenly sported on the Sea Islands. They were taught to tie up comforts, since bedding was scarce; to cut down garments for children; to make special quilts for the aged, and the ill. Refreshments were served. There was singing and good feeling. Clara initiated this work personally by crossing to a little church at Coosaw, listening with enjoyment to the "sweet plaintive melodies" the congregation sang, then setting up a central sewing circle of twenty-five women as a model to be copied all over the islands.

Enola Gardner was known as "Mistress of the Robes." Slender, wiry, a hard worker at every disaster field, she stood at her table opening barrels and sorting out clothing from seven in the morning until far into the night. Before Clara left the region, 20,000 garments had been distributed. Thousands of little homes had been repaired or rebuilt. More than 245 miles of ditches had been dug, reclaiming large tracts of land. Nearly 5 tons of garden seeds, in addition to 800 bushels of peas and beans, had been provided.

The newly dug ditches improved the crops, reclaimed much wasteland, and were a healthful asset. Half a million feet of Southern pine were rafted down to accessible sites for houses. Tools were handed out in rotation, all marked with a Greek Red Cross on the handles and metal. Nails, lumber, and hardware were distributed through local committees. Gardens were fenced to protect them from wandering fowl and pigs.

Many had laughed at the idea of making truck gardeners of the Sea Islanders. But Clara had genuine success with the idea. The Department of Agriculture sent seeds direct to the Red Cross, and nurserymen in New York and Philadelphia augmented the supply. She bought nine hundred bushels of Early Rose potatoes for planting and welcomed seed corn from the Ohio Valley. She soon had forty women cutting up potatoes for seed, and learning to their astonishment that an eye or sprout would give them another crop. The potatoes flourished and a double crop of corn was raised where only one had grown before. Soon lettuce, onions, and peas were added to pork and grits.

Clara and Dr. Hubbell between them conducted this agricultural experiment, once the immediate misery of the people was relieved. "They must not eat the bread of idleness," Clara ruled, repeating one of the fundamental principles of her organization. "We must not leave a race of beggars, but teach them the manliness of self-support and methods of self-dependence."

The workers were paid fifty cents a day, which they took in the form of provisions. Clara told Harris that "we have made one element of the needy strengthen and maintain another element, and all in the direction of the rigid economy that we are compelled to observe." She functioned at headquarters like a magistrate, interviewing committeemen who came from all parts of the devastated region with their problems. Here she was at her best—practical, judicial, moderate in her judgments, knowing about the crops, understanding the people, frugal in her disposition of limited supplies, and always ready with the needed touch of humor. When two rival committees sought to bargain with her, she cut off the supplies of both.

She warned the Islanders not to get into debt. She showed them many ways of making practical use of materials that lay around them. She let the women study her own calico-draped quarters, since Clara had learned to work wonders with dry-goods boxes and a few yards of cotton. She became something of a personal missionary, followed about by the children. Babies were named after her. When asked what he depended on for the winter, one Negro replied: "God and Miss Barton." In Beaufort four middle-aged Negroes showed her their battle scars. She had nursed all of them on Morris Island. Aunt Jane, an aged Negress who had cooked for her at Hilton Head, traveled thirty miles to see her.

By Christmas the churches were open again. Clara celebrated her seventy-second birthday with the knowledge that she had never done a better or more rounded job. With hearty good will her new-found friends sang the Christmas carol she wrote for them that year. It was dedicated to her "Thirty Thousand Sea Islands Friends" and one verse read:

> Forget your night of sad disaster,
>   Cast your burdens all away,
> Wait the coming of the Master,
>   For the Lord is born today.
> Shout then, children; shout and pray,
>   For the blessed Lord is born today.

The Sea Islanders shouted and they prayed, and when spring came they called on Clara with flowers from the woods and fields. They offered her early vegetables from their burgeoning gardens. The sidewalks of Beaufort were by this time bright with garden produce. But by June Clara left them, feeling that the time had come to close up her work on the Sea Islands. Their homes, boats, and farms were in repair. They were well clothed and had adequate food. The phosphate industry had revived. She felt that they were now a "prosperous and self-helping people," and were better left alone.

Her farewell was a circular letter to each clergyman and committeeman on her list, giving detailed instructions on planting, crop rotation, the care of the ditches, general hygiene, productivity, fertilization, and fencing. She urged the cultivation of fig and grape cuttings. With good ditches everywhere, with plenty of vegetables from the gardens, with figs and grapes, there should be almost no sickness on these prosperous islands, and everyone should be happy, Clara concluded with high optimism.

While still at Beaufort she received the news that the bill to protect Red Cross insignia had passed the House. At the same time she had an ugly shock in March, when the *Review of Reviews* published a sharp attack on her, written by Sophia Wells Royce Williams, a free-lance contributor to the magazine. The central idea was that the Red Cross was not a national organization in the true sense of the word; that it should be headed by men like Bishop Henry C. Potter, J. Pierpont Morgan, Philip D. Armour, and other leading figures across the country; that it should have strong medical representation from coast to coast; and, finally, that it needed a "national organization, a national board, and reports which would stand as model and guide for all relief work, the country over." Instead, said Miss Williams:

The country has Miss Clara Barton, industrious, indefatigable, persistent and enthusiastic. . . . For thirteen years since the United States signed the Geneva Convention the National Red Cross Association in this country has been Miss Clara Barton and Miss Clara Barton has been the National Red Cross Society.

Miss Williams had found Clara "rapid, quick and voluble" when she went to see her—"a slight woman rather under-sized, with soft brown eyes, thin gray hair and a large mouth—rather strong withal." She pressed her for reports and documentation on the work of the Red Cross and claimed she got no satisfactory response.

Clara protested behind the scenes and in May the *Review of Reviews* retracted the story to some extent and gave a different presentation of her status. But Miss Williams had stirred up trouble and Bishop Potter was to carry on the feud some years later because of his dissatisfaction with her handling of the funds. Clara began to think along different lines herself and on August 26, 1895, wrote to George M. Pullman, president of the Pullman Palace Car Company, pointing out that the Red Cross could survive but not grow without "the prestige and interest of strong leading citizens behind it." She had worked among its foundation stones, she said, and had not called the attention of the "great master builders" of the nation's institutions to its possibilities. He was the first to whom she had turned. "Unlike most organizations the Red Cross does not mean national help for people's needs, but *people's help for national necessities*," Clara wrote.

Pullman did not respond at this time to her appeal. His nephew, George H. Pullman, had recently joined her entourage of workers and on their return from Sea Islands they visited the home of his father, the Rev. James Pullman, in the Thousand Islands. Young George had been a jovial assistant both at Johnstown and the Sea Islands. He now called Clara the Queen. She liked him greatly although he was forgetful and easygoing, and she could not always regard him as an asset.

But before she had time to pursue the master builders any further she became interested in a new field of action and sailed off for Constantinople with nephew George and a small staff which was further augmented on her arrival by missionaries, teachers, and other Americans concerned with Armenian relief.

## CHAPTER XVI

## *A YANKEE IN STAMBOUL*

THE SUMMER of 1896 found Clara Barton in Constantinople, in a tall narrow house on the shore of the Bosphorus "a pistol shot from the water, but high above it." The view was magnificent, the air balmy, the streets dirty and noisy, and every few days she was drawn inevitably to the window to watch soldiers marching down the street on their way to the Sultan's palace. Their band played strange airs and, as she put it, they "stood under arms to protect him while he went to the mosque to pray."

Immediately after her arrival Clara appeared in the native markets, a determined figure in blue serge, threading her way among the veiled women of Stamboul and "taking up the role of a merchant." She bought large quantities of supplies from wholesale houses to be taken by caravan into the interior. Clara was adept at such work from long experience and had a shrewd eye for a bargain.

She was soon directing the operations of four relief expeditions sprayed out through Turkey and Armenia. It was the first extensive foreign relief program she managed personally and was a new kind of disaster for her—not war, nor flood, nor hurricane, but a man-made massacre, with delicate political elements involved. She was under the enemy's roof, accepted as an individual famous for philanthropic work. Only by grace of this circumstance was she able to function so successfully on behalf of the Armenians. The Red Cross work in Russia had been confined largely to the distribution of food and tools. Here medical care was involved, the restoration of property and the rehabilitation of artisans and farmers.

Clara had reached her goal by way of many complications. For months the American press had been carrying stories of massacre, pillaging, and religious warfare between Moslem and Christian.

Indignation meetings had whipped up hot feeling. The missionaries and Christian teachers in the field had suffered, and Alexander W. Terrell, United States Minister to Turkey, had asked protection for Americans residing there. Business firms with Turkish connections were deeply concerned. Dr. George Washburn, president of Robert College, had sent home a graphic story of slaughter.

The American Board of Commissioners for Foreign Missions, and Spencer Trask, who had formed a National Armenian Relief Committee in New York, both appealed to the Red Cross to distribute funds in the field. At least 350,000 persons were reported to be destitute and starving. Clara agreed to go, when assured that adequate funds would be forthcoming, that the full sentiment of the people was behind her, and that the missions and church societies would be represented. In the final analysis the Red Cross spent $116,326 on Armenian relief, contributing approximately $5,000 of this amount from its standing funds.

Immediately on her arrival Clara went to call on Tewfik Pasha, Turkish Minister of Foreign Affairs. She was still unsure of her status. Just before sailing from America she learned that she would be denied entry to the Sublime Porte, and that Turkey would take care of its own. But in London word had reached her that the Red Cross could distribute supplies, and that its workers would receive protection.

The Pasha must have regarded the intrepid Miss Barton in her prim bonnet and plain blue serge with some curiosity as she stood before him, seventy-four years old, bright-eyed, and the symbol of some distant and, to him, inexplicable drive. "We know you, Miss Barton," he said. "We have long known you and your work. We would like to hear your plans for relief and what you desire."

Humanity alone would be her guide, said Clara, speaking through an interpreter. Many of the Armenians had friends and relatives in America. She had brought skilled agents to furnish aid. They would try first to get the people back to their deserted fields and provide them with farming implements. From this would spring the crops that would feed them. If the agents did not find any need, they would depart. Then Clara added:

We have brought only ourselves, no correspondent has accompanied us, and we shall have none, and shall not go home to write a book on

Turkey. We are not here for that. Nothing shall be done in any concealed manner. . . . I shall never counsel nor permit a sly or underhand action with your government, and you will pardon me, Pasha, if I say that I shall expect the same treatment in return—such as I give I shall expect to receive.

The Pasha quickly responded: "And you shall have it. We honor your position and your wishes will be respected. Such aid and protection as we are able to, we shall render."

They chatted for the better part of an hour. Clara decided that he was a "manly man, with a kind, fine face and genial, polished manners." He kept his word and protection was provided for the four expeditions at all points—the only reason, according to Clara, that her agents returned, "tired and worn, but saved and useful still." Their adventures proved to be fantastic, as they traveled over mountain passes by horseback, mule, and donkey; skidding down rocky ledges; encountering brigands and epidemics; sleeping in stables with the horses or in springless covered wagons; coming close to drowning in the Euphrates when a scoop-shovel ferryboat struck a rock; weathering heavy snow storms and parching drought. The missionary stations were widely scattered, mostly from three to fifteen days' travel from the Mediterranean or the Black Sea.

Back in Constantinople, Clara could visualize it all, receiving letters six weeks old from Dr. Hubbell. It was an exotic, difficult, and much-criticized adventure ranging over Harput, Urfa, Maras, Diyarbekir, Arapkir, Sivas, Alexandrette, Malatya, Samsun, Zeytun, Amasya, and other points. Many of the accounts, receipts, and vouchers, handled by Pullman, were in Greek, Italian, Arabic, Kurdish, Turkish, and Armenian. At the outset their gold was weighed and packed in stout canvas cloth, enclosed in sheepskin, and heavily sealed with wax. Strong cords bearing the Turkish and American seals bound these bundles. After they were dispatched into brigand-infested country, there was a wait of three or four weeks before the pony express arrived at its destination. As time went on drafts were used in the interior, simplifying one of Clara's early problems.

This was the only large-scale expedition in which she did not take to the field, but even as hardy a septuagenarian as Clara would have been an embarrassment in this type of sojourning. Besides, she was badly needed in Constantinople, to act as intermediary with the Turkish Government, to direct the distribution of funds and supplies, to control the field operations, and to handle the criticism that almost snowed her under for a time.

Dr. Hubbell headed the main expedition. But she ordered its route diverted when Sir Philip Currie, the British Ambassador, urged her to send her agents through the Mediterranean instead of the Black Sea, in order to get quickly to Maras and Zeytun, where ten thousand persons were ill with typhoid, typhus, dysentery, and smallpox. They were without doctors, medicine, or food.

Clara soon was telegraphing Dr. Hubbell to take in other areas as well. At Arapkir he found that six hundred were dead and nearly all the homes were destroyed. Here he supervised the most extensive project the Red Cross undertook on this expedition. Dr. Ira Harris, working in Syria at that time, was commandeered by Clara to direct operations at Maras and Zeytun. The death toll was more than a hundred a day when he arrived. His patients had to be fed broth before they could retain their medicines. "Keep the pot boiling. Let us know your wants," Clara telegraphed him. A hospital was opened. Food stations were established for the distribution of meat and soup. The victims had been living largely on boiled leaves from shrubs, weeds, and grass. There were seventeen hundred cases of dysentery and three hundred cases of typhus, while some seven thousand refugees had been jammed into already overcrowded dwellings.

Clara's other agents were assigned the northwestern route through Urfa and Diyarbekir. All met again at the end of April in Harput, which the missionaries referred to as their "bottomless pit." Clara had earmarked her Boston and Worcester funds for this region. Early in June the fine grain crops of the valleys of the Harput and Diyarbekir regions "grew golden and bowed their heavy spear-crowned heads in waiting for the sickle," Dr. Hubbell reported. But the natives lacked scythes and even knives. They were pulling up grain by the roots with their toughened fingers when a flood of harvest tools was offered them by the Red Cross. The blacksmiths were put to work manufacturing tools with iron and steel provided by the American agents. All bore the initials C. B., since the Turks did not welcome the sign of the cross. The cattle were branded in the same way. All the oxen, cows, horses, goats, and sheep had been driven to the Kurdish mountains. When Clara heard of this, in her own words, she "loosened her grasp on the bank account" and sent a draft of $22,000 to missionary head-quarters at Harput to be divided among the three expeditions "for the purchase of cattle, and the progress of the harvest of 1897."

Clara was greatly hampered by clumsy communication. Letters took six weeks to reach their destination. Telegrams, when transmissible at all, took days, and were usually dispatched in Greek, Arabic, or Turkish. Criticism now hummed around her ears. A wave of disapproval had broken free in America over the Red Cross expedition to Turkey. Was she being duped by the Sultan into playing the Turkish game? Why had she ordered the change in route and mission? Was she operating in fields where help was not needed? Was the Turkish Government seeing to it that aid went only to those on officially approved lists?

"I have not only the ministers but my own staff against me," Clara noted on March 5, feeling that Terrell was not supporting her as he should. Clara had said she would assist a Turk if necessary, and Dr. Washburn wanted to know if this were so. "I plead guilty," said Clara, "said I should, I so said before I left, that charity recognized no race, creed, sex nor color. He did not differ with me."

Although well used to criticism by this time she was cut to the quick by so concentrated an attack. She felt betrayed on all sides. Funds were no longer being subscribed. Even her own Red Cross officials in Washington, embarrassed by all the charges, gently proposed that she close up the mission and come home. She wrathfully cabled back: "We will finish the field without further aid." Even had she wished to break up the mission she could not have drawn in her agents from their distant posts within six weeks' time.

All this hostility had sprung from charges that she was collaborating with the Turkish officials at the expense of the Armenian cause. She was "astonished and pained beyond measure" to learn that it was taken for granted in America, England, and even by the missionary boards of Turkey, that she had "pledged herself and signed papers, to distribute the funds entrusted to me, under Turkish inspection and from lists furnished by Turkish officials." She insisted on a public denial of this charge, and wrote to P. V. DeGraw that she "*believed* she had done her best, and she *believed* the best that could have been done under the circumstances." No restrictions had been imposed or offered. There was much agitation in the American newspapers by the friends of Armenia until Clara's explanation cleared the atmosphere.

In the end she accomplished her purpose and the tide of criticism subsided. Thousands received medical care before she had finished. Homes were rebuilt. Farmers were equipped with tools, seeds, and the means of rehabilitation. Craftsmen reopened their shops. She did not claim any miracles. But the Red Cross had brought restoration and rehabilitation into many dark areas, and had proved itself in the foreign field. It had started a chain of production that would carry into the future. On June 10, she wrote to M. Moynier that the record of Dr. Harris and his doctors was better than anything she had encountered in the "contagion-smitten cities of civilization." She detailed with pride the other phases of restoration.

It was another version of the Sea Islands relief, a pattern now well established by Clara and smoothly executed by Dr. Hubbell and her other associates. On June 10 she wrote to Stevé that in spite of all the horror of it, she considered it in many respects her most successful field. "I feel that we are doing so much for humanity that no one else could do, and that there is so much gratitude on all sides, that it is almost a comfort to know that we have suffered something for it."

Clara kept Frances Willard well informed of every move made in this missionary field. With her heavy correspondence and various administrative functions, she had little time for any diversion in Constantinople. But she went to Scutari to speak to the students of Miss Patrick's School for Girls, a missionary college just under the shadow of the hospital where her famous contemporary, Florence Nightingale, had worked. The girls were Athenian, Armenian, Montenegrin, Austrian, Russian, and Serbian. They were training to teach in their own countries and were learning English. But each in her own way had caught the spirit of Scutari, Clara thought. She paid tribute to Florence Nightingale and humbly added: "To bring my tame story of hackneyed, everyday life, to lay beside this altar of history and renown is a thought at which my whole being shrinks into nothingness."

This was Clara in one of her moments of humility but there was nothing either hackneyed or negative about the story she had to tell. After this ceremony she drove to the English cemetery by way of the Florence Nightingale Hospital. She also attended the commencement exercises at Robert College, took tea with Dr. Washburn, and "returned a little party by ourselves in the legation yacht down the Bosphorus just as the evening shades were settling down."

Another of Clara's few social forays was the Fourth of July picnic given in her honor by her missionary friends at Proti, one of the Princes Islands. It was a patriotic luncheon, with American flags, and dashes of red, white and blue "flecking the tasteful viands." Clara thought it strange to be in Constantinople on the Fourth of July. She was deeply moved crossing the Sea of Marmora and dashed off one of her poems. "The day was exquisite; the sea was blue, and always rolling," she noted. Little black ducks, resembling sea gulls, moving restlessly along the shore caught her eye. But she found Constantinople cold and wondered why the residents crossed to the Princes Islands for summer residence while just back of them lay "Mount Olympus white as a ghost."

Mea was planning to join her and Clara wrote urging her to bring only simple, warm clothes with her. She had donned nothing but blue serges since her arrival, she said, although she much admired the large-figured Turkish silks worn by the Turkish women. "They are works of art to my eye," she wrote. Dr. Hubbell had not yet come in from the field but Clara assured Mea that she would like Mr. Pullman. "He is good as refined gold to me. I feel so safe with him." This comment, no doubt, was evoked by the news she had just received of Kate Field's death. Brilliant Kate, whose life had been full of variety and excitement, had died from the effects of being blown off her horse's back while she rode through a hurricane in the Hawaiian Islands. She was a valued friend to Clara, who now wrote illuminatingly to Mrs. J. Sewall Reed, a Boston acquaintance who would help her to introduce first aid in America: "How sad it was, dying all alone with only a stranger to take her last words and feel that last weak clasp of her dying hand. It would have been better and safer if she had had one of my strong boys along. All things considered, I think they are not a bad investment."

One by one the expeditions closed and left their alien territory, coming out by the Black Sea over so dangerous a route that a brigand chief was selected as the most likely escort. When Clara and her party sailed for home, the quay was crowded with people of many races, "the strange costumes and colors commingling in such variety as only an Oriental city can produce." Farewells were shouted in a babel of tongues.

They sailed up the Danube and visited Budapest, taking in its Millennial Exposition. Clara was charmed by the natural beauties and vistas along the way, but was outraged to see women being used as draft animals, yoked to carts. "Europe needs many of our Susan B. Anthonys and Elizabeth Cady Stantons to bring 'tyrant man' to a realizing sense of his duty, and women to their rights," she commented.

From Vienna she hastened on to visit the Grand Duke and Grand Duchess of Baden at their island of Mainau on Lake Constance. This time, on parting, Louise gave her a knot of gold, which Clara put away with her decorations. As usual, she paid a nostalgic visit to Strassburg, then traveled on to London and sailed for home, arriving in New York on September 12, 1896, after eight months of foreign service.

Several months later she received through the State Department the Sultan's decoration of Shefaket, with an accompanying diploma in Turkish. Armenia awarded her the Ordre des Chevaliers de Mélusine, a rare decoration dating back to 1186 and conferred only for humanitarian, scientific, or other services of distinction. These were among the rarest and most cherished of Clara's unique collection of decorations.

Her own people honored her on her return with a dinner at the Shoreham Hotel in Washington. Again the tables were arranged in the form of red crosses, with scarlet chiffon on white damask and American Beauty roses mirrored in mock lakes. Clara sat under the American flag, a high comb rising at the back of her hair, her decorations pinned to her dark silk. She was close to her seventy-fifth birthday, but to spectators she seemed years younger as she smiled up at B. H. Warner, one of the Red Cross officials who later would help to oust her, while he told of watching her at work in one of the Washington hospitals thirty years earlier, with all the wartime din around her. "She came to be known as the mother, not only of one regiment, but of the common soldiery," he said. "Reticent, constant and efficient in all she had undertaken, she has won the confidence of every government under whose flag she has labored, not for any selfish purpose, but in order that she might render aid and succor to those who suffered and were powerless to obtain relief from any other source."

Clara had touched another mountain peak but she experienced the usual collapse that followed great effort on her part. Criticism of her operations kept springing up in the most unexpected places and was now getting close to the inner body of the Red Cross. Spencer Trask complained of delayed accounting for funds sent to Turkey. For a time her health was poor after her return from the Near East. Her voice failed her and her eyes troubled her so much that she dictated her diary entries to Pullman.

But she drew fresh vigor from the Sixth International Conference of the Red Cross held in Vienna in the autumn of 1897. Dr. Hubbell, Pullman, and Dr. Lucy Hall, now married to R. G. Brown, were in her entourage. Clara outpaced them all striding the deck as they crossed the Atlantic, even though "it was like walking on a steep roof." For once she was not seasick, and Pullman reported such items as: "We three Red Crossers . . . went to the extreme bow this morning with our rugs and papers and put in three hours of good work. . . . The Queen was the first lady at breakfast this morning. . . . An hour of story telling, declamation, etc. in the Queen's room closes the day." Clara with Pullman was preparing reports in French on the Sea Islands and Armenian relief to read at the conference and was rehearsing them in advance. Passing through Paris they saw Sarah Bernhardt in *Fédora*, heard *Faust* at the opera, shopped in the Bon Marché, visited the Jardin des Plantes and the Eiffel Tower.

By this time Clara was thoroughly familiar with the delegates who gathered from all the signatory countries. She was warmly received among them, and was invariably given a front seat. They had become not only old friends, "but alas old as well," she noted, "but so wise, dignified and liberal, all narrowness of views seemed to have been worked out of them by the expansive field of thought in which their minds had labored."

Clara modestly described her disaster work. "We spoke little, but laid before them our written reports of the work of the five years," she commented. This made its own impression on the delegates and was followed by much discussion of this aspect of Red Cross work, in which the United States now unmistakably led the field. Clara had not only effected it, but her work had attracted notice, and was to have a profound influence on the ultimate scope and variety of Red Cross activities around the world.

She attended a court reception in Vienna, and was dazzled anew by uniforms and decorations, by the stately bodyguard of the Emperor Franz Josef, and the Gobelin tapestries in the marble halls. She had a long chat with Archduke Ludwig Victor, representing the absent Emperor. She went by special train to the Kahlenberg and looked down on the gentle stretches of the Danube and the Vienna woods. The Mayor of Vienna led the procession of delegates into the Jubilee Hall of the Rathaus with Clara Barton on his arm. These were mellow, unforgettable hours for her, and her troubles at home were briefly forgotten.

On their return Pullman resigned. His going troubled Clara, but his actions had embarrassed her greatly. He had a history of intemperance, and a romantic entanglement in Europe, about which she knew nothing, led to further complications when he returned home. Clara sustained him for as long as she could. He had done useful work for her organization. He wrote well and could function capably when he chose. But he proved to be one of her more disastrous associations. Samuel Ramsey was still in the background silent as a ghost, but urging Clara by letter to help him get a post in the Library of Congress.

Temperance reform was in the air, and the Keeley cure was much discussed. Frances Willard wrote to Clara at this time urging her to say a few "strong words" for the New York *Voice* in its campaign to have the authorities of Yale protect their students from "saloon influence." Miss Willard argued that if the governors and professors of Yale understood that the *mothers* throughout the land "were revolting from sending their sons to an institution so exposed to temptations as young men are at Yale" they would soon do something about it.

By the end of 1897 Clara had settled in the home of her choosing at Glen Echo. It still stands outside Washington, buried in a grove of trees on a bank above the Potomac. It faces the sloping bluffs of Virginia and overlooks the old canal built by George Washington. Clara always enjoyed the view and the fine oak, hickory, and sycamore trees that grew on her property. She cherished her garden, her strawberry beds, her shrubs, and her cows. Nor did she object to the worldly echoes of a near-by amusement park and the clank of the merry-go-round. Bit by bit Dr. Hubbell improved the property, grafting plants, adding to the stock, carrying out Clara's wishes for beauty and utility. It was a source of constant refreshment to her in the closing days of her life, and was the headquarters of the Red Cross until she resigned in 1904.

The house is a white clapboard building, with two steeple-roofed turrets, one of which had a vault built into it for the protection of Red Cross documents. The interior suggests a ship, with its long central hall, its paneled walls, railed balcony, and apartments opening off both floors. Three penthouse rooms are set in the lantern roof, and tinted light streams in through the colored glass of its Red Cross windows. The balcony railing was traditionally hung with Clara's international flags. Oriental rugs, silks, trophies of various kinds from different parts of the world showed up against the dark paneling. A gold settee from the Grand Duchess Louise and an onyx-topped gold-leaf table were among her treasures. Today Glen Echo still has the huge oak desk on which she wrote so many letters, made countless diary entries, and transacted much of her Red Cross business.

## CHAPTER XVII

## "I AM WITH THE WOUNDED"

"YOU NEED no looking after. You will stand without hitching," President McKinley told seventy-five-year-old Miss Barton on a July day in 1897 when she called on him to discuss relief operations for the *reconcentrados* of Cuba. She was soon to be involved in the Spanish-American War but at the moment was considering her status under the Treaty of Geneva.

Clara moved cautiously, sensing international complications, with three countries involved, but she was deeply concerned over the menacing situation in that small island of which she had prophesied as far back as 1874: "It will be history by and by, to whom Cuba belongs."

Her hand had been forced by a group of women she called the "Court Ladies" who had already reached the President with a plea for aid for the large number of Cubans who had been herded into concentration areas. Actually, these women worked under the name and insignia of the Red Cross, so she felt some responsibility for them, although she did not approve of their headstrong course. They had impinged on her authority and Clara went straight to the President. She was wheezing and puffing from her recurrent bronchitis and Mr. McKinley bent close to hear her whispered tones.

His sympathy was with Clara. He told her that in the excess of their zeal, and scarcity of knowledge, they might do real mischief. He laughingly proposed that she advise the Court Ladies to consult their husbands. Clara told him that this was exactly what she had done.

She had gone far beyond this and had been conducting some delicate negotiations of her own. She had had a long talk with M. Moynier on her way home from Vienna. Complaints had

reached him from a group in Tampa,            , calling themselves
the Cuban Patriots, that the head of the Red Cross in America was
obstructing relief work in Cuba. Clara had laid her case in detail
before the President of the International Red Cross until he "thoroughly understood the situation."

She now proposed consultation with the Army and Navy Departments and President McKinley agreed. This was the first time
that the Red Cross had officially sought the advice of its full official
board of consultation. War was in the air. On other occasions, Clara
had cleared matters direct with the President. Now she wished to
go further. Before long she was back at the White House for an
impromptu call which proved to be timely. She found the President and William R. Day, his Secretary of State, discussing an appeal for funds for the *reconcentrados*. They told her she had come
at the perfect moment. They had chosen her as the "most efficient
source of aid," and were about to send for her.

She showed the President a letter she had written to Señor
Dupuy De Lôme, Spanish Minister to the United States, suggesting that she go quietly to Cuba to study the situation at first hand.
President McKinley thought the letter excellent. He asked her if
she would go to the field personally. Without hesitation she said
she would, and left the White House with a brisk step, reflecting
that she had "never expected such thanks from the head of the
nation as I received in that chamber."

Just before Christmas the President appealed to the public for
civilian relief and on New Year's Day, 1898, the Central Cuban
Relief Committee was formed in New York. Clara would not serve
as chairman but nominated her nephew Stevé to act with Charles
A. Schieren, representing the New York Chamber of Commerce,
and Louis Klopsch of the *Christian Herald*, which was raising a
fund. The committee would solicit aid in money and supplies and
the Red Cross would handle the distribution in Cuba.

On February 6 Clara left for Havana with J. K. Elwell, nephew
of her old friend, Colonel Elwell. He spoke Spanish, had been a
merchant in Santiago, and she thought him ideally suited to take
charge of her warehouse and supplies. Thus, six weeks after she
had celebrated her seventy-sixth birthday, Clara was heading into
the Spanish-American War. Her work in Cuba fell into three

phases: *Reconcentrado* relief in the spring of 1898; Spanish-American War relief in the summer of 1898; and Cuban orphan asylum and hospital relief in the spring and summer of 1899.

President McKinley's introductory letter, dated February 4, 1898, backed her up in characteristic fashion:

Miss Barton's well known ability, her long devotion to the noble work of extending relief to the needy and suffering in different lands, as well as her high character as a woman, commend her to the highest consideration and good will of all people.

I bespeak for Miss Barton, wherever her mission may take her, such assistance and encouragement as she may need in prosecuting the work to which she has devotedly given so much time and service.

Other official letters commended her to General Fitzhugh Lee, United States Consul at Havana, and to the commanding officers of the U.S. Navy, in each case making the point that Clara Barton needed no introduction. Once again, she had mustered impressive support and had carte blanche to make her own way. But the world had changed since the days of the Civil War, and a solitary woman could no longer crash a remote and complicated fighting front. Moreover, the status of the Red Cross in time of war had not yet been clearly defined by practice in America.

An amendment to the Treaty of Geneva in 1868, extending its protection to hospital service at sea, had not been ratified by all other treaty nations. Neither the United States nor Spain was covered by these Additional Articles. This left Clara literally floating between earth and sea in her operations. But she did not lack for confidence as her ship sailed into Havana and she noted the "polished, shining battleship Maine" towering above her.

Clara's first collision with the *reconcentrado* problem was at Los Fosos, a degraded hospital where men, women, and children were dying at the rate of a dozen or more every twenty-four hours. She noted the crudely made coffins piled at the entrance, and the patients lying on the floors, some mere skeletons, others bloated grotesquely from malnutrition. The massacres of Armenia "seemed merciful in comparison."

By the time she had toured five buildings where the *reconcentrados* were quartered, her sense of organization was in full play.

Flour, meal, rice, potatoes, canned meat, fruit, bacon, lard, malted milk, and quinine were distributed fast from the newly established warehouse. Arrangements were made with Cuban bakers to turn the flour into bread. Centers were established for the distribution of food by ticket. It was doled out in paper bags as the starving stormed the relief centers.

Clara went to work herself in the warehouse. William Willard Howard, a newspaperman who had assisted in the Armenian field, found her opening and sorting supplies. He said the picture of the president of the American National Red Cross with her skirts pinned up, peering into barrels, would make a fine cartoon for a New York paper. The press usually appreciated Clara's original ways. Even at seventy-six she could laugh with them at her own expense, and did.

As usual, she was pitched into sudden drama. On February 13 she lunched with Captain Charles D. Sigsbee, commander of the *Maine*, and two days later she was working late at her writing table with Elwell when, to quote her own words:

. . . The table shook from under our hands, the great glass door opening onto the veranda, facing the sea, flew open; everything in the room was in motion or out of place—the deafening roar of such a burst of thunder as perhaps one never heard before, and off to the right, out over the bay, the air was filled with a blaze of light, and this in turn filled with black specks like huge spectres flying in all directions. Then it faded away. The bells rang; the whistles blew, and voices in the street were heard for a moment; then all was quiet again.

Clara thought some mammoth mortar had burst, or a magazine had exploded. She quickly learned that the *Maine* had blown up. Elwell went out scouting and brought her such details as he could gather.

"I am with the wounded," Clara cabled to Washington, and went at once to the hospital where the injured had been taken. She approached their bedsides in the old familiar manner, jotting down names, only to have one man peer up at her through the bandages covering his scorched face:

"Isn't this Miss Barton?" he asked.

"Yes," said Clara.

"I thought it must be. I knew you were here, and thought you would come to us. I am so thankful for us all."

This particular sailor was dead two days later. But first Clara had telegraphed at his request to his fiancée: "Wounded, but saved."

She distributed comforts among the injured as in days long past, and did what she could to supplement the "excellent Navy care" they received. The Cubans gave her a "deep plate of choice flowers" and a black-bordered envelope inscribed "For the Dead of the *Maine*." She wrote to Stevé: "Great pieces of that beautiful ship lie on my table charred and splintered. God knows how it happened." She had been an observer of the incident that touched off the Spanish-American War.

Soon she was installed in the villa belonging to the wife of the Cuban Minister to Madrid. But she did not linger long in its exquisite gardens, with their fountains, flowers, and palm and banana trees. With Dr. Hubbell she went from one *reconcentrado* center to another, visiting Matanzas, Artemisa, Sagua la Grande, and Cienfuegos, and finding deplorable conditions everywhere. Practical, urgent, resourceful, Clara moved from point to point, stirring up local officials to action, seeing where land could be utilized, appraising the city ration system, ingenious in her plans for the care of the sick, urging the use of local facilities, pressing the benefits of lime and whitewash for hospital and hovel.

When Senator Redfield Proctor and M. M. Parker arrived from Washington to investigate the situation for Congress, Clara accompanied them to the worst areas. At Artemisa they found between two and three thousand people almost entirely without food. Ten thousand *reconcentrados* had been jammed into this district and three thousand had already died. Others had strayed away looking for food. Five thousand still remained. They were dying at the rate of 175 a month and there was only one hospital. Clara directed the three local physicians to round up women who would care for the sick, and move them from huts to the hospital. The distribution of food by ticket was begun at once. Spurred into action, the Mayor turned over a thousand acres of land lying within the military lines of fortifications. Back in Havana, Clara announced that she "had arranged for food for all." Nothing seemed more urgent at the moment.

It was from information gathered on this trip that Senator Proctor stirred the country with his dramatic speech before the Senate in March on the condition of the *reconcentrados*. He charged that 200,000 out of a population of 1,600,000 had died in the concentration centers within a few months from actual starvation or diseases due to malnutrition.

In passing, he paid tribute to Clara. He had been quietly observing her activities in the course of his tour, and found them good:

Miss Barton and her work need no indorsement from me. I had known and esteemed her for many years, but had not half appreciated her capability and devotion to her work. I especially looked into her business methods, fearing there would be the greatest danger of mistake, that there might be want of system, waste and extravagance, but found she could teach me on these points. In short, I saw nothing to criticize, everything to commend. The American people may be assured that the bounty will reach the sufferers with the least possible cost and in the best manner in every respect.

The first impact of the Red Cross medical and nursing service built up by the New York committee of German origin was felt when Dr. A. Monae Lesser and his wife, Mrs. Bettina A. Hofker-Lesser, better known as Sister Bettina, arrived with a staff and applied the expert medical touch needed for Clara's operations. An orphanage was established and some of the worst cases were moved from Los Fosos into a handsome Cuban home with tropical gardens and swimming pool.

But Los Fosos, too, was improving, with the regular distribution of American food, medicines, clothing, and bedding. There were enough beds for everyone now. Clara felt she was making real headway when Klopsch arrived suddenly from New York, and gave every indication of having come to supervise her operations. Their relations were frigid when he insisted that there should be no more visits to outside cities or villages; that Elwell should devote all his attention to the warehouse; and that Clara should concentrate on her negotiations with the Spanish authorities to permit the *reconcentrados* to cultivate the broad glades of land lying within the *trochas*.

Clara briskly returned the $10,000 contributed by Klopsch's

committee and said she would "no longer be burdened by his gold." She whisked off to Washington to have her status established, leaving Klopsch to run things as he wished. Stevé accompanied her to the State Department for a clarification of procedure. It was then agreed that the Cuban committee in New York would collect and ship the supplies to Cuba. General Lee would receive them. At that point the Red Cross would step in and handle distribution, reporting to the New York committee and, through it, to the United States Government.

Everyone was talking war in Washington. Tension had mounted since the destruction of the *Maine*. On her return to Cuba, Clara felt that her friendly relations with General Erenas Blanco soon must end. When she paid her last call he told her that she had nothing to fear from the regular Spanish troops but that he could not bank on the "irregular and unruly element in the army, the volunteers whose actions could not be controlled." He advised Clara to leave with her staff but offered to be personally responsible for her safety as long as she remained.

He led her into a large salon and pointed to portraits of the Spanish grandees of 1776. "When your country was in trouble," he told her sadly, "Spain was the friend of America. Now Spain is in trouble, America is her enemy."

"I knew no answer for this but silence," Clara observed, "and as we passed out through the corridor of guards, he handing me to my carriage with a farewell and a blessing, I could but recall my experience with the Turkish officials and government, where I entered with such apprehension and left with such marks of cordiality."

At this point Clara moved Red Cross headquarters to Tampa, incurring criticism for her precipitate action. Part of the trouble was Klopsch, who had taken firm hold in Havana during her absence and had spread the "most insinuating and harmful remarks of me, personally, that were decent to utter," Clara wrote to Stevé on April 14.

But the outbreak of war eleven days later changed the face of everything. Clara immediately offered the services of the American National Red Cross for supplemental service. She made two trips to Washington and New York in quick succession, to straighten out complications. Two days before war was declared the *State of*

*Texas*, a Red Cross ship laden with supplies for the *reconcentrados*, had sailed from New York.

Now Clara fortified herself with a letter to Rear Admiral William T. Sampson from John D. Long, Secretary of the Navy, describing her aims. The Treaty of Geneva did not cover naval warfare at this time and Clara was alive to the technical issues involved. She wrote to M. Moynier, detailing each move she had made:

Also you have doubtless seen that the American Government called her citizens home, and that we dutifully obeyed the call, not, however, without the fullest consultation with the Spanish Government on the island and leaving them as friendly as we could have left our own people. They could not guarantee protection against the ungovernable element of the island, and in accordance with the wishes of our government it was considered prudent for the Red Cross to withdraw.

We are, however, the first to return. Our Relief Committee, under the direction of President McKinley and his Cabinet, have laden this relief ship with fourteen hundred tons of general provisions and have asked me to take the direction of the vessel and proceed to Cuba.

But it took Clara some time to reach her destination. The Navy was blockading Cuba and the *State of Texas* was tied up for nearly two months at Key West. Admiral Sampson felt it his duty as chief of the blockading squadron to keep food out of Cuba. Clara saw it as her duty to get it in for the *reconcentrados*. Their viewpoints were irreconcilable, although the letters they exchanged were polite.[9] Clara forwarded them to Stevé to place personally before the Cabinet.

She had moved from Tampa to Key West at the end of April, joining Dr. Hubbell and other members of the party on the *State of Texas*, which she described as a "snug little ship," well built, but by no means new. Its dull black hull could in no way compare with the "snow-white, green and red-striped hospital ships, those heralds of relief that afterwards graced the waters of that bay."

The weeks that followed were tedious for all concerned. Clara wrote reports, spurred her staff to study Spanish, and gave food and tobacco to the crews of captured Spanish vessels who had been living off fish from the holds. They were permitted under Red Cross auspices to correspond with relatives in Spain. Medical treatment was offered them, too. The smoking room of the ship was fitted up as an operating room. The purser's room was converted into a dispensary. The impression prevailed that the *State of Texas* was a hospital ship. Actually, its supplies were designed for the *reconcentrados,* and at this point it was aiding Spanish sailors.

On May 23 General William R. Shafter called on Clara. She found him a "large, short, desperately swelled out man, still a rather fine-looking person." She was to have more dealings with the General in the months that followed, and his ultimate verdict on her was that she "made us do all sorts of things, but she's the greatest woman in the world."

Newspaper correspondents boarded the *State of Texas* to talk to Clara. She found them "all pleasant but *starved for news.*" They journeyed back and forth in rowboats, picking their way among the idle vessels. She had one of the brightest on her own ship and attached to her staff in George Kennan, who was not only a famous correspondent but was vice-president of the American Red Cross at this time. He had been asked to report the work of the organization for the *Outlook* and he sent off dispatches from time to time.

She needed his aid when she learned through the *Herald* that without her knowledge all Red Cross affairs had been placed under the control of George M. Sternberg, Surgeon General of the United States Army. "If we have no status under the Treaty, let it be known, and let us retire," she observed.

Red Cross relations with the military branches of the Government were obviously not well defined, and Kennan dampened Clara's spirits by suggesting that her papers were not in order. He had done research in the various departments and could not find the official documents needed. "Our War Department," commented Kennan, "does not want or accept us. It does not realize our position, is not informed in its relation to the Treaty of Geneva, and is acting adversely in the dark of ignorance."

It was plain why Kennan had not been able to find any of the documents in Government departments. "Good reason—the Govt. never did anything about the *work,*" Clara wrote. "I did it all, and have all the proofs and papers." She steamed off for Tampa and hurried to Washington with Kennan to show him her official papers. On May 25 she was up until three o'clock in the morning at Glen Echo searching through her hidden vault for her original documents. Clara was outraged by his skepticism. "To convince him I brought to light the old credentials so long ago given, with such labor, and toilsome patience," she noted. At last he was satisfied.

Next she called at the War Office, accompanied by Corporal M. L. Tanner, one of the Red Cross officers, who hoped she had not lost her "old time vigor" and would succeed in making herself felt. Actually, Clara was close to tears as she told Secretary of War Russell A. Alger that a clique in the Surgeon General's Office was working against her. But action on her behalf had already been taken. That same day Secretary of State Day, at the President's direction, had firmly established her status by announcing that her organization was the sole and official link in the United States with the International Committee of the Red Cross. He notified the Army and Navy Departments to give full recognition to the Red Cross and make use of its services.

"It was all done for me," said Clara thankfully. "The strain of years had been taken off. The recognition, the Bill and all explanations. I looked at me to see if it is me."

Clara had won a major victory, and the Red Cross had met its first challenge in the area of war. Actually she traced part of her trouble to the powerful Red Cross Relief Committee in New York which on May 24 had offered its services to the President as an independent unit. At the same time Clara was notified that it would "furnish all necessary money and material to support the work of the national body."

It was made up of a group of influential citizens already engaged in extensive relief operations, and was headed by Levi P. Morton. Among its members were Bishop Henry C. Potter, William T. Wardwell, Mrs. Anna Roosevelt Cowles, Dr. George F. Shrady, and Mrs. Whitelaw Reid, who built up the early nursing service of the Red Cross. This committee organized ninety-two auxiliary societies, and spent roughly $300,000 on supplies for camps and hospitals in the United States, Cuba, and Puerto Rico. It furnished everything from a tent to a toothbrush, from an ambulance to a cake of soap. It maintained courteous relations with Clara, sent her abundant supplies, but was not wholly satisfied with her administration.

Chafing under inaction, she was relieved when the order came on June 20 to steam ahead. At last the deadlock was broken. The *State of Texas* was covered with barnacles and made slow progress in choppy seas. It still had its cargo of fourteen hundred tons virtually intact, its working corps of twenty, its crew of thirty-five. It had the Red Cross near its prow and on the smokestack, but it was a dingy hulk in an anomalous situation—"as we smite with one hand we feed with the other"—distinguished only by having the star of the Red Cross on board. Clara was always a personal force to be taken into account.

Admiral Sampson had advised her to proceed to Guantánamo, where the Marines had made a landing. They sailed into the quiet harbor, ringed by wooded hills, and dropped anchor in still waters. American warships were all around them. The Marines were camped along the brow of a hill. Clara was invited to visit the Navy hospital ship *Solace*, which flew the Red Cross flag and had fifty wounded Marines on board. She was much affected by the sight of that "first naval relief ship in American waters," operating under the Treaty of Geneva. It recalled her early battles and she left feeling grateful that she had lived "to see the fruition of the work I had so cherished."

She was drawn into action almost at once. No one now remembered that she was there to help the *reconcentrados*. Her medical staff, consisting of the Lessers, their nine nurses and three surgeons, were summoned to the Reserve Divisional Hospital of Siboney, and Clara was asked to assist with the war victims. She learned that the Rough Riders had been "hardly dealt by" at the battle of Guásimas. Hamilton Fish and Allyn K. Capron were dead, and the wounded needed help. After two newspaper correspondents had graphically described the way in which they were pitched into Spanish houses along the beach and lay in their bloodstained garments on bare, dirty floors, she made up her mind quickly.

"It is the Rough Riders we go to," Clara announced, "and the relief may be also rough, but it will be *ready*. A better body of helpers could scarcely be gotten together."

She set them to work in the hold bringing out medical supplies and dressings. They reached Siboney after dark on the night of June 26 and found the little cove and the neighboring roadstead alive with shifting strings of glitter, marking the uneasy roll of the transport steamers. The sea was rough but Clara's medical staff went ashore as soon as a boat could be lowered. They visited both American and Cuban hospitals during the night, and reported back that the patients lay on the floors without blankets or pillows and no attempt had been made to clean or disinfect either of the buildings.

At daybreak Clara watched the soldiers filing over the hill, "forming in lines by ones and twos, winding up, in and out among the hills, higher and higher, like a great anaconda." American surgeons called on her but did not welcome the idea of women nurses in soldiers' hospitals. Clara reminded them that she had spent a good deal of time there herself in her day. "They appeared to understand that perfectly, or were so polite as not to criticize it," she noted, "but there seemed to be a *later* line which could not be crossed."

The Cubans, who had just come into camp, were more receptive. They wanted all the help they could get from Clara and her staff. Before long Major Louis A. Lagarde sent her an urgent plea for aid, too. Clara responded gladly, saying that although hers was not a hospital ship she had good supplies, intelligent workers, and the "true spirit of the Red Cross, that seeks to help humanity wherever its need exists." After that, aid was given impartially.

Clara had undertaken a stiff task in getting her supplies ashore at Siboney. Everything had to be rowed or floated on two flat scows in the brief hours when the surf was not too high. Bedding and hospital supplies were dumped in the ocean when one of the scows turned over. On another trip it took Dr. Hubbell half a day to get back from the shore to the ship, less than a quarter of a mile. The men waded, waist deep, pulling the scows up out of the surf, landing meal, flour, condensed milk, tea, coffee, and canned goods. Clara stood on the deck, directing loading operations, as she used to stand in the mud on Civil War battlefields. The woman of forty had become the woman of seventy-five. Her sight was less keen. There were wrinkles around her eyes and mouth. She seemed to have shrunk a little in stature, but her lively sense of order, system, and authority remained the same.

It did not surprise her to be called into fast action when word came through from George Kennan, who was at General Shafter's headquarters, that she was needed at the front. The message reached her at the hospital in Siboney where her medical force was at work. She was relieving the first of the American Red Cross sisters to do battle duty. Her supplies were now desperately needed, since from July 1 to 3 the battles of El Caney and San Juan raged and General Shafter's forces lacked even the most basic items. He had penciled an order for Miss Barton to seize any empty wagons coming in and to load them with blankets, clothing, tents, food, and medical necessities.

Clara had her staff work all night getting out supplies and shipping them ashore. When the last had gone she followed herself. The surf had risen so that her yawl was nearly swamped as she clambered ashore to a pier already splitting down the middle. Two six-mule army wagons had been commandeered and had already gone ahead, well loaded with their Red Cross supplies. There was no other suitable conveyance in sight. But Clara promptly halted the first hay wagon that came in view, and climbed on top of the bales, along with Dr. and Mrs. Gardner and Major James A. Mc-Dowell, an assistant in whom she put much trust because he had served in twenty-six battles during the Civil War. Patient Dr. Hubbell trailed along on foot. After four hours of rocky riding they reached the First Division Hospital of the Fifth Army Corps, if hospital it could be called. There Clara came on one of the worst after-battle scenes in her large experience. "If there was anything more terrible in our Civil War, I am glad that I was not there to see it," Kennan remarked.

The hospital was about three miles east of Santiago and lay in an open glade of a wooded valley, bounded by mountains and flanked by dense jungle. It consisted of three large tents with operating tables, half a dozen smaller ones for the wounded, and a scattering of "dog kennels," as the low shelter tents were called. All around the tents, as well as in them, lay men fresh from the battlefield and the operating table. There were no blankets or covering of any kind. Most of them lay in a tangle of tall wild grass in soaking ground, or under clumps of piñon bushes. As soon as a strip of thatching was stretched across a group of the wounded, fresh casualties would come in and attention would shift. Eight hundred men had already been brought in when Clara arrived. Most had been stripped to the waist for examination farther up the line. Others, who had been operated on, lay stark naked, because of the lack of supplies. Their misery was dreadful to behold. They suffered from the blazing tropical sun in the daytime and the chilly dew at night.

Clara was hailed with a shout: "My God, boys. It's Clara Barton. Now we'll get something to eat."

She went straight to the cook house and took charge. She saw from a glance at the fireplace that it was set up by men who knew nothing of making a camp. She and McDowell gathered stones and bricks and built a proper fireplace, found water, and soon had agate kettles filled. The wood was green and burned slowly. A heavy drizzle fell. Clara had tarpaulins spread over her supplies as they were brought from the wagons. Soon she was stirring her famous gruel. "I had not thought to ever make gruel again over a camp-fire," she noted. As she saw the men lap it up, she reflected: "I felt it was again the same old story and wondered what gain there had been in the last thirty years. Had anything been worse than this?"

Her gruel was still the staple item, but milk, chocolate, rice, and tea soon were added. Most welcome to the parched and fevered soldiers was Clara's "Red Cross cider," made from stewed apples and prunes, mixed with the juice of limes and cooled in a near-by stream.

That first night she had no blankets, since she had concentrated on food and medical supplies, but she tore off strips of unbleached muslin to cover the nakedness of the men. Seventeen died in the night. In the morning the ambulances were loaded with the wounded being taken along the "rough, pitiless road to Siboney" where they were received by the hospitals there or were put aboard transports. The casualties were 1,475 killed and wounded before the heights were won. Emergency quarters were improvised along the way, since no preparations had been made. Those who could walk at all came limping and scrambling over the hilly road. The others lay in their tracks or were brought in by wagon or in the few ambulances available. Clara always maintained that the slaughter would have been reduced if artillery instead of infantry had been used. The men were mowed down with rapid-fire guns.

Dr. Hubbell soon arrived with more tarpaulins, charcoal braziers, and food—"another contribution from the surf of Siboney." Clara moved her small Red Cross emergency station close to the headquarters tent of Major Marshall William Wood, Chief Surgeon of the 1st Division, who helped her to protect her supplies from the rain, and gave her a tent for herself. But suddenly the weather cleared and there was moonlight.

She was never to forget these few strange nights passed on the edge of the jungle, with the "sea like waves of silver, the camp on the shore, the horses standing motionless, the hospital tents with the occasional flickering light of a candle, the sound of the surf brought back on the cool breeze, and over all the tragedy of life and death, of pain and sorrow."

The operating tables were lined up in front of the few tents, and the surgeons worked eerily in a "flood of silver moonlight." Lights were banned lest guerrilla sharpshooters fire from the trees, but when the surgeons found they could not work successfully by moonlight they had their candles relit and took chances. It made Clara think of Antietam. Two Red Cross men had been killed earlier by sharpshooters firing at wagons.

While she was in this area her quarters were visited early in the day by an "officer in khaki uniform showing hard service." A bandanna handkerchief hung from his hat, to protect the back of his head from the sun. This was none other than Colonel Theodore Roosevelt. Then, as Clara tells it:

"We were very glad to meet the gallant leader of the Rough Riders. After a few moments conversation he said; 'I have some sick men with the regiment who refuse to leave it. They need such delicacies as you have here, which I am ready to pay for out of my own pocket. Can I buy them from the Red Cross?'

" 'Not for a million dollars,' said Dr. Gardner.

" 'But my men need these things,' he said, his tone and face expressing anxiety. 'I think a great deal of my men. I am proud of them.'

" 'And we know they are proud of you, Colonel. But we can't sell Red Cross supplies.'

" 'Then, how can I get them? I must have proper food for my sick men,' he said.

" 'Just ask for them, Colonel.'

" 'Oh,' he said, his face lighting up with a bright smile. 'Then I do ask for them.' "

The Colonel would not wait to have them sent. A sack was filled with malted milk, oatmeal, canned fruits, rice, tea, chocolate, beef-steak, and vegetables, and then: "Before we had recovered from our surprise, the incident was closed by the future President of the U.S. slinging the big sack over his shoulders, striding off, and out of sight through the jungle."

Clara traveled back and forth three times in wagons over the rough road between the hospital and Siboney, rounding up fresh supplies, until every wounded man was in a tent, wrapped in a blanket, with a rubber poncho beneath him on the sodden ground. During one of her absences the *State of Texas* made a trip to Port Antonio in Jamaica and took on fifteen tons of ice. This was worth its weight in gold. Clara had seen her nurses work miracles with a single chunk of ice for head wounds, chipping it into tiny pieces and husbanding them in a bit of blanket.

On one of her trips the sea was so rough that she could not get back to her ship. Her little party settled in for the night in the local post office, which had been taken over by the American Army. Clara wanted to bivouac in her wagon under the tropical stars but her helpers would not hear of it. It had served her well in old Virginia and on the drifting sands of Morris Island, she told them indignantly. In the end she spent part of the night walking along the beach. Kennan left her "writing orders and telegrams by the light of a flaring, guttering candle" and went out to share the piazza with the sleeping form of Lord Alfred Paget, naval observer for the British Government. Seeing him sprawled in white ducks, Kennan had taken him for a ghost. Dr. Hubbell slept on one of the post-office counters, and Dr. E. Winfield Egan, of Clara's staff, without blanket or pillow, stretched himself on the dirty planks below. Later they were all to learn that they had been badly exposed to yellow fever in this building.

On July 4, as the Stars and Stripes flew from all the mastheads at Siboney after the naval victory, the Red Cross was in operation at various points along the southern coast of Cuba. It had its emer-gency station at the front, its Red Cross hospital in Siboney run by Dr. Lesser, and a ward of thirty beds in the general hospital managed by Major Lagarde. In addition, refugees were being fed at various points along the way.

But relief operations were suspended abruptly on July 10 on account of an outbreak of yellow fever. When Clara attempted to land supplies at Guantánamo Bay for the refugees in that district after the surrender of Santiago she was refused anchorage, since her ship had come from plague-stricken Siboney. On her return from Guantánamo she urged Admiral Sampson, on board the flagship *New York*, to let food go in with the troops, since the people would be in a starving condition. He heeded her advice. "The food shall enter in advance of the forces; you may go in this afternoon," he told her.

Thus the *State of Texas*, flying the flag of the Red Cross, led the naval parade into the vanquished city. Clara took this as a great compliment to the organization she headed. Admiral Sampson gave her a pilot to steer her through the channel, not yet completely cleared of mines. As they swept out into the open and lost sight of all other ships she could scarcely accept the situation. Later she described her emotions:

Leaning on the rail, half lost in reverie over the strange quiet beauty of the scene, the thought suddenly burst upon me—are we really going into Santiago, and alone? Are we not to be run out, and wait aside, and salute with dipping colors, while the great battleships come up with music and banners and lead the way? . . .

Could it be possible, that the commander who had captured a city declined to be the first to enter; that he would hold back his flag-ship and himself, and send forward and first a cargo of food on a plain ship, under direction of a woman? Did our commands, military or naval, hold men great enough of soul for such action? It must be true, for the spires of Santiago rise before us. . . .

At this point Clara, standing in the bow with some of her helpers, asked if someone would lead the Doxology. The "rich full voice" of Enola Gardner burst into "Praise God from Whom All Blessings Flow" and the entire ship's company joined in. This was followed by "My Country 'Tis of Thee" as the ship sought anchorage, facing a bare wind-swept wharf and the stricken city of Santiago, with its red-tiled roofs and Spanish belfries.

It was late afternoon. The mango trees drooped after a heavy thunderstorm. Mountains and belfries were touched with the glow of the sinking sun. Small boats came swarming out, their passengers begging for food. There was nothing in the city to eat except rice. More than half the homes were deserted. The people had fled to El Caney and other suburbs to escape the bombardment.

Next morning the *State of Texas* steamed up to the best pier in the city and a hundred stevedores went to work unloading. A tramway ran along the dock to the customs warehouse. Boxes, barrels, and bales were pitched out of the ship and wheeled away. "It was something to see the lank, brawny little army of stevedores take their first breakfast in line, alongside the ship," commented Clara.

After the flagship arrived both Admiral Sampson and Admiral Winfield S. Schley called on Clara to see how her work was proceeding. As they were leaving she asked Admiral Sampson what orders or directions he had for her.

"You need no directions from me," he responded, "but if any one troubles you, let me know."

When she was thanking him for his courtesy in letting her precede him into Santiago, Admiral Schley jestingly remarked: "Don't give him too much credit, Miss Barton. He was not quite sure how clear the channel might be. Remember that was a trial trip."

When General Shafter appealed to Clara to help the refugees who had fled to El Caney, she urged that they be sent back to Santiago, where she would feed them from her *reconcentrado* supplies. They soon poured in and she worked through a local committee, which divided the city into thirty districts. Written requisitions were made to the Red Cross, and food was furnished to 32,000 half-starved persons in the first five days after the *State of Texas* arrived in port. Clara also worked with a local philanthropist named H. Michelson, who had been running soup kitchens but had been forced to close them for lack of supplies.

Then the American troops arrived and Clara sent supplies to those camped in the surrounding hills. She stocked the Spanish hospitals, arranged for tents to shelter prisoners being shipped back to Spain, and directed the distribution of hundreds of tons of ice from the newly arrived steamer *Mary E. Morse*. There were no facilities for unloading this cargo, but she arranged to have army transports run alongside and take what they needed for their sick and wounded soldiers.

Although there was little yellow fever in Santiago the captain of the *State of Texas* suddenly decided to quarantine the ship after the cargo had been unloaded. Those who left it could not return. Kennan decided to take his chance and stay ashore. He lived at the Anglo-American Club and went each day, to the wharf, where Mrs. J. Addison Porter, wife of President McKinley's secretary and one of Clara's helpers, sent him down baskets of food by rope, meanwhile exchanging news with him while he ate in the sunshine. Kennan thought it all very foolish, since the crew went ashore freely and returned to the ship. He was angry with Clara for refusing to take the Lessers on board when they came down with a sickness which he believed to be calenture but which was diagnosed as yellow fever. However, the Army medical authorities later blamed the Red Cross for the spread of yellow fever by opening its hospital in a condemned building, and Clara was in rather a delicate situation.

When the *State of Texas* sailed off for New York she was left without a ship. She had no water transportation during the five weeks she remained in Santiago, and kept agitating for a Navy ship to give her flexibility of movement. Finally, on August 21, she left for Havana on a commercial ship, with thirty-four mules and three hundred tons of general stores. Much as she loved them, her mules had given her much trouble, escaping from time to time. She wrote to Stevé on August 6: "They are splendid great fellows, full of life and handsome as mules can be. I love every one of them, and as you say, if we could have had them at Siboney they would almost have saved the army. There never was anything needed so much as these mules and a few heavy wagons."

Like many of the army officials, Clara had learned by this time that aside from the shortage of supplies, better landing arrangements and more ambulances and wagons might have made all the difference to the suffering endured by the soldiers of the Spanish-American War. "Cuba was a hard field, full of heart-breaking memories," she wrote. "It gave the first opportunity to test the co-operation between the government and its supplemental handmaiden, the Red Cross."

Before she had finished the Red Cross had distributed roughly six thousand tons of provisions in Cuba, with an estimated value of half a million dollars. Her operating expenses, with thirty men and women, for seven months, were $11,706. This included maintenance for her entire staff and her mules.

But she found no welcome in Havana, where she had expected to distribute supplies. The city was under the old Spanish rule. Her captain, trained in the merchant marine, had committed a technical solecism by entering the harbor without proper clearance papers. A $500 fine and duties almost exceeding the value of the cargo were imposed. The fine was paid and Clara sailed for America, profoundly depressed by the dispatches she had been getting from Stevé. All pointed to heavy clouds at home.

When she reached Glen Echo the storm began to break around her head. Had she sought self-glory, pursued her old traditions, not insisted on strict accounting, and diverted supplies intended for the *reconcentrados* to the use of the army? Much was made of her advanced age, her stubborn will, her refusal to co-operate with the committees at home, her army negotiations, and the fact that at a time when the head of the Red Cross should have been in residence in Washington, directing war relief, she was held up idle for two months on her ship and later went to the field when she was needed behind an administrative desk at headquarters. Her other "crimes" included failure to have her ship properly striped—a circumstance she later explained by pointing out that it had set off as a relief ship for the *reconcentrados*.

Actually, the *State of Texas* had become something of an embarrassment to the Army and Navy. It had sailed on its mission a few days before war was declared, but sympathy for the *reconcentrados* was lost sight of when fighting began. Clara, as usual, pursued an unorthodox course, helped the captive men on Spanish ships, distributed her supplies as she saw fit, and was indignant when Admiral Sampson curbed her activities until the war was won. The decision had been left to him, as commanding officer in that area.

Clara's various moves incurred official criticism, although President McKinley continued to view her with a sympathetic eye. He never forgot her age or that she had worked wonders in the past with her impromptu methods. But she was now confronted with formidable opposition from the New York committee, which criticized her lack of system in handling accounts and believed she was bungling matters with the military authorities and was diverting supplies to the enemy. The early whispers of dissatisfaction about the Russian Famine Fund and her operations in Turkey grew to a steady chorus of attack during the Spanish-American War.

It was a new experience for Clara to find every move she made being questioned. She had never had to handle a wartime operation, or one on such a large and diffused scale, and she had not been required in the past to report to the Government. She did not welcome all the red tape emanating from New York along with the floods of superior supplies. Her traditional sense of organization had been a personal matter when she could handle things directly. Clara was never at her best working in harness and would brook no criticism where Red Cross matters were concerned. At this point she leaned heavily on her helpers for her bookkeeping and was in considerable confusion over the different committees bombarding her with instructions from New York. Stevé begged her to co-operate more fully with these important bodies but Clara was growing more autocratic with age. Her will was law and a tart message from Mrs. Anna Roosevelt Cowles annoyed but did not move her.

Finally Joe Sheldon rushed to her side at Glen Echo when he heard there was "some intrigue going on about the command and control of the National Red Cross." He had a long talk with Clara and tried to clarify some of the things that had puzzled her about the different New York committees. After this interview she wrote to Stevé on October 3:

I cared so little about all that money business that I never understood it at all. The committees have been all a mixture to me, and the explanation given me by Judge Sheldon today is the first tolerably clear comprehension I have had of what committee was which, or which committee was what. . . . You who have known so well all your life how little I cared for money, so it was not wasted, you know I never cared who had it, so it did some one some good.

Both Schieren and Stevé pulled out of the Central Cuban Relief Committee that autumn. Attacked on the one hand, Clara had many powerful defenders and received Congressional thanks as well as the personal appreciation of the President, who received her with his usual cordiality on her return from Cuba and offered her a furlough as he would have done to "the most gallant of his soldiers."

In his message of December 6, 1898, he said:

. . . It is a pleasure for me to mention in terms of cordial appreciation the timely and useful work of the American Red Cross, both in relief measures preparatory to the campaigns, in sanitary assistance at several of the camps of assemblage, and, later, under the able and experienced leadership of the president of the society, Miss Clara Barton, on the fields of battle and in the hospitals at the front in Cuba.

Clara was soon on his doorstep again, insisting that the Red Cross return to the field and finish its relief operations for the orphan children of the *reconcentrados*. But the New York relief committee offered opposition at once and questioned the advisability of sending a woman in her late seventies into this complicated field, where wartime animosities had not yet subsided. Finally the President approved her plan and she sailed early in April, 1899.

This trip proved to be an unhappy one. The organization she had left had deteriorated in plan and purpose and her vision of caring for fifty thousand "shelterless, unfed, unclothed, uncared for little children of the dead *reconcentrado* mothers' shrank in scope. However, a hospital was opened outside Havana and two thousand children received Red Cross care.

But business matters were in a muddle and on July 10 she wrote to Dr. Gardner that the man she had sent to investigate reports that the Army of Occupation was interfering with Red Cross work had usurped her power. The field was without first aid. The treasury was empty or, in Clara's own words:

We are I think ruined, there are so many grasping at us that it is impossible to stand. . . . Our work here is good and successful. The great N.Y. Committee take all our money and will of course swallow us. . . . Shall we step out and let it go? . . . Shall I let them take it and turn me out? I don't care much. I am heart broken.

The entire operation ended in November, 1899. Clara's work was long remembered by the Cubans. In July, 1951, a marble bust of her was unveiled in Santiago de Cuba, a tribute by the Cuban Red Cross to the woman who had given such unique service in the Spanish-American War. After she left the island she was presented with an album inscribed with the names and tributes of five hundred leading Cubans.

The Red Cross nurse came to the fore during the Spanish-American War, but the growth of the service was controlled largely by the New York committee and Clara did not feel that she had much to do with it. Hospitals across the country were canvassed for trained nurses of the best caliber and thus the service was built up. The majority worked in army camps. By the end of the war approximately seven hundred Red Cross nurses had served the army in one way or another.

But it was some time before Surgeon General Sternberg was convinced that volunteer nursing service had any place in time of war. He refused transportation to Red Cross nurses in the beginning but worked with Dr. Anita N. McGee, who was director of the D.A.R. Hospital Corps. In organizing an Army Nurse Corps Dr. McGee became a relentless enemy of Clara's, and was still assailing her in 1916, four years after her death. Discord first arose over precedence in the field. Dr. McGee, under the wing of the army, was critical of Clara's unorthodox approach to military regulations and in the long run was acid over her support of Dorence Atwater, who was still in disgrace with the War Department.

Under pressure Dr. Sternberg finally co-operated with the Red Cross committee on the question of nurses. But there was no dampening the flame of antagonism that flashed from Dr. McGee to Miss Barton. However, a strong Red Cross nursing service was in the making. Miss Delano would bring it to fruition. More than 29,000 Red Cross nurses were enrolled in the First World War and in 1945 nearly 153,000 registered nurses held "active status" on the Red Cross roster. Clara never failed to uphold the nursing service and she gave it its early impetus, but a statement given out from her headquarters on an August day in 1897 suggested that the image of Clara Barton as a nurse existed only at that time in the hearts of the soldiers, thousands of whom had "felt her tender care and soulful pity." She was pictured as a buffer "between the bullets and the hospitals" and the point was made that army nurses did not receive "tons of stores, pack them in wagons, trail over mountains and through deep valleys in heat and cold, to where a battle raged."

Clara seemed to be trying to dissociate herself from the Barton legend, possibly because she had a sound understanding of her own professional limitations. She has been described as the "gifted amateur in nursing before there were professionals" and the public has continued to view her as a nurse. "I never claimed to be a nurse," she said of her Civil War work. "There were hundreds of women who could nurse as well or better than I could."

But the fact is that there was only one Clara Barton and, with her, all battles were measured against the immensity of Antietam and Fredericksburg. At a nurses' rally in Washington in 1928 Major General C. P. Summerall, Chief of Staff of the United States Army at that time, evoked the image of Clara in terms she might have approved:

A distinguished General of the Civil War declared that a picture of Clara Barton would be the picture of an angel of mercy hovering over a field of carnage and slaughter; enveloped in the smoke of battle as in a cloud and bringing succour and hope to the wounded and effectually performing the last sad rites to the dead. . . . This would be a true picture. This . . . in short, would be Clara Barton.

Thus the image of Clara Barton as a nurse on the battlefield remains a historic reality, although it was only one phase of her many-faceted life.

## CHAPTER XVIII

## *MISS BARTON MEETS THE CZAR*

THE NAME Clara Barton spread like wildfire as a panic-stricken crowd parted to let a spry old lady nearing her seventy-ninth birthday board a small ferryboat bound from Texas City to Galveston on a September day in 1900. They were fleeing a stricken city. She was heading toward it with Red Cross relief.

A great hurricane and tidal wave had swept over Galveston and the city was in chaos. Between five and six thousand of its thirty-eight thousand inhabitants were dead. Three thousand homes had been destroyed and nearly every building in the city had been damaged.

Sailing close to this wreckage, Clara noticed flashes of flame along the shore. The bodies of storm victims were being cremated. Funeral pyres at Galveston, she reflected, giving passing thought to the many different forms of disaster she had viewed. As she walked ashore she took mental notes, later transferred to paper:

The streets were well nigh-impassable, the animals largely drowned, the working force of men diminished, dazed, and homeless. The men who had been fathers of the city, its business and its wealth, looked on aghast at their overwhelmed possessions, ruined homes, and worse than all, mourned their own dead. . . . Scores of persons came alive out of that wreck with simply the band of a short or a nightdress held by its button about the neck. . . .

City squares had disappeared or were reduced to rubble. Corpses were still being dug from under the ruins, where houses had crashed on entire families. Hundreds more had been borne out to sea. Trees lay strewn in crazy patterns. Chimneys, telegraph poles, and church spires had broken off like pipestems. Many of the survivors fled to Houston and martial law was declared.

No sooner had Clara arrived than word got out that the head of the Red Cross had collapsed and was dangerously ill. Mrs. Ellen Spencer Mussey, who had become Red Cross counsel after the death of her husband, General R. D. Mussey, loudly proclaimed Clara's illness to the world and said that she should be taken home. She had opposed her going in the first place and would soon be one of the small group of her associates bent on ousting the founder from office.

When Clara learned of this she got up with dignity and anger, marched out of her room at the Tremont Hotel, and took personal charge of relief operations. Mrs. Mussey went back to Washington and Clara squelched the alarm about her health by functioning without a break for the next two months. She wrote firmly to General Edward W. Whitaker, who had urged her in a kindly way to return because of her health, that she could no more conduct the relief of Galveston from Washington headquarters than "you could have chased into Richmond after Kilpatrick, facing the Confederate Army as you did—with your cavalry troops safe in corral in Washington City."

It was true that her name still worked magic in a disaster area. The governor of Texas wrote to her that her very presence, even without the substantial aid she had rendered, "would be indeed a benediction, and it has served to inspire our people with energy, self-determination and self-confidence."

Dr. Hubbell was in Iowa and Clara called in General Sears to function as her chief agent. She reminded him of a general giving battle commands, he testified in 1916 when backing up an unsuccessful movement in Congress for a memorial to Clara Barton. The General took over the Santa Fe building, which she quickly converted into a storehouse and workshop. She followed her usual procedure of appealing for funds and supplies, and worked with the local committees and army helpers already on the scene. She asked for hardware, lumber, building materials, and household goods, as well as for food and clothing. Her first thought always, after resuscitation, was rehabilitation.

Late in October the public distributing agencies were closed. Clara transferred the Red Cross activities to Houston where many of the victims of the hurricane had fled, and were now worse off than those who had stayed in Galveston. In two days, supplies were doled out to seven hundred persons in distress. Stoves and heaters were given to families on the mainland who had been cooking out in the open. Here Clara made one of her more memorable gestures when she supplied a million and a half strawberry plants to take the place of those that had been washed away in the strawberry section of southern Texas. The plants bloomed by Christmas. Large ripe berries were being picked in February and the first fruits were sent to Clara, who shared them with Mrs. Mussey and other members of her board, fighting at that moment over her operations in Texas. Seed corn, cottonseed, and seed potatoes were freely distributed, so that in sixty days the farmers had an abundant supply of food for the markets. At Sea Islands Clara had learned her lesson well of leaving a disaster field with sustenance for the future.

She wrote to President McKinley praising the "fortitude, the courage, the calm judgment, the self-forgetfulness and tender solicitude of the people left after the awful destruction." But she warned the White House against crackbrained and costly schemes for rebuilding the devastated city. "Galveston does not need a ship load of portable houses, nor steel ribbed structures; but some plain common sense cheap pine tenements," she wrote.

The Red Cross gave $120,000 in money and supplies for relief at Galveston. The New York *World* raised a fund which Clara distributed. All goods were conveyed free by the Wells Fargo Express, and the Pullman Palace Car Company brought the Red Cross party home by private car on the personal order of August Belmont. "It is one of the innumerable proofs you must have received of the universal admiration and esteem for you and your work," wrote Bradford Merrill, of the *World*.

Captain Edwin Goudge, master of a British tramp steamer blown from its pier in Galveston to Texas City, turned the ship into a relief center of his own and took orders from Clara. He was amazed when he met her, and reported in the Galveston *News*:

I expected to find a commanding sort of person, but I was mistaken. On the contrary she was one of the most genteel women I ever met. Sat quietly at her desk listening calmly to reports from all kinds of people, and issuing orders in the most ladylike manner imaginable. I was astonished at her appearance of frailty, but impressed by her face. It was a face of character—alive, alert, gentle.

This was Clara's last important venture into a disaster area. She returned to face increasing dissension in the ranks of her own organization. It had been gathering momentum for several years. She had achieved one of her great objectives in June of that year when the Red Cross at last obtained its federal charter from Congress. This put it on a sound and permanent footing in the Convention of Geneva and cleared up its status in time of war. President McKinley gave Clara the pen with which he signed the bill, at the same time thanking her for what she had done in Cuba.

Under the new charter a Board of Control was appointed, annual financial statements were to be submitted to Congress, the Red Cross insignia would have full protection, and brassards to neutrals would be distributed at the discretion of military powers in time of war. But as things developed, the measure for which she had worked so hard brought her more personal grief than satisfaction. She was faced at once by opposition from newcomers who thought her too old, too autocratic, too slack in administrative detail to carry on her functions as head of an organization capable of massive growth. Its work in the Spanish-American War had established its importance.

But she had strong support at the White House until a September day in 1901 when, for the third time in eighty years, she made a diary entry on the assassination of a President with whom she had worked. None had been more courteous to her than McKinley. "Our good President has gone," she wrote. "All the world mourns with us. . . . What it is to have lived through the slaying of three Presidents."

Clara resumed her accustomed eminence and had her last flash of glory in the summer of 1902, reaching the height of her world acclaim at the Seventh International Red Cross Conference in St. Petersburg. There she was the most honored of guests. "Everybody was so kind to us all, but I felt they were especially kind to me," she noted.

On a May day, her troubles forgotten, she was riding by train through Holland, observing the tidy countryside with a sympathetic eye, pleased to find the fields so green, the waterways so full, the cows covered with gray blankets and feeding in grass up to their eyes. It always delighted her to see livestock "fat, well-groomed and happy." Getting closer to Russia the "geese, the storks, the good flocks of sheep" also were reassuring.

Clara recorded the moment when Germany gave place to Russia and a "small man with a fine silk hat and big Red Cross on his collar" welcomed Miss Barton and her entourage. She found the atmosphere congenial at once, although she confessed herself confused by the Russian twilight. She went to the Hotel de France, unpacked and laid out her "black and yellow bonnet" and her various costumes for the many functions she was called on to attend. The first was a reception at the Palace de la Tauride, given by the Empress Dowager Dagmar. Clara wore brown silk but hesitated about her medals. "All the world in decorations except me," she noted. "I had left mine off, not knowing if it were well to wear them or not."

She was much impressed by the Empress and watched her walk into the magnificent reception room through doors guarded by two blackamoors:

At length she entered, a small, lovely lady, like the Princess of Wales, now Queen of England, dressed in entire black with jet. She spoke to me first . . . and so on around the entire room, near 100 persons and said a proper thing to each, then returned to me, bade goodby, wished a pleasant journey and left the hall gracefully. She must have occupied three quarters of an hour in this reception. Each man kissed her hand. It was an elegant reception.

After this encounter the delegates dined in a room larger than "our East Room, filled with round tables, set with taste and hospitality," Clara observed. But it was also used by the children as a playroom and had a swing and toboggan in view. Later they all admired the vases, pictures, and tapestries adorning the palace and walked "through the hall of tapestry given to Emperor Paul by Marie Antoinette."

Clara visited the Summer Garden. She sailed through the islands and observed the homes of the Russian nobles. At night she watched a troop of gypsies sing and dance at the Palace Yelaguine. She was much impressed by the Russian Opera, although on the whole she was indifferent to music. On a June day she visited the Winter Palace and took stock of the crown jewels, which included the larger section of the Kohinoor diamond. Still the army buff, and a good judge of a well-packed box, Clara cheerfully commented: "The Queen's jewels, diamonds, are in a box on the floor beside the crown jewels—the box is nearly as large as one of my army boxes and is said to be full."

On June 2 the delegates were received by the Czar and Czarina in the amber room of Tsarkoïe-Sélo. They were presented in national groups, and in Clara's party were Mrs. J. Ellen Foster, Dr. Nicholas Senn, and Admiral William K. Van Reypen. She bowed low as the Russian rulers each in turn addressed a few words to her. But she also took a close look at them and was impressed by the Czar. "He is young, handsome, looks like a mature college graduate," she noted. She admired the Czarina and commented on the affection both seemed to feel for their children.

But Clara nearly came a cropper at the feet of the Czar. During the reception little pots of fruit, fish, and meat were passed around as hors d'oeuvres. She found an orange one delicious, then took a second, which proved to be lobster. One bite was sufficient. Dinner at the Palace that night passed in a haze. She went to bed deathly ill, having found for the fiftieth time in her life that "*I* and *lobsters* don't agree."

Clara had quite recovered by morning, but was annoyed to find that Mrs. Foster had sat by her bed all night. She already knew her to be in the enemy camp along with Mrs. Mussey and realized that any sort of physical collapse would be used against her. "I am always so sorry I cannot trust her, sorry that I have been made to know so much," she wrote.

On the day after the banquet the Czar sent Clara a decoration by the Court Chamberlain, with a letter accompanying it. She was the only delegate thus honored. The festivities were overwhelming, but the conference itself, lasting eight days, was a "great and harmonious affair." The delegates were all old friends and she felt the full impact of this international association. When her name was introduced by General O. B. Richter, president of the Russian Red Cross and aide-de-camp to the Czar, they all rose and gave Clara special acclaim. She was reaping honors abroad, if not at home.

This conference may also have served to show her that her own organization was not keeping pace with the Red Cross in other countries. On June 18 she wrote to Mrs. John A. Logan, widow of the Civil War general who ran for the Vice-Presidency with Blaine, and now one of her warmest defenders:

The seventh International Red Cross Conference belongs to the past. It was a great gathering of the representatives of many nations, all unselfishly working to bind the powers more closely together in the name of humanity. For once Uruguay stood on the level with England and Spain with the United States. No one delegation sought to take any advantage of another. Each did its best to promote the interests of all in the spirit of brotherhood. We in the U. S. do not know much of the splendid Red Cross organizations of the Old World with their armies of numbers, their resources in treasure and equipment; and their preparedness for calls to duty.

She was struck by the extensive Red Cross work being done in Russia—"all hospital work, all emergency work, nearly all relief work, care of children, orphans, foundlings." She was particularly impressed by the St. Elizabeth Hospital, a Red Cross institution run under the patronage of the Empress. She found it flourishing on the site of an old monastery, and discussed the work with the Lady Superior and the hospital doctors. Next she visited the Life Saving Department and thought it well kept by the State. She commented on the "kind hearts, the universal good-will of the people themselves." In a second letter to Mrs. Logan she observed: "I am glad to know Russia as I have seen it now. It is the coming nation, slow it may be, but it comes."

Clara marveled over the "gilded and gemmed carriages" in the royal coach houses, some of them a hundred and fifty years old, yet "bright and beautiful as yesterday." The Czar's horses, however, were her greatest treat on this expedition. She had specially asked to visit the royal stables and she quickly decided that she had never seen any horses to match the black Orloffs and the dapple grays. Both "went like the wind." She studied the way in which the royal stalls were arranged, comparing them with Baba's quarters at Glen Echo. She made detailed diary notes on the Russian horses:

They are not allowed to be *sold* out of Russia, it is said. They weigh from one thousand to fourteen hundred pounds, are jet black, have glossy hair, high arching necks, step as proud as war-horses, with full even tails, trimmed at the bottom to keep them from touching the ground. The Russian harness is not half the weight of ours, and much less of it; the shafts are kept away from the body, and *all* horses are round and fat. I have not seen a poor horse in Russia. . . .

By this time Clara was tired. "Am getting too much of entertainments and get so broken up in the work I must do." Zealous as always, she sat up late at night working on her official report, which involved reading many documents in French. She worried about the correct manner of sending thanks to the Czar for her decoration. She bought an *Almanach de Gotha* to guide her but John Wallace Riddle, acting Chargé d'Affaires at St. Petersburg, stood over her in the American Embassy and approved her letter. She went home to clean her white gloves with benzine and prepare for more festivities—this time in Moscow, a city she found less impressive than St. Petersburg.

Her hotel room was cold and smelled of varnish. The American delegation was lodged all together in the same suite of rooms. But Clara enjoyed the race course, with its Battle of the Flowers and followed up every Napoleonic landmark, from Sparrow Hill to the Kremlin. The Grand Duchess Sergius, wife of the governor general of Moscow, talked to her at length and later sent her an autographed portrait. She was said to be the handsomest woman in Russia and "I think that may be true," Clara conceded.

After this lively burst of international good-will Clara was further exhausted. The conference, the adulation, and all the sight-seeing and feasting had taken their toll. Tired and shaky, with her eyes in trouble, she developed a severe cold on her way back to Berlin. However, she promptly drove to the Palace, viewed statues of the old Emperor and Bismarck, and entered the comment in her diary: "How little time ago I saw them all alive, now only figures in stone. How lonesome the world is getting to be." News of the death of Edward VII reached her at this point, and she found it hard to believe.

Clara bought smoked glasses and a parasol to protect her eyes and set off for the royal stables, but found the horses much inferior to the Czar's Orloffs. She disapproved of their square tails. By the end of June the Grand Duchess Louise was welcoming her affectionately at Carlsruhe, where she stayed for two weeks. "Nowhere in the world would I have been so warmly and lovingly received," Clara commented. They sat in Louise's private sitting room, drinking tea and discussing the education of American women, the Red Cross, and the administration of hospitals. Clara left photographs of herself, both for Louise's private chambers and for the new school she had founded.

She was invited to the prorogation of Parliament. The Grand Duke was to officiate. She wore her purple silk skirt, a white lace waist, and all her decorations. She enveloped herself in a new long wrap, was conducted to the chamber, and sat in a box facing the royal family. She had a long talk that night with the Grand Duke, who reverted to the subject of Strassburg, saying the Alsatians were getting over their prejudice against the Germans and were prospering. He told Clara he thought Theodore Roosevelt "earnest and honest," and said he had great confidence in his administration.

Louise, who must have known of some of the trouble Clara was having with her organization, embraced her on parting and said: "Tell them in America how I love you. Tell them." Clara told her friend that she would never see her again. Louise protested. She reminded her that she had said the same thing twenty years earlier. "Seeing me now," Clara wrote, "she did not believe it at all." This time, however, it was true.

A visit to another friend, Princess Salm Salm, and a trip to Strassburg stimulated Clara and brought back a flood of nostalgic memories. In Geneva, on the other hand, she felt "tired and lonesome—all the world gone." She visited the grave of Minna Kupfer, who had married Abram Golay, brother of Jules, and had died in 1895. "A few leaves of ivy—one little rose—and that is all of my faithful Minnie," she wrote. Anna Zimmermann was long since dead, too, but the ghost of the living Antoinette Margot seemed to walk with Clara in Paris as she visited the Place de la Madeleine where "even the stones of the pavement seemed familiar" from the days of the Franco-Prussian War. She went into a little restaurant once run by her landlord. He was no longer there but Clara nibbled on a sandwich and some *petits gâteaux* and drank hot chocolate.

After this small venture she decided to cut loose in Paris. She was tired of having people always around her, of having every move watched, every word weighed. She had become so much of a public figure that no privacy was left her. So, in her purple skirt and her black-and-yellow bonnet, with her Red Cross brooch and her amethyst pansy, she went flitting about Paris with her own special brand of dignity. "Growing bold," she went straight to the Place Vendôme to admire its column, in place again. She could remember it lying in the mud after the Commune. She took her bearings there and headed for the Tuileries. All seemed to come back to her—"and I walked till nearly three, five good hours without once inquiring a street or the way or taking a carriage. . . . How *had* I remembered it?"

Nor had she failed to notice the "fly-devoured, under-fed, over-driven, sunken creatures" that passed for horses in Paris. Not one had a decent tail. No wonder Russia would not permit its "beautiful intelligent Orloffs to be sold out of the country!"

On her last day in Paris, Clara, ever interested in Napoleon, did some day-dreaming at the Hôtel des Invalides, reflecting on how sound it was to depend on oneself. "I have often felt that I had nearly lost my identity by constant dependence upon others," she commented. "I believe that now I could go and trace all Italy and Corsica after these thirty years, without personal help."

She lunched cheerfully on cherry tart and lemonade, then went home to write of the conference to Stevé before sailing: "Did nothing carelessly, nor in too great haste—wrote my report of the conference—some twenty pages—sent it to President Roosevelt, made out all my accounts. . . . no mistakes have been made, no bad luck. . . . well enough managed, it seems to me, and fortunately ended, if it does end well the rest of the way."

Obviously Clara knew that she would face difficulties on her return. The trip had freshened her viewpoint and she was in a self-analytical mood on the voyage home. Turning the pages of an evocative book in the ladies' lounge of the steamer, her old self-doubts assailed her, although her life was near its end and there was nothing she could change:

I fell into a revery myself as to how much reading I should have done, how much I should have lived with the literary world, if I had never heard of a Red Cross. Would it perhaps have been better if I never had, as it looks now. I almost *feel yes*. I cannot see that I have really established anything that is to *live*, or that is, *perhaps*, needed in a country like ours, and with a people so full of ready adaptation, and quick impulses . . . but if usefulness to the people, and my usefulness to it, have found an end, is to me the question of the moment—the *latter* seems to me very apparent, and the former is not for *me* to decide.

On her return Clara had a small exchange with Susan Anthony on the subject of the Czar and Czarina. Reports of a forthcoming divorce were in circulation, and Susan was stirred up because the motive was supposed to be the failure of the Czarina to produce a son. "Why can't he see that he had better cling to his first love and *get* the *laws changed* so that a woman can succeed to the throne," Susan demanded, fully in character. "He had better remember Josephine and Napoleon. To put Josephine away was the most wicked thing done by him."

Clara expressed the opinion that the story was mere gossip, preposterous and untrue. Besides, she reminded Susan, Josephine was not divorced because she bore only daughters but "because from age she could not bear anything." Clara closed the argument with the comment: "I give Russia credit for better sense."

*CHAPTER XIX*

## END OF AN ERA

ROLLING WAVES of applause greeted the sight of Theodore Roosevelt escorting Clara Barton to a seat beside him on the platform of the Detroit Armory in 1902. Both were guests at the Spanish-American War Veterans Convention. The soldier audience had two of its favorite idols in view and shouted its approval.

"Teddy" was gallant to Clara that day, whatever his thoughts about her may have been. She was eighty years of age. She was under fire, and his sister, Mrs. Anna Roosevelt Cowles, was one of her most determined critics. But Clara was still the demure warrior, in her proper frame at the moment, surrounded by a multitude of soldiers, as she sat with the President of the United States, the governor of Michigan, and the mayor of Detroit.

Her car was next in line to the President's in the city parade. She was just as roundly cheered as he. She sat at his right in the reviewing stand watching her boys go by. That night she was the only woman at the table of honor at the banquet given for Roosevelt. She was asked to speak but "no woman's voice could fill that house already packed full" and her words were completely lost. "I did the best I could and held my notes to give to the *Spanish War Journal*," Clara commented.

Many honors had been paid her in her day, from far-off St. Petersburg to Texas, but this was perhaps the most conspicuous gesture accorded her in her own country. It came late, when Clara's empire was crumbling. She could not fully relish an occasion that would have stirred her in other years. Although the "air seemed to quiver with the weight of human voices" when she and Roosevelt shook hands in public, in actual fact, after half a century of goodwill and the friendship of nine Presidents, her relations with the White House were ebbing and soon would be ended altogether.

Ever since the Spanish-American War Clara had been conscious of the rift within her organization, of censure not only from newcomers with the "varnish not yet dry on them" but from some of her most trusted associates, such as Mrs. Mussey and Mrs. Foster. The immediate attack centered on business methods and the failure of some of her agents to turn in vouchers promptly at Galveston, coupled with the comparatively small sum the Red Cross had handled in comparison with the vast sums spent on relief in that area.

The federal charter exacted a strict system of accountability to Congress. Money was to be handled through the treasurer only, and Clara was expected to consult the new Board of Control before taking off for a disaster area. The spontaneous methods that had served her well for two decades were under fire. When there was a job to be done she had always hurried into the field "regarding neither weather, night nor Sunday, nor waiting for the call of a meeting." In her 1901 report to Congress she wrote:

The Red Cross in its nature, its aims and purposes, and consequently, its methods, is unlike any other organization in the country. It is an organization of physical action, of instantaneous action, at the spur of the moment; it cannot await the ordinary deliberation of organized bodies if it would be of use to suffering humanity; . . . it has by its nature a field of its own.

It was Clara's policy to get first to the victims, organize relief on the spot, raise money and supplies as she moved along, and leave the business details to her assistants. Trustful and loyal by nature, she had implicit faith in the men and women she chose to work for her. But her organization at the turn of the century had only minor resources, a small staff of uncertain status, and the public no longer responded so readily to the personal type of appeal she had found effective in the past. The public criticism that dogged her during the Spanish-American War had had its effect on public opinion. Moreover, she had lived through a changing civilization. Philanthropy was veering from bounty to social service. It would soon be organized and decentralized. These were the broader aspects of a fight that narrowed down between 1900 and 1904 to personalities and political gropings by both sides, ending with the retirement of Clara in 1904 and the rebirth and rapid growth of the organization she had founded and cherished for two decades.

In the course of the reincorporation three new figures appeared, on the recommendation of the New York committee. They were Mabel T. Boardman, Elizabeth J. Kibbey, and Thomas Walsh. Miss Boardman, daughter of William Jarvis Boardman, Cleveland lawyer and businessman, was a capable administrator interested in humanitarian work. Through her strong drive and sincere belief in Clara's incapacity to conduct the affairs of the Red Cross she was an important factor in forcing her resignation.

Although refusing the presidency of the Red Cross, believing that a man should always hold this office, she served as chairman of the executive board and became Clara's successor in power and prestige where the organization was concerned, figuring importantly in its expansion. Clara introduced the Red Cross to America and in her own individualistic way, and with infinite effort, made its values familiar to the American people. Mabel Boardman gave it organizational strength, raised $2,000,000 for its stately headquarters in Washington, built up its nursing, first aid, and wartime services with the help of many able associates, and fortified it with strong financial and social backing.

In questioning Clara's regime she maintained that the American Red Cross had not kept pace with its sister organizations around the world; that it did not truly represent the humanitarian scope of the United States; that, in short, it was a feeble infant in the midst of plenitude; and that much more should be expected and demanded of it. She drew attention to the millions in money, the field hospitals, the doctors and nurses working under the banner of the Red Cross in France, Austria, Italy, Germany, and Japan.

However bitter the feeling between these two women and their protagonists, their names are inevitably linked with the history of the Red Cross in America. They were obviously irreconcilable types by taste, training, and temperament. Clara was a flavorsome pioneer who had given her country more than one woman's share of service but had perhaps outlived her era. Although she was persuaded that Miss Boardman coveted her role she was not blind to her own situation and wrote revealingly to Stevé early in January, 1900, picturing herself as something of an anachronism:

I am the last of my generation—I am strange among the new. We cannot comprehend each other. I have lacked the knowledge of the newer generation, and done my work badly, and naturally grow discouraged and timid and want to escape it all. All these things have made me tired, and the animosities, ambitions, jealousies and bickerings of people about me, make life seem of little value. So I sit here, working hard, looking through the tears day after day. . . .

Clara watched defections on all sides after 1900. Mrs. Mussey was the first to go. B. H. Warner, who on her return from Turkey had publicly called her a "Queen Among Women," next stepped out. Phillips withdrew, but soon was back with Clara, working for her more enthusiastically than ever. Stevé, busy with his insurance business in New York, stayed away after the board had refused to appoint him her business manager. "Stevé is tired and wants to do his own work," Clara noted about her nephew. "Right and best if he prefers." But he, too, would return and help her to the end. He had often stood as a buffer between the insurgents and his aunt.

Various conciliatory moves were made but Clara viewed them all as part of the drive to get her out of office. A small group of the more friendly spirits proposed that she be named honorary president, with all the laurels that could possibly be heaped upon her, but that the active work of the organization should be turned over to others. She quickly nipped in the bud a movement by her friends to have an annuity of $5,000 voted for her in Congress for "distinguished services." She was stung with outraged pride when Miss Boardman also proposed an annuity, which her father and several other businessmen would guarantee for one year until other arrangements could be made, if Clara would step upstairs to the honorary presidency of the Red Cross.

Miss Boardman urged Mrs. Logan to persuade Clara to retire of her own volition. Early in January, 1902, she wrote to her:

Our work is not for today but for the time to come; and we want to prove to the country that we have a complete and fully organized body, not dependent upon a few individuals, but upon a thorough and competent organization. Only in this way can we hope to gain the confidence and receive the substantial aid of business men. First and foremost our work is for the *Red Cross*—and I feel in this interest—we can all pull together with harmony and strength.

Actually, Clara had been ready to step out at the turn of the century. She made the gesture when the federal charter was signed in 1900. At the meeting of the incorporators in the Arlington Hotel she proposed a million-dollar fund, to come from the people, and permanent headquarters for the Red Cross "in keeping with its national importance and the example of other countries." On this occasion she was persuaded to stay.

She offered her resignation again in 1901, when a series of recommendations presented at the annual meeting amounted to a vote of censure for her actions. At that time a new Board of Directors with thirty members was appointed to succeed the Board of Control, but the majority vote of the executive committee was still against Clara. On her return to Glen Echo she remarked: "We came home. I to contemplate the hole in my room to escape through. There are only four of us . . . the others are a clique."

Clara's group was small, but determined. They persuaded her to stay, against her better judgment. Mrs. Logan kept her firmly tethered and spoke up for her, since it was not Clara's custom to defend herself. Then, pushed to the wall and under heavy attack, Clara grew stubborn on her own account and decided she would not be ousted. A committee consisting of Miss Boardman, Warner, and Simon Wolf had been assigned to examine her accounts from the beginning of her operations.

By the end of 1902 she was persuaded that her antagonists "strike to kill, and fight to win." But she was equally certain that she would "never yield an *inch* to them beyond their legal rights as a Board." At this time she wrote to Leonora Halstead that she could not quite let go. She had carried the burden for so long that "in some way the straps still hang under it and I cannot quite pull them out, but the confinement which they entail upon me is, I think, all the connection that I feel."

The situation came to a head after Clara's return from the St. Petersburg Conference, when a bold move was made by her supporters to modify the bylaws in such fashion as to abolish the Board of Directors that had hamstrung her since the 1901 meeting and get her back in the saddle again. Clara foresaw that "ugly remarks" would be made as proxy votes were rounded up in different parts of the country, and the Remonstrants, as the opposition group was known, were kept in the dark about the purpose of the proposed change in the bylaws.

On October 25 she wrote to Mrs. Logan that eighty-three votes were needed at the annual meeting, and as many more as they could muster "to tie the knot *this* time that won't slip—surely it is time that we are able to do *something* for the welfare of our cause." Clara made no secret of the fact that she detested committees, boards, and meetings. In her opinion "the best number for a committee to work well and efficiently was three, when one was dead and the others couldn't come." She was only dimly aware of some of the moves being made by her backers, but the finagling made her uneasy. It was not in keeping with her forthright character and she made a diary entry on the subject:

I try to know as little as possible of it all, this wire pulling and meeting are all so foreign to me, so distasteful that I can scarcely *live* in the atmosphere of them. I am heavy of heart. I see only bitterness and enmity as the result of it all. I don't know how to play the part I am expected to as the president. I still see only my escape from it all if I could get away. It is the same old sadness that took possession of me when Klopsch was sent to Cuba to watch me, and with power to deceive me so far as possible. I could wish today, for my personal peace, that I had left the country then and found quiet in some unknown spot, where I could not be reached nor disturbed by the twists or tricks of other people.

"This is the day of all days to be dreaded," she wrote before setting off for the Arlington Hotel on December 9, 1902. But she showed no outward concern as she walked into the room and a situation charged with dynamite. The Remonstrants, in a countermove, attempted to pack the meeting. The names of fifty new members were proposed early in the day, in the hope that they would be elected at once and would swing the vote against Clara's forces.

The meeting was stormy from start to finish and lasted far into the evening. Clara watched Sara A. Spencer, one of her most valued friends, move over to the other faction and vote against her on every count. Mrs. Logan held her ground firmly for Clara. Miss Boardman and Miss Kibbey were "an angry pair." But her friends had come from various parts of the country to support her. General

Sears had arrived from Kansas, Dr. and Mrs. Gardner from Indiana, Mrs. J. Sewall Reed from Boston, E. R. Ridgeley from Kansas, Joseph Sheldon from New Haven, and Dr. Lesser from New York. At the last moment Samuel M. Jarvis, a Havana banker and one of her warmest supporters, arrived from New York and took his place beside Francis Atwater, Dorr's brother, who edited the Meriden *Daily Journal* in Connecticut and was now acting as Clara's business manager. "I could not express the relief and strength it brought," Clara commented, when Jarvis walked in. Another powerful friend in court.

Her side won all down the line. The bylaw revision was railroaded through. She was elected president for life on Dr. Lesser's motion by a standing vote of twenty-eight to three. Richard Olney, an "old Oxford boy" and Secretary of State under Grover Cleveland, was appointed counselor, Samuel W. Briggs secretary, and William J. Flather treasurer. Flather promptly pulled out, however, pleading excess business of his own.

"Victory after victory was won through the long hard warring day," Clara wrote when it was over. "The Red Cross is free and in the hands of its friends." By this time she had no thought of giving up. Much as she loathed the whole business, she wrote to Mrs. Logan three days after the meeting that "there is strength and determination enough in me to sit down on the lightning struck log and declare that I *will* sit there."

But the course now became rough. Clara had met more than her match on the public front. Seventeen of the Remonstrants prepared a memorial for Congress and wrote to the President protesting the action taken at the annual meeting. They reviewed the entire controversy and drew attention to the "very irregular methods and arbitrary proceedings used by the authors of these by-laws," suggesting that they violated the requirements of the Treaty of Geneva. They enclosed a copy of the bylaws and stated their case as they saw it.

President Roosevelt communicated at once with Clara through his secretary, George B. Cortelyou, informing her that he and the Cabinet could no longer serve as her Board of Consultation. This was a time-honored link, rarely invoked but greatly valued by Clara. Attention was drawn to the fact that Flather had resigned on account of "loose and improper" accountability. Clara later produced his letter of resignation, which referred only to press of business.

She was stunned by the unexpectedness of this public snub. She sought an interview with the President but did not get it. On January 27, 1903, she wrote him a dignified letter, reminding him that great generosity attended great power. She reviewed the official status of the Board of Consultation, pointed out that every administration, including his own, had co-operated fully, and disclaimed any usurpation practiced or discourtesy intended. In characteristic vein Clara wrote:

For twenty years this Red Cross work, so small at first—a mere spark—has grown up under our hands until its welcome blaze lighted the footsteps of relief for an entire and direful contest of nations, and of which none better than your honored self knows the hardships or the needs, or can better judge if this body of relief were aggressive of its conduct, imperious or unjust in its demands, or its president assumed unwonted or unauthorized power or manifested love of distinction, pride of place or greed of spoil.

But the most illuminating paragraphs of this letter, showing Clara's state of mind, were dropped on the earnest pleadings of her friends. They were courteous, but quietly desperate in tone.[10] Mrs. Logan wrote to Cortelyou urging that the President see Clara. "I do not think that he realizes that he has inflicted so serious a wound as he did by his letter," she observed, pointing out that Clara was "absolutely crushed." Cortelyou answered crisply that the President thought an agreement between both sides was "essential to good work." There was no further word from the White House.

The whole affair became a matter of public record when the Remonstrants submitted their memorial to Congress with all the documentation they had sent to President Roosevelt, and additional letters which came as a surprise to Clara's forces, since they revealed some of the opposition's earlier scheming to have the president of the Red Cross retired.

Phillips returned to help Clara at this juncture. "There is not a better pen in the country, a newspaperman from the start," she wrote of him, observing that he had made the gesture voluntarily, apparently "smitten by conscience, to repentance." He prepared a

memorial, entitled *Some Facts Concerning Clara Barton's Work,*
designed to offset the enemy attack. He argued that the President
had been misinformed on the handling of the bylaw situation, and
that neither Miss Barton nor the majority had been given an opportunity to present their side of the case.

The wind blew hotter, however, within the next few days when
the Remonstrants were suddenly suspended from membership on
the ground that they had started internal revolt. Clara did not favor
this drastic move, but she was now being directed by those around
her. The ousted members questioned the authority of the executive
committee to drop them, but conceded that in their advocacy of a
new president for the Red Cross, the question of Miss Barton's integrity was not in any way involved.

Clara showed a conciliatory spirit at once, and the majority voted
to consider a revision of the disputed bylaws. She wrote that if in
initiating these peace measures she seemed to be overlooking "just
grounds of personal offense in imputations wantonly made upon
my honor and integrity" she did it knowingly and willingly because
the cause of the American Red Cross stood first in her affection
and desires. She added:

It would be strange if it did not—if the cause for which I have devoted myself for half a century were not deemed by me worthy of any
possible sacrifice of personal pride or personal interests. It would be
specially strange, if after so many years of earnest effort for the relief
of human suffering, during which I have always lived and moved in
the full glare of the public gaze, I could not now safely trust my character and good name to the care of the American people. I am sure that
I can.

Clara had one deep-rooted characteristic that showed now, as in
nearly every crisis of her life. She had no heart for a fight on her
own behalf, and instead of defending herself under attack, almost
invariably shrank into silence. This mechanism can be traced clearly
through all her diary entries. Instinctively she turned to the thought
of flight, however innocent her situation.

"They will get no 'back talk' from me," she wrote to Stevé. "I
may not be wise in my doings with them, but I shall always be a
lady and shall never feed public gossip."

Dreading unfavorable publicity for her organization, she was deeply concerned to note that the "enemy got things in the papers." This was particularly true in Washington. Clara had always had a friendly press, thanks partly to Phillips and Kennan. Now she reflected sadly that except for the Boston *Herald* and the Davenport *Democrat* she had not seen a single article that "did not malign us one way or another." On April 1, the Washington *Post* reported that "Bishop Potter and other prominent New Yorkers" endorsed the action taken by the minority group in the Red Cross. The same committee was in operation again, working against Clara. In fact, the move to have her supplanted originated in this quarter.

By early April there was no longer any question of an annuity or tactful retirement for Clara. Briggs wrote to Phillips that another stage had now been reached, and she was henceforth "unworthy of any consideration." In great bitterness of spirit Clara wrote to Mrs. Logan on April 3 that her only solace was that they could not "crucify her bodily." She added: "I wonder does our President think he is doing the country a service in standing behind this— he probably does."

But Susan Anthony considered the whole affair a "mean and despicable business" and did not approve of the President's part in it. She wrote to Clara on July 28, 1903:

The old saying that "all things work together for good" is true provided we work them the right way. I am glad if the women who have worked for your dethronement have placed you more firmly in the chair of the Red Cross. It was too bad that the President put his foot in it; not only in that but in the W.C.T.U. and one or two other little affairs that he could not know about, hence should not have taken any part in them. . . . I hope you will get everything in good trim so that your successors will be able to see that you did everything for the best. . . .

Clara told Phillips that she did not enjoy being "cuffed by that big, impulsive boy, who chances, for the time, to be President of the United States." Phillips worked hard to get a friendly press for Clara again. Most of her early supporters had come back to help her and new and potent voices spoke for her. For a time she took heart and she and Mrs. Logan tried unsuccessfully to arrange inter-

views with Andrew Carnegie and John D. Rockefeller. Clara gave
Richard Harding Davis an honorary membership in the Red Cross.
"We must have persons of eminence and distinction whom we
must invite," she wrote to Mrs. Logan. "We must arrange to show
a little elegance, at least good manners as well as 'business principles.'"

Clara was stung by all the talk of social prestige and wrote to
Stevé at this point:

I have never worked for fame or praise, and shall not feel their loss
as I otherwise would. I have never for a moment lost sight of the
humble life I was born to, its small environments, and the consequently
little right I had to expect much of myself, and shall have the less to
censure, or upbraid myself with for the failures I must see myself make.

As Clara's business manager, Atwater now "unmoored" her from
Washington for a time. She rented a seven-room apartment in New
York and in the midst of all her woe took another important step
by introducing first aid into America that summer, a significant
move for the future of the Red Cross. Edward Howe, an English-
man, had approached her about initiating first aid in the manner of
the St. John Ambulance Corps. Clara saw its intrinsic value and
also its possibilities as a source of revenue for the Red Cross. On
June 9 she wrote to Tillinghast: "It will enable the Red Cross to
become self-supporting and in time fund itself, without begging
and without dependence upon the gifts of the wealthy. There is
no reason, under the system established, why the American Red
Cross should not become as rich as Russia. . . ."

From her own funds she supplied little kits and dolls, had classes
started in various cities, publicized the movement, and distributed
diplomas, giving out life-membership certificates to Margaret Carnegie, Marshall Fisk, and Immanuel Kant. But the movement
limped along for lack of resources until the reorganized Red Cross
established it firmly in 1909 and made it a well-recognized national
movement. Again she had applied the match to a fire that burned
without her tending.

"Almost too depressed to exist," she wrote on a hot August day
in 1903, after trailing over to Brooklyn to have her ear treated.

"There are many buds of promise in this thing, but they mostly fall."

She was "lonesome and homesick" early in September as she signed forty first-aid diplomas, put them in tubes, and dispatched them, recording sadly:

These are the first diplomas that go out. It is like commencing anew after twenty years' work. It is a problem which way it goes—up or down. I surely know that if it were twenty years back, and I could read the future, I should never have the courage nor the heart to commence it.

Clara returned to Glen Echo from this dreary interlude to feel a chill in Washington, too. Old friends refused to accept office on her first-aid committee. An "ugly article" appeared in the New York *Tribune*. She dared not "read more for her nerves." She had bronchitis, ear trouble, shooting pains, and was floundering around. "The city was beginning to be alive for the unveiling [of the Sherman statue]. I had no desire to remain nor heart to stay and came home. . . . It is not worth while to say more. I cannot conjecture where this state of mind will lead me, or will end." Mrs. Logan lunched with the President but to no avail.

Early in December Clara responded to a call from Butler, Pennsylvania, where an epidemic of typhoid fever raged, with thirty to forty deaths a day. She was pictured going out on a snowy night from Glen Echo, a small Negro girl lighting her way by lantern, and catching the earliest train to survey this field. She did not wait for permission, or for a pending meeting of her board, but wrote her excuses: "For twenty-five years no call had gone unheeded. I am not unmindful of your courteous notice of a meeting of the officers, to be held tomorrow at our headquarters. But you will readily comprehend that being subject to investigation under no circumstances could I attend meetings of the organization."

Clara and her associates took $2,000 from the Elks with them to Butler. She found that the local nurses were doing well and that money was the primary need. She stimulated local efforts to cope with the epidemic. A newspaper appeal for assistance was issued and $65,567 was raised. Clara was back in Washington for Christmas Day, her eighty-second birthday, and on the last day of 1903 she wrote that a "hard and terrible year" had ended, during which the "scurril of the press has been poured over me, like the filth of a sewer."

But worse was to come. Clara had bowed to the inevitable and at the annual meeting the majority group voted an investigation by a committee appointed by its own counsel, Richard Olney. He named Senator Redfield Proctor, who had worked with Clara in Cuba, General Fred C. Ainsworth, and William Alden Smith. Both sides were to have a hearing. The object was to clear the air, still the controversy, and pave the way for reorganization.

Joe Sheldon, who had served Clara for a lifetime, suggested a younger man to represent her at the proceedings. He was now old and felt unequal to the battle. "You can't fight the *Government, the newspapers and the great combination of able and rich and ambitious men,*" he wrote. "In such an unequal fight I fear you will be left in a sad plight." In the end L. A. Stebbins and Thomas S. Hopkins represented Clara's interests. Leigh Robinson was counsel for the Remonstrants.

Outwardly Clara was calm and cheerful. But the plumes of woe showed clearly in her diary entries. She kept her trunk packed, and thought of going to Mexico. But as usual these flight impulses did not get beyond the stage of depressed diary jottings. Mrs. Mollie A. Hines, a relief worker who was now her constant companion, pictured her on the eve of the investigation rising at five in the morning—"the windows flying open—the sweeper rushing over the floor—clothing being brushed with great vigor" and Clara busy at her desk long before breakfast:

Every day is a new beginning—every day is the world made new— so far as appearance goes. I have never seen her look so well—so young— so full of vigorous life. What she feels or thinks or the way her inner life is lived—I know no more of than you . . . for I know nothing.

A New York *Herald* reporter found her serene and youthful for her years, surrounded by the "trophies and memories of more than forty-three years of active service in the cause which has made her name and fame world-wide." She noted the line drawings and engravings of Clara on the battlefield, the inscribed portraits of

kings and queens, the souvenirs of every campaign from the Johnstown flood to the Armenian massacres. The reporter commented on
her "clear, steady rich voice and soft shining eyes; on her trim,
spare little figure; on the neatness of her black satin gown; on the
amethyst brooch at her neck."

This was Clara at Glen Echo on a February day in 1904. Snow
had just ceased falling, and the canal was a white carpet. She had
her "house in good order," for she was receiving four hundred
suffrage delegates gathered for the annual convention of the American Woman Suffrage Association. The guests came direct from
luncheon at the White House and she greeted them at the parlor
door, with Mrs. Carrie Chapman Catt beside her. Miss Anthony
was too exhausted to make the journey but she urged her old friend
to join her at their closing meeting next day.

Clara hated to go. She dreaded the thought of a speech, or even
a public appearance, but this was Susan Anthony asking her.
Thunderous cheers greeted her appearance on the platform. Susan
had a place reserved for her at her side. She asked Clara to speak
but "I utterly declined."

She then drew me beside her to the front of the stage and stood there
with her arm about me while she told the audience that I was at the
first suffrage meeting in Washington in 1869, that later I sent out my
call to the soldiers to stand by women as I had stood by them—that
there were only us left now to stand together at this last meeting.

Two valiant nineteenth-century pioneers stood embraced while
the assembled women jumped to their feet in acclamation. Then
Clara sat down abruptly. She knew it was a public gesture deliberately staged for her at this time by her old friend. "We both realized
that we should never stand together again before a Washington
audience," Clara commented. "This was Providence's triumph for
the night in 1869, which I so well remember. God's ways are
strange—but sure."

Next came the veterans to show their loyalty three days before
the charges were filed. "Glen Echo is getting to rival the Waldorf,"
she wrote to Stevé, informing him that the "whole city body of
the Spanish War Veterans were to storm Glen Echo." Afterward

she wrote: "The comrades came . . . and left with full and happy hearts. Mine?"

At this point she addressed her nephew with a note of deep appeal. He had been making himself scarce, and she wanted him near her during the investigation. After reviewing the long course they had followed together she wrote:

They have muttered, threatened and stormed a long time, but now they are on the step and their hands are on the knob. We must act *now*, decisively and forever. We either hold and win, or yield and lose, and Stevé, it is you and I, just you and I, that can turn the scale, and settle it all, forever, as the chance of its beginning was given to us alone, so is the choice of its continuance, and its future. There are just two roads for us to take. We were never up to the forks before.

In this same letter Clara admitted that the opposition was strong. She would wait for the decision to be made, she said. Then she would resign and leave the country forever.

On March 16, 1904, the formal complaint was filed with Senator Proctor, involving: Failure to create an organization comparable to those existing in Europe and Japan; diversion of funds given for specific purposes to other causes; the unwarranted use of proxies and violation of the bylaws; and a lack of "authoritative and legal financial reports of receipts and expenditures." There was no suggestion of personal malfeasance on Clara's part.

By the end of March she and her associates had a fifty-three-page reply to the charges ready to turn in, and two thousand copies awaited distribution. They defended the handling of relief funds by field agents, objected to the investigation of accounts dating back to the 1880's, upheld the accounting of recent years, and denied violation of the existing bylaws. They charged that behind the action of the Remonstrants was a conspiracy against Miss Barton by a group "who have boldly, insolently demanded that she retire from the presidency under a cloud, and place them in control."

The committee held three sessions in all and at the second, on April 26, Morlan appeared as a witness, staggering the Barton forces with the tale he told. He charged that $20,000 raised for the Russian famine relief fund had been largely diverted to other uses by Clara, some of it for aid in Texas; and that $12,000 of it had gone for

Red Cross Park, one half the value of the property, instead of the token dollar payment claimed by Clara.

When she heard of Morlan's testimony she stayed up all night at Glen Echo hunting for old records to disprove his charges. As she ran through the vouchers she noted: "Find a world of better bookkeeping than I can imagine where we got the time to do."

Morlan quickly collapsed as a witness and was shown up for the shifty and unreliable character he was. He failed to reappear for cross-examination with the documentation he had promised. Mrs. Hines produced a letter he had just sent her, with a thinly veiled threat that suggested an attempt to blackmail Clara. Counsel for the defense instantly denied that any Red Cross money had ever been invested in Red Cross Park, and showed that the title was allowed to lapse because of the accumulation of taxes and charges for maintenance, the property then reverting to its original owners.

Morlan had shown the Remonstrants a letter which he said Clara had written him when the property ownership lapsed. In it she expressed shock and alarm over the charges he made, asked him to give her time "to withdraw from the entire concern by surrendering the deed, annulling the charter and returning the property to its original owner," and begged for time to arrange the matter so as to "avert *disgrace and scandal.*"

To Clara's enemies this letter was tantamount to an admission of guilt in the Red Cross Park affair. To her protagonists it was the letter of a distressed but completely innocent woman, seeking to shield the Red Cross from scandal.

A letter signed by Bishop Potter and his influential associates in New York, condemning the operations of the Red Cross and demanding reorganization; and a deposition from Spencer Trask, chairman of the Armenian Relief Committee, saying that the figures sent from Constantinople were "not such as any good business would consider entirely satisfactory," were laid before the committee.

The investigation ended abruptly and inconclusively. Proctor refused to proceed when Morlan disappeared. He called it "the most outrageous proceeding that has ever come under my observation," leaving the impression that Clara had been exonerated. Although the hearings were closed, much that transpired leaked out to the press, and she felt that she was left "hanging between earth and heaven." She bore no rancor to Morlan and mildly noted in her diary on the day he made his charges: "He seems to be working for revenge. . . . I have no hardness towards him. He is, as he is, and cannot help it. He has great kindness in his nature. He was dear to me and I loved and trusted him."

This was typical of her approach to a number of men and women who betrayed her. But Dr. Gardner was outraged. "The blackmailing rascal!" he exclaimed a few weeks later, recalling that Morlan had handled the Russian famine funds in Washington. "He must have dipped into the checks and drafts that came in, pretty deeply, to have gotten the amount of funds he seems to have had to fritter and gamble away."

Clara resigned on May 14, 1904. "A fine day—cool," she wrote, with what emotion the entry barely suggests. "Only an ordinary day. The *Post* has the resignation as of the Associated Press. . . . I clear up the last of the letters in the little desk." A world had ended for her and although sought for interviews she remained silent. But her work spoke for itself, and as the Chicago *Inter-Ocean* phrased it, in commenting on her retirement: "Clara Barton cannot resign her place in the world as the one real, true representative of the Red Cross in this country."

Without budget or endowment she spent an estimated $2,000,000 for relief during the twenty-three years in which she steered the Red Cross along its humanitarian course, the prelude to $2,352,000,000 invested by the American people in Red Cross relief at home and abroad between 1900 and 1955. She made few comments ever on her frugality or the amount of her own time, money, and lifeblood that she put into the work, but shortly before her death she wrote revealingly to Mrs. Logan:

For the multitude of failures I have encountered, I am sorry. . . . I might add, that in all my life, and its various activities, I had never received, nor had desired, remuneration for services, and with the exception of the $15,000 returned to me by the Thirty-seventh Congress, nothing for personal expenditures. Economy, prudence, and a *simple life* are the sure masters of need, and will often accomplish that which, their opposites, with a fortune at hand, fail to do.

Mrs. Logan functioned as president of the Red Cross until June, 1904, when reorganization began. In autumn the old association was dissolved and a new corporation was created by an act of Congress signed by President Roosevelt on January 5, 1905. The Red Cross then came under Government supervision, with an annual report required by Congress, and an audit by the War Department. As Miss Boardman put it: "For the first time the American Red Cross became truly national in its scope and standing."

William Howard Taft was the new president. Rear Admiral William K. Van Reypen, former Surgeon General of the Navy, was appointed chairman of the central committee. Clara's name headed a list of sixty incorporators, and was on the roll call at all annual meetings. But she severed her links decisively with the Red Cross and had nothing further to do with the organization she had founded.

"When I can get out of my house and my hands all that belongs to the new organization it will be the same as if I had never known it. This will be well," she wrote with resignation as the summer advanced and she worked with Dr. Hubbell at Glen Echo, separating her own from the Red Cross records. Her life had been so lived that it was almost impossible to dissociate the two.

When the roses bloomed in June Clara's depression lifted as she headed West for a G.A.R. encampment at Mason City, Iowa, where she was feted with all the old-time enthusiasm. She attended the university commencement, sat at the campfire with her soldier friends, and dressed up in her mulberry silk for the evening gathering. She feared she would be asked to speak, so slipped away, but the soldiers saw her and clamored for her to return and address them. With great diffidence and a weak voice Clara did, and the audience warmed her with their shouts. The governor, the mayor, all the local celebrities honored her on this occasion and she felt so elated that she wrote one of her impromptu poems on the train traveling between Mason City and Cedar Rapids.

Uncertain of the course to pursue at this point, she was finally persuaded by Dr. Hubbell to make a Clara Barton home at Glen Echo. This appealed to her. By November her spirit was more or less restored. The wound that Theodore Roosevelt had inflicted was healing. All "spoils in the way of records" had been parceled out.

Just before the meeting at the end of the year that snapped the last thread she had with the Red Cross, Clara wrote to Stevé: "I am done fearing them. I deal with them with dignity and composure, and an annoying good-will and spirit." Then, with a touch of mischief, she added: "If he dared to say, the new secretary is a warmer friend to me, than to them. He is the son of a Civil War soldier and doesn't forget it."

## CHAPTER XX

## *TWILIGHT*

HER OWN sun all but set, Clara leaned over her much-used desk
at Glen Echo on a March day in 1905 to exchange brief courtesies
with the man who had given the idea of the Red Cross to the world
at large. Dunant, who had received the first Nobel prize in 1901
for this gift to mankind, had sent her with "respectful homage"
from Heiden, Switzerland, a booklet on the Red Cross movement in
Europe. Silent about her own troubles, Clara wrote in response:

> None of us living today will ever comprehend the full value of the
> thought you gave to the warring world; but if the seed be sown some-
> where and garnered in other fields by reapers yet unborn, its worth is
> all the greater, and in centuries to come the name of Henri Dunant
> will be written higher on the scroll and in broader letters than today.

She knew how severe Dunant's sufferings had been and rejoiced
with him in his ultimate recognition. From great wealth he had
sunk to pauperism, and was bankrupt and despondent after lighting
the torch that Clara had borne across the Atlantic. He was lost to
the world for fifteen years, then was found in an old men's home in
Heiden, ill and broken. After that the Empress of Russia assured
him a life pension. The stigma of bankruptcy was removed from his
record. He was rediscovered as the man who had started a world-
wide movement of encompassing scope. Just as Clara was stepping
down from her pedestal he shared the Nobel prize with Frédéric
Passy. There had been little or no communication between them
until 1905.

Clara celebrated her eighty-fourth birthday that year by sending
out a holly- and mistletoe-covered booklet rallying her friends to her
new cause, the National First Aid Association. She was careful to

point out that it stemmed from the time-honored St. John Ambulance Corps of Europe. With the prophetic touch she added: "It will become time-honored in America as well, for it has come to stay."

Clara's new venture was an extension of the work she had started in New York with Edward Howe. A year later, depressed by an unfriendly newspaper reference, she wrote: "The First Aid is all that in *any* way reconciles me to the fact that I did not leave the country on the receipt of President Roosevelt's letter. The impulse to do so was almost stronger than the ties of life. . . ."

Clara might be in eclipse on the national scene but she was not forgotten abroad. A message reached her from the Eighth International Red Cross Conference, held in London in the summer of 1907. The delegates regretted her absence and cited the "grateful remembrance in which she is still held for her cooperation of former times and for the example which she has given to the old European world."

When this message reached her Clara was at Glen Echo, the dairymaid with the Quaker bonnet, and the scintillant decorations pinned to her scarlet shawl. She churned, made Dutch cheese, and cheerfully milked her Jersey cows. But she craved the time for other uses. Her old-time retinue of satellites and helpers no longer surrounded her. The court over which she had presided for years was broken up. She was all alone at last except for Dr. Hubbell. It was difficult to get ahead with her first-aid work under these conditions.

Clara was still the perfectionist in household affairs, and was up every day soon after five, washing, ironing, cleaning, or writing letters, for she was at all times a champion correspondent, never failing to send out Valentines, Christmas and Easter cards; to remember birthdays and anniversaries; and to keep alive her strings of communication around the world.

In the summer of 1907 *The Story of My Childhood* was published. She intended it to be one of a series of "little books" covering the span of her life and designed for the young. But her second, dealing with her teaching days, was never finished. In the year that followed she spent much time putting together a home for herself in her native Oxford, but she was seriously ill on her eighty-seventh birthday. She had stepped on a broken board in a garden walk and injured a vertebra. A German woman doctor treated her by manipulation and by the spring of 1908 she was her old vigorous self again, sitting straight as a ramrod beside her old friend Admiral Sigsbee at a memorial service held in Washington for the men blown up on the *Maine*.

That autumn she watched electric lights being installed at Glen Echo. She was making brisk entries in her diary again. There had been long gaps in the preceding two years, and her handwriting was spidery now, although still quite clear. She autographed a thousand greetings for Christmas, 1909, her eighty-eighth birthday, and two months later set out on a wintry day "to read a little paper on the death of Lincoln" before a Washington club. She thought she could have added much to the reminiscences of Stanton retailed by one of his former clerks. The Civil War was ever green in Clara's heart.

By this time she was considered something of an oracle herself. She had seen and experienced so much that she was a natural target for reminiscence. Had any living woman shared in as much human drama as Clara Barton, between battlefields and disaster areas? To quote herself:

. . . What armies and how much of war I have seen, what thousands of marching troops, what fields of slain, what prisons, what hospitals, what ruins, what cities in ashes, what hunger and nakedness, what orphanages, what widowhood, what wrongs and what vengeance. And yet one lives and laughs as if nothing had happened and thanks good fortune that it is as well as it is.

Still the "mammoth newspapers brought in the slough of the world" and Clara found them "full of accidents, murders and divorces and the country full of intrigue." Reporters traveled to Glen Echo to get her opinion on subjects ranging from divorce to the Thaw case, which she followed with close attention. She disagreed with Professor William James on the subject of war. "Man's nature requires *something* to keep up its nobility," said Captain Barton's Clarissa.

After a long stretch of reading magazines on a winter day early in 1910 she commented on "how much work it is to keep up with the world." She was preparing herself for a visit from Ida M.

Tarbell, who was writing a series on famous women for the *American Magazine*. A great blizzard raged and Clara was snowed in on the day of the interview. She took two beaten eggs, a little hot milk, and read Elbert Hubbard—"so kindly, so well done"—as she waited. She was apprehensive about Miss Tarbell. "I fear I shall disappoint her, as I have taken little or no part in the progress of women as a factor. I hope I have not retarded, and have opened some doors, if I did not push them through."

She left no record of her impression of this interview but Miss Tarbell's cut-and-dried account of Miss Barton appeared in the April issue of 1910.[11] A few days later Clara was energetically making up a list for the New York *World* of eight women, dead ten years, who in her opinion qualified for the Hall of Fame. She chose Harriet Beecher Stowe, Lucretia Mott, Frances Dana Gage, Abigail Adams, Mary A. Bickerdyke, Dorothea Dix, Maria Mitchell, and Lucy Stone Blackwell, forgetting what made Lucy Stone famous when she added her husband's name.

Clara was beginning to feel alone in a world of shadows. Susan Anthony had died in the spring of 1910. By winter she was mourning Julia Ward Howe, for whom she wrote a memorial which was read at a public meeting in New York. The next to go was Dunant —"one more of the great and the good gone," she commented. Mary Baker Eddy, whom she had come to regard as "our greatest living woman," was next on the list. Then Abby Sheldon, one of her oldest and dearest intimates, and Dorence Atwater. Dr. Lucy Hall Brown had died in 1907.

"It is very remarkable how many persons of prominence, known to the world, are just now passing on," Clara wrote toward the end of 1910. "One scarcely can think on which side to place a friend at first thought. This world begins to seem empty to us who have known and had them so long."

All this had its effect on Clara. More and more she was attending spiritualistic sittings, and the shades of the famous were being invoked, chiefly by a medium named Mrs. Julia Warneke. Clara had always been drawn to the occult, a fashionable interest among the feminist pioneers. Now her personal sorrows and the deaths of friends had deepened her belief that the veil between life and death was thin. Dr. Hubbell was heavily committed to the parlor séances and when Clara was not well enough to attend, he took exhaustive notes on her behalf. This had been going on for some time and she had been "advised" by the spirits in the first place not to retire from the Red Cross; and in the second place to abandon her first-aid work because the organization she had founded was fast becoming so strong and prosperous that she could not hope to succeed in her solitary venture.

At a séance held at the Oxford Hotel on a March day in 1910 Clara was momentarily persuaded that Lincoln "made a prayer over her head," and that President McKinley "came so warmly and directed me to go on with my work." Dr. Hubbell was the ruling influence in this temporary manifestation of Clara's old age. At the end she passed out of it but after her death he handed over the house at Glen Echo and all of Mamie's possessions to Mrs. Mabelle Rawson Hirons, granddaughter of the Barton family physician in North Oxford. He was persuaded to make this move when Mrs. Hirons supposedly went into a trance and told him that Clara was commanding him from beyond the grave to give her the house. Finding later that he had been duped and that Mamie's possessions were being scattered in all directions, he sued and eventually recovered the property.

While Clara was still alive the sittings involved a wide range of celebrities, with Theodore Parker the most constant adviser. Grant, Sherman, Susan Anthony, all figured in the "messages." But although drawn into this curious world for a time through the associations around her, Clara still showed her native tough skepticism. "If it *is* really true," she wrote on March 30, 1910, "where are all the myriads of all the years? If all delusion, how is it done, how does the medium get her knowledge?"

Long before she dabbled in spiritualism she had become interested in Christian Science through Miss Rena D. Hubbell, Julian's niece, and the Rev. William Schoppe, her Universalist pastor who had become a reader and practitioner. With her strong belief in the influence of mind over matter, Clara was drawn to "Science and Health." She used practitioners from time to time and advised them for her friends. Her sympathies were with Mrs. Eddy in her historic lawsuit. She sympathized with her deeply when calumny touched her.

Clara was letting go a little in the spring of 1910. She rarely had what she called a "give away" or idle day, but the first-aid movement was beyond her failing strength. Stevé was tackling the Rockefeller Foundation in its behalf, but "it all seems so far beyond me that I cast it away from me," she wrote. "It is a good work, useful and needful, but I am not able to supply its needs."

However, Clara was contented that spring in other, simpler ways. She loved Glen Echo—"the hills and the trees and the birds, the water, and the moon which always seemed to be shining there." The woods were starred with spring flowers, the air was fragrant with blossoms, and Clara reported to Stevé that she had a "new milch cow, a big bossy calf, a door-yard full of little chicks and Baba, sleek and nice in his new coat. We must have a million strawberry blossoms and expect fruit in a few weeks."

Clara trimmed the ivy, and snipped at shrubs until the "poor burdened bushes held up their relieved heads and seemed glad." She reflected that she was "made for the country." She had never wanted anything but a plain house, one or two good horses, a carriage, a saddle, books, and the God of nature. "All this strife and struggle in cities is wrong," she wrote. "I dislike it all and am so tired of it that it *must* be wrong for me to pursue it."

Dr. Hubbell helped Clara at every turn. He plowed the garden, candled the eggs, canned raspberries, cherries, and currants under her supervision. He built her a little sun porch and put a lounge in it, which Clara said was like having a settee in the woods. "I surely have a world of luxuries—and *such* kindness," she wrote of Dr. Hubbell, who had never failed her in sickness or in health, in good or ill fortune.

As the sun set in a "fleece of gold" on an April day in 1910 she wondered if she had done right to accept an invitation to speak before the Social Economics Club of Chicago, attend a May breakfast there, and initiate a first-aid branch. It was a long journey to take alone at the age of eighty-nine. But she stayed up until four in the morning packing, then left three hours later for the West. The hall in Chicago was large and crowded. Faces shimmered around Clara. She shook hands until she could scarcely stand. She felt her heart giving out as she rose to say a few words. Finishing abruptly, she sat down. "The day came to an end," she noted in her diary that night. "Pulse all out of tune, just a wreck. But it was a glorious day and none knew how *I* made it."

She went on to Oak Park, to speak on Scutari, and eleven hundred persons listened with close attention. This time she stayed with her distant cousin, the Rev. Dr. William E. Barton, who was to write a detailed biography of Clara after her death. But she caught a severe cold and for the next five weeks there were no entries in her diary.

She decided that she would make her Christmas greetings that year a "kind of closing up of personal correspondence." Then she would settle down to her oldest letters and records, concentrate on writing her life history, and "let the present be buried in the past." But by January 14 she exploded: "I am so tired of all this writing."

Clara well might be. Millions of words had flowed from her pen and pencil—in letters, in diaries, in articles, in documents, in books. Her first history of the Red Cross was published in 1898. Another edition was issued in 1904. She never went to bed without her candle, pad, and pencil beside her, and it was her habit to wake up at unearthly hours and make notes. Few women have left so rich a store of personal memorabilia behind them. "I have never destroyed my letters," she wrote toward the end, "regarding them as the surest chronological testimony of my life, whenever I could find the time to attempt to write it. That time has never come to me, and the letters still wait my call."

When Leonora Halstead pressed her about an autobiography as she retired from the Red Cross in 1904, Clara wrote in a crushed vein:

It is too late—the world is too dark for any thought ahead. *Others* are writing my biography, and let it rest as they elect to make it. I have lived my life, well and ill, always less well than I wanted it to be but it is, *as* it is, and as it has been; *so small* a thing, to have had so much about it!

But in actual fact Clara had every right to a proud belief in her own enduring importance, since she had earned the confidence of so many men of stature. At Sherborn she called herself a "national woman" but in every sense of the word she was an international figure when she gave up the presidency of the Red Cross. After her death Julian Hubbell, the person who had known her best, observed that "it was the great minds that appreciated her most and gave her greatest credit." He viewed her as "quiet, conscientious, simple, sensitive, just, sensible, diffident, yet physically and morally brave; deliberate in her actions, considerate of the feelings of others, and infinitely patient." Often she let the waters roll over her head where her interests were concerned rather than defend herself. "Wait, wait for the wheels to turn," she would tell Julian under stress. "When you don't know what to do, do nothing."

Clara frequently went into Washington for meetings, to pay calls, or to sit once more in the galleries of the "Great Stone House." On a blustery day in January, 1911, she set off for the Capitol in that new wonder, the automobile, to hear a debate on the bill "Medical Freedom." She had decided views on this. "The committee was evidently allopathic," she commented. "I hardly think the bill will pass."

She took up Esperanto for a time, more to help friends who were inaugurating classes than from any deep interest in it herself. Wholly in character, she wrote: "While I am sure it will never be of the smallest use or gratification to me, personally, I am willing to give the time and influence if it will benefit others, which I think it may." Early in 1911 she collapsed suddenly, "plunging at the first moment" into the narrow cot in her workroom. She thought she read her own death sentence on the face of the doctor who attended her, and scrawled out her last wishes on loose sheets of paper, since she was too hoarse to speak. Anticipating her own end, she wrote: "I don't want [you] to be sentimental nor sad—but I wish that with no ceremony all in the house . . . gather and sing a few of the little old hymns that David loved best and would help sing." Actually, there was only one hymn on Clara's list—"Jesus, Lover of My Soul." The other songs she wanted were: "America," "Tramp, Tramp, Tramp," "Darling Nellie Gray," "Lilly Dale," "My Old Kentucky Home," "Juanita," "Her Bright Smile Haunts Me Still," and "Wings of a Dove."

But Clara finally picked up strength and on March 11 was able to write: "I get into my purple princess and feel more like myself." Two weeks later she "fitted collars or yokes to my ten suits and put them all in order," showing that she now felt far from the grave.

She made scathing comment on the "present craze for extraordinary costumes indulged in by women . . . huge hats, dangerous hat-pins . . . hobble and harem skirts. . . ."

Next day she went outdoors for the first time since January and visited her beloved Baba. She treated his eye, left him free in his stable, and a few days later padded the partition "to save the further wearing off of his tail." Before her death Clara had Baba shipped to the rich pastures of a friend in Virginia. She thought this would be a happy hunting ground for him when she was gone.

As the days went on she watched Dr. Hubbell seed a white-clover lawn below the house for the hens, and graft the Clara Barton rose to another variety. She worked over her hydrangeas until she felt so tired that she had to subside with a book on Charlotte Brontë. "I cannot read a line of the printed facsimile," Clara complained, peering through her tiny spectacles and wondering how any publisher managed to cope with the Brontë script. But her own fine copperplate was failing her at last and was becoming difficult to decipher.

From this she turned to sterner fare—the Greek philosophers—while she did a little carpentry on some broken boxes in her bureaus. "I took them resolutely in hand and gave them all the strength I had to spare," she wrote. At each pause she read "The Trial of Socrates" and decided that his arguments would do credit to a contemporary court. Next she took up the speech of Xenophon after the defeat of Cyrus the Younger, observing that "his generalship was most remarkable and recalls the old lessons of Anabasis." Clara had tackled Demosthenes and studied his enemy Aeschines before the boxes were again "handsome, firm and useful to last me always." She often regretted how little time she had had in her busy life for reading.

On July 10 she took note of the great suffrage parade in London—thirty thousand women marching in line. With an unwonted touch of bitterness she wrote:

It is all right—grand, and means success, for womanhood. I only regret that the course of women toward me personally has been so hard, as to take the sweet from the triumph I should so much enjoy. I hope this is not selfishness. I have no ill will. I wish the best to come but memory holds me passive.

A week later she looked longingly at a typewriter and wished that she had learned years earlier to use it. "Oh, the things we might have done, and did not, and the things we did, that we ought not! Could an all-knowing life rectify these?" She sat down at the typewriter, knowing nothing of its workings. She studied the book of directions and in "two hours wrote a passable letter." Clara was elated, remarking: "This gives me an idea. I can at least so fit myself as to be able to copy an article that needs it." Her delicate hands that had supplied the needs of so many suffering human beings punched feebly at the keys.

Only a few weeks earlier she had roughly penciled her will, leaving an estate of $15,000 to be divided among her legal heirs. She left the Glen Echo house to Dr. Hubbell, who loved it dearly and planned to make it a permanent memorial to Clara. That year she summered peacefully at Oxford where French River lapped its wooded shores, reminding her of her childhood days of play, of Stephen and David, and her galloping colts.

On her return to Glen Echo in September she complained of the "heated spine" that always indicated serious trouble. She moved restlessly between her easy chair and her green velvet hourglass footstool, getting "faint, short-breathed, and nervous." By this time the pigeonholes of her tall desk were packed with neatly arranged letters, and her papers had been put away in secret places. "I have left no choice articles lying about in envelopes, but all are in delicate colored dresses and laid away forever," Clara wrote.

Actually, she had tucked some of them away so secretly that it was not until the 1930's that Miss Rena D. Hubbell, who, with her twin sister, Mrs. Lena Hubbell Chamberlain, had inherited the Barton home from Dr. Hubbell when he died in 1929, noticed a blank space between two adjoining clothes closets. Investigating, they found it packed with Clara's diaries, with intimate papers, manuscripts, letters, pictures, clippings, and other memorabilia destined later for the Library of Congress. This, with the carefully annotated material given by Miss Saidée F. Riccius and Hermann P. Riccius, Clara's great-niece and great-nephew, give the rounded picture of her life that she never had time to write. They, in turn, had inherited it from Ida Barton Riccius, David's daughter, who edited it for Dr. Barton.

As her end approached Clara felt that she had made good disposition of her affairs. Her last letter was written to the Grand Duchess Louise on February 26, 1912, six weeks before her death. It shows that she knew she had reached the end of the road:

Dearest, dearest Grand Duchess,

They tell me I am changing worlds, and one of my last thoughts and wishes is to tell you of my unchanging love and devotion to you. I have waited long to be able to tell you of better news, but it does not come.

Thanks, oh, such thanks for your letters and your love. Dr. Hubbell will write you of me when I am gone and I commend him to you. May God bless and keep you forever more.

Blessings ever,
[Signed] Clara Barton

When the moment came Clara was not reluctant to die. The weariness of great age had settled on her at last; the rigors and pains of her years overwhelmed her. "Let me go! Let me go!" were her last words, as Dr. Hubbell and Stevé stood by her bed.

It was Good Friday, April 12, 1912, and Clara had rounded her ninety-first birthday. She died without rancor, her place in history assured. The medical verdict was that she had simply succumbed to old age. Her last hours were passed with the spring verdancy of Glen Echo around her and her two most faithful friends by her side. She had made her last diary entry in 1910, but had busied herself almost up to the end and her mind was clear.

Clara's wishes for a simple funeral were honored. She had never believed in ceremonial mourning. While the newspapers from coast to coast and in foreign countries carried tributes, only a few friends gathered at Glen Echo for the funeral rites. The White House was silent. So was the official Red Cross. But the Red Cross flag was displayed, along with those she had used in twenty fields of disaster. One had floated from the masthead of the State of Texas as she sailed into Santiago. A eulogy by Mrs. Logan was read at her bier.

Stevé, Dr. Hubbell, and Dr. Eugene Underhill of Philadelphia, accompanied Clara's body from Glen Echo to North Oxford. A dense fog cut off ferry service from Jersey City and in order to get from one station to the other in New York and make their train connection they had to hire a covered express wagon. When the driver learned that he was conveying Clara Barton he dropped his reins and threw up his hands. All three men thought that she would have appreciated what followed.

"My God, is this the body of Clara Barton?" he exclaimed. "Why, my father was a Confederate soldier and at the battle of Antietam he was wounded in the neck and was bleeding to death when Miss Barton found him on the battlefield and bound up his wounds in time to save his life."

Soldiers waited at Worcester to escort the cortege to Memorial Hall, Oxford. Seventeen members of the family shared in the services with diverse memories of their unforgettable Aunt Clara. Old pupils, old friends, old soldiers stood at attention. A silk flag from the Woman's Relief Corps was draped over Clara's breast as the thinning ranks of old soldiers in blue stood at attention. She was buried beside her father and mother on a knoll in the wooded cemetery of North Oxford, in the family plot which she had preserved with care, and where flags fly perpetually around the plain granite monument. A soldier she had nursed at Morris Island watched the Rev. Dr. William E. Barton drop red roses over her coffin at the moment of committal.

Clara was not forgotten. She became an enduring legend to the youth of the land, as one generation after another grew up to view her in the image of an American heroine. Nearly a century after the Civil War her name was among the first in any popularity poll involving famous women. Her personality was still a living force in the American National Red Cross itself—with its 44,000,000 members, its 3,713 chapters, its world-wide links with seventy independent national Red Cross societies around the world. She had faith in its future, even as she was stepping out. Her parting message on the day she resigned summed up her feeling:

Although its growth may seem to have been slow, it is to be remembered that it is not a shrub, or plant, to shoot up in the Summer and wither in the frosts. The Red Cross is a part of us—it has come to stay—and like the sturdy oak, its spreading branches shall yet encompass and shelter the relief of the nation.

Neither Clara nor Dunant lived to see the branches spread in all directions as they do today. But the spirit of both had infused the virgin soil.

# Appendix

❋

(Letter from Clara Barton to Count Bismarck, December 9, 1870.)
Count Bismarck
    Governor-General of Alsace

Honored Count:

Through the politeness of your adjutant and his amiable lady, I learn that Your Highness will kindly permit me to communicate with you in reference to the work I am endeavoring to perform among the destitute people who are so fortunate as to fall under your protecting care. But speaking no German, lacking confidence to attempt a conversation in French, and fearing that English may not be familiar to you, I decide to write, subject to translation, the little explanation I would make of my work, its origin, progress, and design.

I entered Strassburg the second day after its fall, and, observing both the distress of its inhabitants and their bitterness toward their captors, who must always remain their neighbors, I deemed it wise, while they should receive the charity so much needed, that something of it be presented by German hands. In this view I was most cordially met by that noblest of ladies, the Grand Duchess of Baden, to whom I am also indebted for this introduction to you, and immediately under her generous patronage, I returned with an assistant to do what we could in the name of Germany. At first, we could only give indiscriminately to the hundreds who thronged our doors. But directly, I perceived that a prolonged continuance of this system would be productive of greater disaster to the moral condition of the people than the bombardment had been to their physical; that in a city, comprising less than eighty thousand inhabitants, there would shortly be twenty thousand confirmed beggars. Only a small proportion of these families had been accustomed to receive charity, but one winter of common beggary would reduce the larger part to a state of careless degradation from which they would scarcely again emerge. It seemed morally indispensable that remunerative employment in some form should be given them. Again I consulted Her Royal Highness, who kindly approved, generously making the first contribution of materials, and we opened our present "Workrooms for Women" in the month of October. To say that the results have surpassed my most sanguine expectation is little, the facts are much more; but a stranger both to people and language, it is not singular that my work, which depends entirely upon public patronage, has often lacked the necessary means to attain the full measure of success.

My original design was to aid not only the inhabitants of Strassburg, but those in other portions of Alsace who are equally destitute. I thought that to be just to all and produce the best moral influence, the employment, and the payment, should be given to Strassburg, thus making of the inhabitants workers, instead of beggars, but that the warm garments made by them should be sent to the half-naked peasants of the villages, and little country homes where the harvest has been lost, and neither money nor clothing comes within reach. And to the extent of my means I have done this. The peasants have heard of the rooms, and often walk two and three leagues to ask for garments, and the clergymen from around the old battlefields, and from Bitche are making appeals in behalf of their half-naked and shivering people. Both my sympathy and my judgment would favor the hearing of these appeals so far as possible. This population must always be the neighbors, if not a part, of the German people; it will be most desirable that they should be also friends; they are in distress—their hearts can never be better reached than now; the little seed sown today may have in it the germs of future peace or war.

But pardon my boldness, Honored Count; I am neither a diplomatist nor political counselor; I am only a maker of garments for the poor.

I have objected to the purchasing of materials for my work from magazines, believing that, if the attention of some large manufacturers of stuffs were called to the subject, materials could be supplied in a much better manner.

Other noble societies, I rejoice to say, have sprung up later, all of which I believe will confine their praiseworthy efforts to the city of Strassburg, and in every respect but that of affording employment will, I trust, prove sufficient for the necessities. My little work has been the pioneer, that ploughed through the earliest and deepest drifts, and which, though often weary and disheartened, still seeks to push beyond the beaten track, over the fields, and along the hillsides, and gather the sufferers out of the storm.

After this, I fear too lengthy, explanation, will Your Highness kindly permit me, for the sake of perspicuity, to arrange under two or three distinct heads the prominent features of my work.

1st. I desire to give employment, and payment therefor at the usual rates, to some portion of the destitute families of Strassburg.

2d. To distribute the garments made by them among the people of the surrounding districts which have been reduced by the calamities of the war.

3d. That, beyond this, I design to make no appropriations of charities, but to refer all such applicants residing within the city to the various societies and committees of the same.

4th. To attain this object and carry on the work is required, material, in warm stuffs of both wool and cotton, suitable for clothing for working-men, women, and children.

5th. Money to pay the workers,—sufficient for the number employed.
Strassburg, Dec. 9th, 1870.

## 2

International Committee for the
Relief of Wounded Soldiers
Geneva, August 19, 1877

To the President of the United States, at Washington:

Mr. President:

The International Committee of the Red Cross desires most earnestly that the United States should be associated with them in their work, and they take the liberty of addressing themselves to you, with the hope that you will second their efforts. In order that the functions of the National Society of the Red Cross be faithfully performed, it is indispensable that it should have the sympathy and protection of the Government.

It would be irrational to establish an association upon the principles of the Convention of Geneva, without the association having the assurance that the army of its own country, of which it should be an auxiliary, would be guided, should the case occur, by the same principles. It would consequently be useless for us to appeal to the people of the country, inasmuch as the United States, as a Government, has made no declaration of adhering officially to the principles laid down by the Convention of the 22d August, 1864.

Such is, then, Mr. President, the principal object of the present request. We do not doubt but this will meet with a favorable reception from you, for the United States is in advance of Europe upon the subject of war, and the celebrated "Instructions of the American Army" are a monument which does honor to the United States.

You are aware, Mr. President, that the Government of the United States was officially represented at the Conference of Geneva, in 1864, by two delegates, and this mark of approbation given to the work which was being accomplished was then considered by every one as a precursor of a legal ratification. Until the present time, however, this confirmation has not taken place, and we think that this formality, which would have no other bearing than to express publicly the acquiescence of the United States in those humanitarian principles now admitted by all civilized people, has only been retarded because the occasion has not offered itself. We flatter ourselves with the hope that appealing directly to your generous sentiments will determine you to take the necessary measures to put an end to a situation so much to be regretted. We only wait such good news, Mr. President, in order to urge the founding of an American Society of the Red Cross.

We have already an able and devoted assistant in Miss Clara Barton, to whom we confide the care of handing to you this present request.

It would be very desirable that the projected asseveration should be under your distinguished patronage, and we hope that you will not refuse us this favor.

Receive, Mr. President, the assurance of our highest consideration.

For the International Committee:

G. Moynier, President.

# 3

## THE RED CROSS OF THE GENEVA CONVENTION: WHAT IT IS

### By Clara Barton

To the People of the United States, Senators and Representatives in Congress:

Having had the honor conferred upon me of appointment by the Central Commission holding the Geneva Convention, to present that treaty to this Government, and to take in charge the formation of a national organization according to the plan pursued by the committee working under the treaty, it seems to me but proper, that, while I ask the Government to sign it, the people and their representatives should be made acquainted with its origin, designs, methods of work, etc. To this end I have prepared the following statement, and present it to my countrymen and women, hoping they will be led to endorse and sustain a benevolence so grand in its character, and already almost universal in its recognition and adoption by the civilized world.

Clara Barton
Washington, D.C.

## What the Red Cross Is

A Confederation of relief societies in different countries, acting under the Geneva Convention, carries on its work under the sign of the Red Cross. The aim of these societies is to ameliorate the condition of wounded soldiers in the armies in campaign on land or sea.

The societies had their rise in the conviction of certain philanthropic men that the official sanitary service in wars is usually insufficient, and that the charity of the people, which at such times exhibits itself munificently, should be organized for the best possible utilization. An international public conference was called at Geneva, Switzerland, in 1863, which, though it had not an official character, brought together representatives from a number of Governments. At this conference a treaty was drawn up, afterward remodeled and improved, which twenty-five Governments have signed.

The treaty provides for the neutrality of all sanitary supplies, ambulances, surgeons, nurses, attendants, and sick or wounded men, and their safe-conduct, when they bear the sign of the organization, viz., the Red Cross.

Although the convention which originated the organization was necessarily international, the relief societies themselves are entirely national and independent; each one governing itself and making its own laws according to the genius of its nationality and needs.

It was necessary for recognizance and safety, and for carrying out the general provisions of the treaty, that a uniform badge should be agreed upon. The Red Cross was chosen out of compliment to the Swiss Republic, where the first convention was held, and in which the Central Commission has its headquarters. The Swiss colors being a white cross on a red ground, the badge chosen was these colors reversed.

There are no "members of the Red Cross," but only members of societies whose sign it is. There is no "Order of the Red Cross." The relief societies use, each according to its convenience, whatever methods seem best suited to prepare in times of peace for the necessities of sanitary service in times of war. They gather and store gifts of money and supplies; arrange hospitals, ambulances, methods of transportation of wounded men, bureaus of information, correspondence, etc. All that the most ingenious philanthropy could devise and execute has been attempted in this direction.

In the Franco-Prussian War this was abundantly tested. That Prussia acknowledged its beneficence is proven by the fact that the Emperor affixed the Red Cross to the Iron Cross of Merit.

Although the societies are not international, there is a tacit compact between them, arising from their common origin, identity of aim, and mutual relation to the treaty. The compact embraces four principles, viz., centralization, preparation, impartiality, and solidarity.

1. *Centralization.* The efficiency of relief in time of war depends on unity of direction; therefore in every country the relief societies have a common central head to which they send their supplies, and which communicates for them with the seat of war or with the surgical military authorities, and it is through this central commission they have governmental recognition.

2. *Preparation.* It is understood that societies working under the Red Cross shall occupy themselves with preparatory work in times of peace. This gives them a permanence they could not otherwise have.

3. *Impartiality.* The societies of belligerent nations cannot always carry aid to their wounded countrymen who are captured by the enemy; this is counterbalanced by the regulation that the aid of the Red Cross societies shall be extended alike to friend and foe.

4. *Solidarity.* This provides that the societies of nations not engaged in war may afford aid to the sick and wounded of belligerent nations without affecting any principle of non-interference to which their Governments may be pledged. This must be done through the Central Commission, and not through either of the belligerent parties; this ensures impartiality of relief.

That these principles are practical has been thoroughly tested during the fifteen years the Red Cross has existed.

The Convention of Geneva does not exist as a society, but is simply a treaty under which all the relief societies of the Red Cross are enabled to carry on their work effectually. In time of war, the members and agents of the societies who go to the seat of war are obliged to have their badges viséed by the Central Commission, and by one of the belligerents—this is in order to prevent fraud. Thus the societies and the treaty complement each other. The societies find and execute the relief, the treaty affords them the immunities which enable them to execute.

And it may be further made a part of the raison d'être of these national relief societies to afford ready succor and assistance to sufferers in time of national or widespread calamities, such as plagues, cholera, yellow fever and the like, devastating fires or floods, railway disasters, mining catastrophes, etc. The readiness of organizations like those of the Red Cross to extend help at the instant of need renders the aid of quadruple value and efficiency compared with that gathered hastily and irresponsibly, in the bewilderment and shock which always accompanies such calamities. The trained nurses and attendants subject to the relief societies in such cases would accompany the supplies sent and remain in action as long as needed. Organized in every State, the relief societies of the Red Cross would be ready with money, nurses, and supplies, to go on call to the instant relief of all who were overwhelmed by any of those sudden calamities which occasionally visit us. In case of yellow fever, there being an organization in every State, the nurses and attendants would be first chosen from the nearest societies, and, being acclimated, would incur far less risk to life than if sent from distant localities. It is true that the Government is always ready in these times of public need to furnish transportation, and often does much more. In the Mississippi flood, a few years ago, it ordered rations distributed under the direction of army officers; in the case of the explosion at the navy yard, it voted a relief fund, and in our recent affliction at the South, a like course was pursued. But in such cases one of the greatest difficulties is that there is no organized method of administering the relief which the Government or liberal citizens are willing to bestow, nor trained and acclimated nurses ready to give intelligent care to the sick; or, if there be organization, it is hastily formed in the time of need, and is therefore comparatively inefficient and wasteful. It would seem to be full time that, in consideration of the growth and rapidly accumulating necessities of our country, we should learn to economize our charities, and ensure from them the greatest possible practical benevolence. Although we in the United States may fondly hope to be seldom visited by the calamities of war, yet the misfortunes of other nations with which we are on terms of amity appeal to our sympathies; our southern coasts are periodically visited by the scourge of yellow fever; the valleys of the Mississippi are subject to destructive inundations; the plains of the West are devastated by insects and drought, and our cities and country are swept by consuming fires. In all such cases, to gather and dispense the profuse liberality of our people, without waste of time or material, requires the wisdom that comes of experience and permanent organization. Still more does it concern, if not our safety, at least our honor, to signify our approval of those principles of humanity acknowledged by every other civilized nation.

# 4

(Letter from Gustave Moynier to James G. Blaine.)

Geneva, June 13th, 1881

The Honorable Secretary of State
   James G. Blaine
      Washington.

Sir:

Miss Clara Barton has just communicated to me the letter which you did her the honor to address to her, dated May 23rd, 1881, and I wish to express to you the great satisfaction which it has given me. I have no doubt that, thanks to your good dispositions and those of President Garfield, the United States may soon be counted among the signatories of the Geneva Convention, since you allow me to hope that a proposition to that effect will be submitted to Congress by the Administration.

I wish to thank you and President Garfield for your willingness seriously to consider the request conveyed in my letter of August 19th, 1877—a request the more natural, as it tends to associate your country with a work of charity and civilization for which it is most highly qualified.

Since my letter of 1877 was written there have been several additional Governmental adhesions to the Convention of Geneva, and I believe these examples will be the more encouraging to the United States in that they are afforded by America—it being under the influence of the events of the late war on the Pacific Coast that Bolivia joined on October 18th, 1879, Chile on November 15th, 1879, the Argentine Confederation on November 25th, 1879, and Peru on April 22nd, 1881.

This argument in favor of your country's adhesion is the only one that I can add to my previous solicitation and the printed documents transmitted to you by Miss Barton to enlighten your judgment and that of Congress.

I await with complete confidence the result of your sympathetic endeavors; and I beg, Sir, that you will accept the assurance of highest consideration.

G. Moynier,<br>President.

## 5

### THE AMERICAN ASSOCIATION OF THE RED CROSS
### ARTICLES OF INCORPORATION, OCTOBER 1, 1881

**I.**

The name of this association shall be The American Association of the Red Cross.

**2.**

The term of its existence shall be for twenty years.

**3.**

The objects of this association shall be:

1st. To secure by the United States the adoption of the Treaty of August 22d, 1864, between Italy, Baden, Belgium, Denmark, Holland, Spain, Portugal, France, Prussia, Saxony, Würtemberg, and the Federal Council of Switzerland.

2d. To obtain recognition by the Government of the United States, and to hold itself in readiness for communicating therewith at all times, to the end that its purposes may be more wisely and effectually carried out.

3d. To organize a system of national relief and apply the same as mitigating the sufferings caused by war, pestilence, famine and other calamities.

4th. To collect and diffuse information touching this progress of mercy, the organization of national relief, the advancement of sanitary science, and their application.

5th. To cooperate with all other similar national societies for the furtherance of the articles herein set forth, in such ways as are provided by the regulations governing such cooperation.

The number of this association, to be styled the "Executive Board," for the first year of its existence, shall be eleven.

Clara Barton
William Lawrence
Jos. K. Barnes
A. S. Solomons
Alex. Y. P. Garnett

## 6

(Letter from Dr. Henry W. Bellows to Clara Barton.)

New York, 232 E. 15
Nov. 21, 1881

My dear Miss Barton:

It has been a sore disappointment and mortification to those who inaugurated the plan of organized relief, by private contributions, for sick and wounded soldiers in our late war, since so largely followed by other nations, that they should still find the United States the only great Government that refuses to join in the treaty, framed by the International Convention of Geneva, for neutralizing battle-fields after the battle, and making the persons of surgeons and nurses flying to the relief of the wounded and dying free from arrest. This great international agreement for mitigating the horrors of war finds its chief defect in the conspicuous refusal of the United States Government to join in the treaty! The importance of our national concurrence with other Governments in this noble treaty has been urged upon every administration since the war, but has thus far met only the reply that our national policy did not allow us to enter into entangling alliances with other powers. I rejoice to hear from you that our late President and his chief official advisers were of a different opinion, and encouraged the hope that in the interests of mercy and humanity it might be safe to agree by treaty with all the civilized world, that we would soften to non-combatants the hateful conditions that made relief to the wounded on battle-fields a peril or forbidden act. I trust you will press this matter upon our present administration with all the weight of your well-earned influence. Having myself somewhat ignominiously failed to get any encouragement for this measure from two administrations, I leave it in your more fortunate hands, hoping that the time is ripe for a less jealous policy than American self-isolation in international movements for extending and universalizing mercy towards the victims of war.

Your truly
H. W. Bellows

## 7

(Editorial from the Chicago *Inter-Ocean* of March 31, 1884.)

The day is not far distant—if it has not already come—when the American people will recognize the Red Cross as one of the wisest and best systems of philanthropic work in modern times. Its mission is not accomplished when it has carried the generous offerings of the people to their brethren who have met with sudden calamity. It does not stop with the alleviation of bodily suffering and the clothing of the destitute— blessed as that work is, when wisely done, so as not to break down the manly spirit of self-help. The Red Cross has become a grand educator, embodying the best principles of social science, and that true spirit of charity which counts it a sacred privilege to serve one's fellowmen in time of trouble. The supplying of material wants—of food, raiment and shelter is only a small part of its ministry in its work among suffering humanity. When fire or flood or pestilence has caused widespread deso- lation, the Red Cross seeks to carry to people's hearts that message which speaks of a universal brotherhood. It is all the time and every- where sowing the seed of brotherly kindness and goodwill, which is destined in time to yield the fruits of world-wide peace. Once let the love of doing good unto others become deeply rooted and practiced as an international custom, and arsenals and ironclad navies will give way to the spirit of equity. War will cease as a relic of barbarism, and peace will shed its benedictions over all nations.

## 8

### The Women Who Went to the Field

The women who went to the field, you say,
The *women* who went to the field; and pray
What did they go for? just to be in the way!—

They'd not know the difference betwixt work and play,
What did they know about *war* anyway?
What could they *do?*—of what *use* could they be?
They would scream at the sight of a gun, don't you see?
Just fancy them round where the bugle notes play,
And the long roll is bidding us on to the fray.
Imagine their skirts 'mong artillery wheels,
And watch for their flutter as they flee 'cross the fields
When the charge is rammed home and the fire belches hot;—
They never will wait for the answering shot.
They would faint at the first drop of blood, in their sight.
What fun for us boys,—(ere we enter the fight;)
They might pick some lint, and tear up some sheets,
And make us some jellies, and send on their sweets,
And knit some soft socks for Uncle Sam's shoes,
And write us some letters, and tell us the news.
And thus it was settled by common consent,
That husbands, or brothers, or whoever went,
That the place for the women was in their own homes,
There to patiently wait until victory comes.
But later, it chanced, just how no one knew,
That the lines slipped a bit, and some 'gan to crowd through;
And they went,—where did they go?—Ah; where did they not?
Show us the battle,—the field,—or the spot
Where the groans of the wounded rang out on the air
That her ear caught it not, and her hand was not there,
Who wiped the death sweat from the cold clammy brow,
And sent home the message;—" 'T is well with him now"?
Who watched in the tents, whilst the fever fires burned,
And the pain-tossing limbs in agony turned,
And wet the parched tongue, calmed delirium's strife
Till the dying lips murmured, "My Mother," "My Wife"!
And who were they all?—They were many, my men:
Their record was kept by no tabular pen:
They exist in traditions from father to son.
Who recalls, in dim memory, now here and there one.—
A few names were writ, and by chance live to-day;
But's a perishing record fast fading away.
Of those we recall, there are scarcely a score,
Dix, Dame, Bickerdyke,—Edson, Harvey, and Moore,
Fales, Whittenmeyer, Gilson, Safford and Lee,

And poor Cutter dead in the sands of the sea;
And Frances D. Gage, our "Aunt Fanny" of old,
Whose voice rang for freedom when freedom was sold.
And Husband, and Etheridge, and Harlan and Case,
Livermore, Alcott, Hancock, and Chase,
And Turner, and Hawley, and Potter, and Hall.
Ah! The list grows apace, as they come at the call:
Did these women quail at the sight of a gun?
Will some soldier tell us of one he saw run?
Will he glance at the boats on the great western flood,
At Pittsburgh and Shiloh, did they faint at the blood?
And the brave wife of Grant stood there with them then,
And her calm, stately presence gave strength to his men.
And Marie of Logan; she went with them too;
A bride, scarcely more than a sweetheart, 'tis true.
Her young cheek grows pale when the bold troopers ride.
Where the "Black Eagle" soars, she is close at his side,
She staunches his blood, cools the fever-burnt breath,
And the wave of her hand stays the Angel of Death;
She nurses him back, and restores once again
To both army and state the brave leader of men.

She has smoothed his black plumes and laid them to sleep,
Whilst the angels above them their high vigils keep:
And she sits here alone, with the snow on her brow—
Your cheers for her comrades! Three cheers for her now.
And these were the women who went to the war:
The women of question; what did they go for?
Because in their hearts God had planted the seed
Of pity for woe, and help for its need;
They saw, in high purpose, a duty to do,
And the armor of right broke the barriers through.
Uninvited, unaided, unsanctioned ofttimes,
With pass, or without it, they pressed on the lines;
They pressed, they implored, till they ran the lines through,
And this was the "running" the men saw them do.
'T was a hampered work, its worth largely lost;
'T was hindrance, and pain, and effort, and cost:
But through these came knowledge,—knowledge is power.—
And never again in the deadliest hour
Of war or of peace, shall we be so beset

To accomplish the purpose our spirits have met.
And what would they do if war came again?
The scarlet cross floats where all was blank then.
They would bind on their "brassards" and march to the fray,
And the man liveth not who could say to them nay;
They would stand with you now, as they stood with you then,
The nurses, consolers, and saviors of men.

# 9

(Letter from Rear Admiral W. T. Sampson to Clara Barton.)

U.S. Flagship "New York," First-Rate
Key West, Florida, May 2, 1898

Miss Clara Barton, President American National Red Cross:

1. I have received through the senior naval officer present a copy of a letter from the State Department to the Secretary of the Navy; a copy of a letter from the Secretary of the Navy to the commander-in-chief of the naval force on this station; and also a copy of a letter from the Secretary of the Navy to the commandant of the naval station at Key West.

2. From these communications it appears that the destination of the steamship *State of Texas,* loaded with supplies for the starving reconcentrados in Cuba, is left, in a measure, to my judgment.

3. At present I am acting under instructions from the Navy Department to blockade the coast of Cuba for the purpose of preventing, among other things, any food-supply from reaching the Spanish forces in Cuba. Under these circumstances it seems to me unwise to let a ship-load of such supplies be sent to the reconcentrados, for, in my opinion, they would be distributed to the Spanish army. Until some point be occupied in Cuba by our forces, from which such distribution can be made to those for whom the supplies are intended, I am unwilling that they should be landed on Cuban soil.

Yours very respectfully,
(Signed) W. T. Sampson
Rear-Admiral U.S.N.,
Commander-in-Chief U.S. Naval Force, North Atlantic Station.

## 10

Extract withheld on advice of friends from letter written by Clara Barton to President Roosevelt on January 27, 1903.

It need not be said that no person of sufficient prominence (I do not say importance) to be worthy of such notice from the highest potentate of a great nation, could ever remain in that country after that. Let me say then for your satisfaction and my own that after such announcement I must leave the country not to return, and I beg you to understand that I do this in good faith and patriotic loyalty. If disturbing elements will be more at rest and act in better harmony in my absence than with me present, it may be my duty to go.

Again, let it be understood that I do not go abroad to mingle with the people of distinction I may chance to know, thus creating another avenue of discontent or disturbance. My retirement shall be absolute, out of the influence of all, and I will live out in another country the good faith I have always sought to cherish in my own. This is not written, Mr. President, to burden you with a reply; it asks nothing and needs no answer. My little affairs have already occupied too much time so important as yours. I trust to trouble you no further. With no word of remonstrance or complaint and in perfect good will and loyalty, I have the honor to subscribe myself,

Your obedient countrywoman

## 11

Ida M. Tarbell on Clara Barton, *American Magazine*, April, 1910.

Irregular and dangerous as the practice was, a large number of women did attach themselves to the armies quite independent of all authority and of all organization and did valiant service. Clara Barton was practically a free lance—going where she would, furnishing her own supplies, doing uninstructed and unimpeded what she found to do. She served the wounded of both armies indiscriminately, a practice which at first amazed and sometimes angered the Union officers from whose headquarters she worked. But opposition never swayed her purpose and before the war was over Miss Barton's individual efforts had established the right of the wounded or suffering, irrespective of uniforms, to all the aid which could be commanded. This was really Miss Barton's greatest service to the country in this period, though not the only one.

## 12

Clara Barton's personal list of public figures with whom she had dealings, and many of whom were her friends. She omitted Theodore Roosevelt's name.

Presidents:
  Abraham Lincoln
  Andrew Johnson
  Ulysses S. Grant
  Rutherford B. Hayes
  James A. Garfield
  Chester A. Arthur
  Grover Cleveland
  Benjamin Harrison
  William McKinley

Vice-Presidents:
  John C. Breckinridge
  Schuyler Colfax
  William A. Wheeler
  Hannibal Hamlin
  Henry Wilson
  Garret A. Hobart

Chief Justices:
  Salmon Portland Chase
  Morrison R. Waite
  Stanley Matthews

Secretaries of State:
  William H. Seward
  Elihu B. Washburne
  Hamilton Fish
  William M. Evarts
  James G. Blaine
  T. F. Frelinghuysen
  Thomas F. Bayard
  John W. Foster
  Walter Q. Gresham
  Richard Olney
  John Sherman
  William R. Day
  John M. Hay

Secretaries of War:
  Edwin M. Stanton
  John M. Schofield
  William T. Sherman
  Robert T. Lincoln
  William C. Endicott
  Redfield Proctor
  Daniel S. Lamont
  Russell A. Alger

Secretaries of the Navy:
  Benjamin F. Tracy
  Hilary A. Herbert
  John D. Long

Secretaries of the Treasury:
  Salmon Portland Chase
  George S. Boutwell
  William Windom
  Charles J. Folger

Secretaries of Agriculture:
  Norman Jay Colman
  Jeremiah M. Rusk
  J. Sterling Morton
  James Wilson

Secretaries of the Interior:
  Zachariah Chandler
  Henry M. Teller
  John W. Noble

Postmasters General:
  James N. Tyner
  John Wanamaker
  Wilson S. Bissell
  William L. Wilson

U.S. Army:
  Major General Nelson A. Miles
  Major General Wesley Merritt
  Major General John R. Brooke
  General Daniel E. Sickles
  Brigadier General James F. Wade
  Brigadier General M. I. Ludington
  Brigadier General Adolphus W. Greely
  Brigadier General John M. Wilson
  Brigadier General Joseph C. Breckinridge
  Brigadier General C. C. Augur
  Brigadier General Richard N. Batchelder
  Brigadier General W. A. Hammond
  Brigadier General H. D. Rucker
  Lieutenant General John M. Schofield

General Officers U.S. Volunteers:
  Major General William R. Shafter
  Major General Leonard Wood
  Brigadier General James H. Wilson
  Brigadier General Fitzhugh Lee
  Brigadier General William Ludlow
  Brigadier General Fred D. Grant

U.S. Navy:
  Rear Admiral Winfield S. Schley
  Rear Admiral William T. Sampson

Miscellaneous:
  Surgeon General Joseph K. Barnes
  General Philip H. Sheridan
  General R. D. Mussey
  George B. Loring
  E. G. Lapham
  Surgeon General George H. Crum
  General Benjamin F. Butler
  Sumner I. Kimball, U.S. Life Saving Corps
  Walter Weyman, Surgeon General, Marine Hospital Service

European Sovereigns:
  Czar of Russia
  Francis Joseph, Emperor of Austria
  Grand Duke and Duchess of Baden
  William I, Emperor of Germany

Empress of Germany
Natalie, Queen of Serbia
Abdul Hamid, Sultan of Turkey

## *13*

### Newspaper Tributes to Clara Barton

*New York Times,* September 10, 1931:

Clara Barton died nearly twenty years ago—two years before the World War came—but she is among America's immortals. She owed that immortality to the enduring institution which she founded fifty years ago. It is hardly conceivable that the American Red Cross will not live as long as the Republic. It is essential in the life of a people enjoying individual liberty. . . . Thanks to her zeal and the ever-widening horizons which the guidance of other leaders and the service of hundreds of thousands in all parts of the world have been given the Red Cross, America now takes the lead in this movement of mercy.

New York *Sun,* April 13, 1912:

General Scott called Kearny the bravest man he ever knew; certainly Miss Barton was one of the bravest of women, and she deserved the laurel no less than the famous soldiers of the Civil War. But Clara Barton was more than brave. She devoted her life to humanity. She was one of the most useful of women, self-sacrificing to a degree, generous to a fault. Health and fortune she devoted to her great cause; . . . Into the span of what other life have more mercy, tenderness and love entered? Is it not the finest kind of glory that when the American Red Cross is seen or mentioned the name of Clara Barton comes to the mind like a benediction?

New York *Post,* April 13, 1912:

Surely, in all fields relating to the humanitarian side of life, the nineteenth century produced no finer figures than Florence Nightingale and Clara Barton.

New York *Globe,* April 13, 1912:

More justly than the man who first made the remark, Clara Barton could have said: "The world is my country, and do good my religion." Her religion ran to the whole of mankind. She was a true cosmopolite, although in visible aspect seemingly a New England provincial. She not only preached but practiced the new internationalism. She represented the spirit that knows not race, nor color, nor country, nor creed, nor sex, nor any other thing when the cry of human need is heard. . . . Give the world enough Clara Bartons and the brotherhood of man will be ushered in.

Brooklyn *Standard-Union*, April 13, 1912:

The whole world today, to its remotest corner, is paying reverence to Clara Barton. . . . When men went forth with banners to kill, Clara Barton followed to undo their work under the Cross. . . . Doubtless, she must be classed as a genius, for genius is the intuitive capacity for overcoming insuperable difficulties.

Boston *Transcript*, April 12, 1912:

In all wars and in all battlefields, wherever the Red Cross may carry comfort and healing, it will also carry the name of Clara Barton. Nor are wars to be the ultimate limit. Wherever calamity, plague, famine, flood or fire are combatted there also will be felt the influence of this woman's immortal work. . . . All the great disasters of the last twenty-five years are milestones in the life of this noble woman, who took up the work of Florence Nightingale and developed it, from a merely national movement on the part of England for the benefit of English troops, to an international movement for the benefit of humanity itself.

Rockford *Register-Gazette*, Rockford, Ill., April 15, 1912:

Considerable comment was caused at the funeral of Clara Barton Sunday by the absence of any representative of President Taft or of the American National Red Cross, the organization which Miss Barton founded. Nor were any flowers from either the organization or the White House in evidence. . . . The principal floral tribute was a canopy of American beauty roses from the Woman's Relief Corps.

Worcester *Gazette*, April 13, 1912:

The sign of the cross, in crimson red, had come nearer its true significance under her direction than it ever did before, whether by Constantine named or borne by Crusader bands in assaults upon the Crescent. Thus far in the world's history, no other has come so near the Christ spirit in the union of all kindreds, tongues and people in one universal bond of brotherhood as this mild-mannered, softly-spoken woman.

Richmond *Journal*, April 17, 1912:

. . . Clara Barton was a woman of large vision and great heart. She answered the call of the world for service in its broadest, truest sense and when the infirmities of age were upon her, and her ability to serve was restricted, she sent this message, which needs no comment and no interpretation, to her soldiers: It says:

"When you were weak and I was strong, I toiled for you.

"Now you are strong, and I am weak. Because of my work for you, I ask your aid. I ask the ballot for myself and my sex. As I stood by you, Pray you stand by me and mine."

Detroit *Free Press*, April 15, 1912:

She was perhaps the most perfect incarnation of mercy the modern world has known. She became the founder of the most significant and widespread philanthropic movement of the age, a movement that already has become an intrinsic part of world civilization.

Albany *Press-Knickerbocker*, April 14, 1912:

No nobler service than hers is recorded in history.

# BIBLIOGRAPHY

Adams, Elmer C., *Heroines of Modern Progress*. New York: Sturgis and Walton Company, 1913.

Anthony, Katharine, *Susan B. Anthony: Her Personal History and her Era*. New York: Doubleday and Company, 1954.

Atwater, Francis, *Memoirs of Francis Atwater*. Meriden, Connecticut: Horton Printing Company, 1922.

Bacon-Foster, Mrs. Corra, *Clara Barton, Humanitarian*. Washington: The Columbia Historical Society, 1918.

Barton, Clara, *A Story of the Red Cross: Glimpses of Field Work*. New York: D. Appleton and Company, 1904.

——. *The Red Cross. A History of This Remarkable International Movement in the Interest of Humanity*. Washington: American National Red Cross, 1898.

——. *The Red Cross in Peace and War*. Washington: American Historical Press, 1899.

——. *The Story of My Childhood*. New York: The Baker and Taylor Company, 1907.

Barton, William E., *The Life of Clara Barton*. 2 vols. Boston: Houghton Mifflin Company, 1922.

Bicknell, Ernest P., *Pioneering with the Red Cross*. New York: The Macmillan Company, 1935.

Boardman, Mabel T., *Under the Red Cross Flag at Home and Abroad*. Philadelphia: J. B. Lippincott Company, 1915.

Boylston, Helen Dore, *Clara Barton. Founder of the American Red Cross*. New York: Random House, 1955.

Brockett, L. P., and Mrs. Mary C. Vaughan, *Woman's Work in the Civil War*. Boston: R. H. Curran, 1867.

Butler, Benjamin F., *Autobiography and Personal Reminiscences of Major-General Benjamin F. Butler*. Boston: A. M. Thayer and Company, 1892.

——. *Private and Official Correspondence of General Benjamin F. Butler, During the Period of the Civil War*. Norwood, Massachusetts: The Plimpton Press, 1917.

Catton, Bruce, *A Stillness at Appomattox*. New York: Doubleday and Company, 1953.

————. *Mr. Lincoln's Army*. New York: Doubleday and Company, 1951.

Commager, Henry Steele, *The Blue and the Gray*. Indianapolis: The Bobbs-Merrill Company, 1950.

Dana, Charles A., *Recollections of the Civil War*. New York: D. Appleton and Company, 1899.

Donald, David, edited by, *Divided We Fought: A Pictorial History of the War, 1861–1865*. New York: The Macmillan Company, 1952.

Dulles, Foster Rhea, *The American Red Cross, A History*. New York: Harper & Brothers, 1950.

Dunant, J. Henri, *A Memory of Solferino*. Washington: The American National Red Cross, 1939.

————. *Un Souvenir de Solferino*. (Third edition). Geneva: Jules Fick, 1863.

Epler, Percy H., *The Life of Clara Barton*. New York: The Macmillan Company, 1941.

Gaeddert, Gustave R., *The History of the American National Red Cross. Vol. II. The Barton Influence, 1866–1905*. Washington: The American National Red Cross, 1950.

Harper, Ida Husted, *The Life and Work of Susan B. Anthony*. Vol. III, Indianapolis: The Hollenbeck Press, 1908.

Hendrick, Burton J., *Lincoln's Wartime Cabinet*. Boston: Little, Brown and Company, 1946.

Howe, Mark Anthony De Wolfe, *Causes and Their Champions*. Boston: Little, Brown and Company, 1926.

Johnson, R. U., and C. C. Buel, *Battles and Leaders of the Civil War*. New York: The Century Company, 1844–1887.

Kellogg, Sanford C., *The Shenandoah Valley and Virginia, 1861–1865: A War Study*. New York: Neale Publishing Company, 1903.

Kennan, George, *Campaigning in Cuba*. New York: The Century Company, 1899.

Kite, Elizabeth S., *Antoinette Margot and Clara Barton*. Philadelphia: American Catholic Historical Society of Philadelphia Records, 1944.

Livermore, Thomas L., *Numbers and Losses in the Civil War*. Boston: Houghton Mifflin and Company, 1900.

Logan, Mrs. John A., *The Part Taken by Women in American History*. Wilmington, Delaware: The Perry-Nolle Publishing Company, 1912.

————. edited by, *Thirty Years in Washington*. Hartford, Connecticut: A. D. Worthington and Company, 1901.

Long, E. B., edited by, *Personal Memoirs of Ulysses S. Grant*. New York: The World Publishing Company, 1952.

Mann, Jonathan B., *The Life of Henry Wilson, Republican Candidate for Vice-President.* Boston: J. R. Osgood and Company, 1872.

Margot, Antoinette, *"The Three Stitches." A Story of Strassburg.* 1871.

*Memorials and Funeral Tributes.* Worcester: N. A. Pearson, 1912.

*Memorial to Clara Barton.* U.S. Library, Committee on House. Washington: Government Printing Office, 1917.

Miller, Francis Trevelyan, edited by, *Photographic History of the Civil War.* 10 vols. New York: The Review of Reviews Corporation, 1911.

Millis, Walter, *The Martial Spirit.* Boston: Houghton Mifflin Company, 1931.

Moore, Frank, edited by, *The Rebellion Record: A Diary of American Events.* 12 vols. New York: G. P. Putnam's Sons, 1862.

Nason, Rev. Elias, *Life and Public Services of Henry Wilson.* Boston: B. B. Russell, 1876.

Nevins, Allan, *The Emergence of Lincoln.* New York: Charles Scribner's Sons, 1950.

Page, Charles A., *Letters of a War Correspondent.* Boston: L. C. Page and Company, 1899.

Parker, John Lord, *Henry Wilson's Regiment: History of the 22nd Massachusetts Infantry.* Boston: Rand Avery Company, 1887.

Randall, James G., *The Civil War and Reconstruction.* Chicago: D. C. Heath and Company, 1937.

Sellers, Leila, *Commissioner Charles Mason and Clara Barton.* Journal of the Patent Office Society, Vol. XXII, November, 1940.

Stillé, Charles J., *History of the United States Sanitary Commission.* New York: Hurd and Houghton. Cambridge: Riverside Press, 1869.

*The Red Cross of the Geneva Convention, What It Is.* Rufus H. Darby, 1878.

Tiffany, Francis, *Life of Dorothea Lynde Dix.* Boston: Houghton Mifflin and Company, 1890.

Walcott, Charles F., *21st Regiment Massachusetts Volunteers 1861–1865.* Boston: Houghton Mifflin Company, 1882.

Williams, Blanche Colton, *Clara Barton, Daughter of Destiny.* Philadelphia: J. B. Lippincott Company, 1941.

Woodbury, Augustus, *Major-General A. E. Burnside and the Ninth Army Corps.* Providence: 1867.

Young, Charles Sumner, *Clara Barton, A Centenary Tribute.* Boston: Richard G. Badger, 1922.

## Magazines

American Magazine
Arena
Harper's Weekly
Home Journal
Illustrated Home Journal
Ladies' Home Journal

Leslie's Popular Monthly
New England and Yale Review
Red Cross Courier
St. Louis Illustrated Magazine
Scribner's Magazine

## Newspapers

Boston Daily Journal
Bordentown Register
Chicago Inter-Ocean
Christian Science Monitor
Cincinnati Inquirer
Dansville Advertiser
Dansville Express
Detroit News
Evansville Breeze
Highstown Gazette
Johnstown Daily Democrat
New York Daily Graphic
New York Evening Sun
New York Sun

New York Times
New York Tribune
New York World
Philadelphia Ledger
Rochester Chronicle
St. Louis Globe Democrat
Toledo Times
Washington Evening Star
Worcester Daily Telegram
Worcester Evening Gazette
Worcester Evening Transcript
Worcester Daily Spy
Youngstown Telegram

# INDEX